ART HISTORY

PORTABLE EDITION   THIRD EDITION

A View of the World
Part Two: Asian, African, and Oceanic Art
and Art of the Americas

MARILYN STOKSTAD

Judith Harris Murphy Distinguished Professor of Art History Emerita
The University of Kansas

CONTRIBUTORS

David A. Binkley, Claudia Brown, Patricia J. Darish,
Robert D. Mowry, and Sara E. Orel

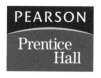
PEARSON
Prentice
Hall

Upper Saddle River, NJ 07458

Editor-in-Chief: Sarah Touborg
Sponsoring Editor: Helen Ronan
Editorial Assistant: Christina DeCesare
Editor in Chief, Development: Rochelle Diogenes
Development Editors: Jeannine Ciliotta, Margaret Manos,
    Teresa Nemeth, and Carol Peters
Media Editor: Alison Lorber
Director of Marketing: Brandy Dawson
Executive Marketing Manager: Marissa Feliberty
AVP, Director of Production and Manufacturing: Barbara Kittle
Senior Managing Editor: Lisa Iarkowski
Production Editor: Barbara Taylor-Laino
Production Assistant: Marlene Gassler
Senior Operations Specialist: Brian K. Mackey
Operations Specialist: Cathleen Peterson
Creative Design Director: Leslie Osher
Art Director: Amy Rosen
Interior and Cover Design: Anne DeMarinis
Layout Artist: Gail Cocker-Bogusz
Line Art and Map Program Management: Gail Cocker-Bogusz,
    Maria Piper

Line Art Studio: Peter Bull Art Studio
Cartographer: DK Education, a division of Dorling Kindersley, Ltd.
Pearson Imaging Center: Corin Skidds, Greg Harrison, Robert
    Uibelhoer, Ron Walko, Shayle Keating, and Dennis Sheehan
Site Supervisor, Pearson Imaging Center: Joe Conti
Photo Research: Laurie Platt Winfrey, Fay Torres-Yap, Mary Teresa
    Giancoli, and Christian Peña, Carousel Research, Inc.
Director, Image Resource Center: Melinda Patelli
Manager, Rights and Permissions: Zina Arabia
Manager, Visual Research: Beth Brenzel
Manager, Cover Visual Research and Permissions: Karen Sanatar
Image Permission Coordinator: Debbie Latronica
Manager, Cover Research and Permissions: Gladys Soto
Copy Editor: Stephen Hopkins
Proofreaders: Faye Gemmellaro, Margaret Pinette, Nancy Stevenson,
    and Victoria Waters
Composition: Prepare, Inc.
Portable Edition Composition: Black Dot
Cover Printer: Phoenix Color Corporation
Printer/Binder: R. R. Donnelley

Maps designed and produced by DK Education, a division of Dorling Kindersley, Limited, 80 Strand London WC2R 0RL.
DK and the DK logo are registered trademarks of Dorling Kindersley Limited.

Credits and acknowledgements borrowed from other sources and reproduced, with permission, in this textbook appear on the appropriate page within text or on the credit pages in the back of this book.

Cover Photo:
    Machu Picchu, Peru. Inca. 1450–1530. Photo: Danny Lehman / Corbis.

Pearson Education LTD.
Pearson Education Australia PTY, Limited
Pearson Education Singapore, Pte. Ltd
Pearson Education North Asia Ltd

Pearson Education, Canada, Ltd
Pearson Educación de Mexico, S.A. de C.V
Pearson Education—Japan
Pearson Education Malaysia, Pte. Ltd

10 9 8 7 6 5 4 3 2

ISBN 0-13-605408-0
ISBN 978-0-13-605408-5

CONTENTS

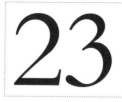

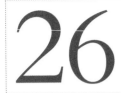

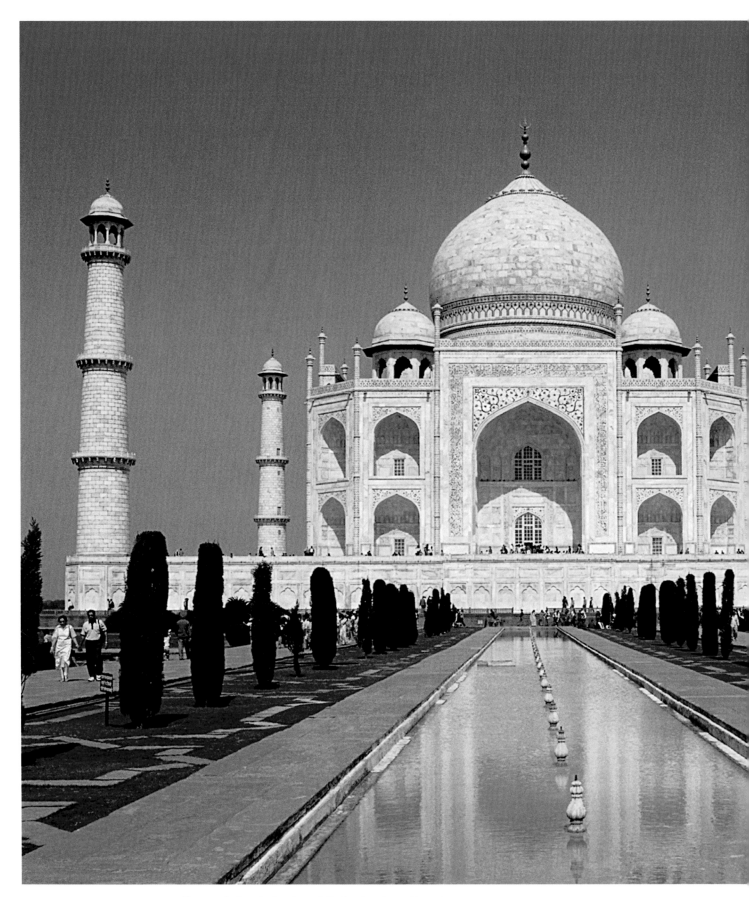

23–1 | **TAJ MAHAL**   Agra, India. Mughal period, reign of Shah Jahan, c. 1631–48.

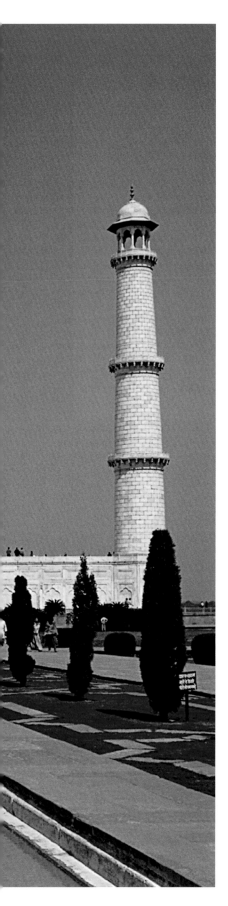

CHAPTER TWENTY-THREE

ART OF SOUTH AND SOUTHEAST ASIA AFTER 1200

23

Visitors catch their breath. Ethereal, weightless, the building before them barely seems to touch the ground. Its reflection shimmers in the pools of the garden meant to evoke a vision of paradise as described in the Qur'an, the holy book of Islam. Its façades are delicately inlaid with inscriptions and arabesques in semiprecious stones—carnelian, agate, coral, turquoise, garnet, lapis, and jasper. Above, its luminous, white marble dome reflects each shift in light, flushing rose at dawn, dissolving in its own brilliance in the noonday sun. One of the most celebrated buildings in the world, the **TAJ MAHAL** (FIG. 23–1) was built in the seventeenth century by the Mughal ruler Shah Jahan as a mausoleum for his favorite wife, Mumtaz-i-Mahal, who died in childbirth.

Inside, the Taj Mahal invokes the *hasht behisht*, or "eight paradises," a plan named for the eight small chambers that ring the interior—one at each corner and one behind each *iwan*, a vaulted opening with an arched portal. In two stories (for a total of sixteen chambers), the rooms ring the octagonal central area, which rises the full two stories to a domed ceiling that is lower than the outer dome. In this central chamber, surrounded by a finely carved octagonal openwork marble screen, are the exquisite inlaid cenotaphs of Shah Jahan and his wife, whose actual tombs lie in the crypt below.

A dynasty of Central Asian origin, the Mughals were the most successful of the many Islamic groups that established themselves in India beginning in the tenth century. Under their patronage, Persian and Central Asian influences mingled with older traditions of the South Asian subcontinent, adding yet another dimension to the already ancient and complex artistic heritage of India.

INDIA AFTER 1200

By 1200 India was already among the world's oldest civilizations (see "Foundations of Indian Culture," page 815). The art that survives from its earlier periods is almost exclusively sacred, most of it inspired by the three principal religions: Buddhism, Hinduism, and Jainism. These three religions continued as the principal focus for Indian art, even as invaders from the northwest began to establish the new religious culture of Islam.

Buddhist Art

After many centuries of prominence, Buddhism had been in decline as a cultural force in India since the seventh century C.E. By 1200, the principal Buddhist centers were concentrated in the northeast, in the region that had been ruled by the Pala dynasty (c. 750–1199). There, in great monastic universities that attracted monks from as far away as China, Korea, and Japan, was cultivated a form of Buddhism known as Tantric (Vajrayana) Mahayana.

ICONOGRAPHY OF A TANTRIC BODHISATTVA. The practices of Tantric Buddhism, which included techniques for visualizing deities, encouraged the development of images with precise iconographic details such as the gilt-bronze sculpture of the **BODHISATTVA AVALOKITESHVARA** in FIGURE 23–2. *Bodhisattvas* are beings who are well advanced on the path to buddhahood (enlightenment), the goal of Mahayana Buddhists, and who have vowed out of compassion to help others achieve enlightenment. Avalokiteshvara, the *bodhisattva* of greatest compassion, whose vow is to forgo buddhahood until all others become *buddhas*, became the most popular of these saintly beings in India and in East Asia.

Characteristic of *bodhisattvas*, Avalokiteshvara is distinguished in art by his princely garments, unlike a *buddha*, who wears a monk's robes. Avalokiteshvara is specifically recognized by the lotus flower he holds and by the presence in his crown of his "parent" *buddha*, in this case Amitabha, *buddha* of the Western Pure Land (the Buddhist paradise). Other marks of Avalokiteshvara's extraordinary status are the third eye (symbolizing the ability to see in miraculous ways) and the wheel on his palm (signifying the ability to teach the Buddhist truth).

Avalokiteshvara is shown here in the relaxed pose known as the posture of royal ease. One leg angles down; the other is drawn up onto the lotus seat, itself considered an emblem of spiritual purity. His body bends gracefully, if a bit stiffly, to one side. The chest scarf and lower garment cling to his body, fully revealing its shape. Delicate floral patterns enliven the textiles, and closely set parallel folds provide a wiry, linear tension that contrasts with the hard but silken surfaces of the body. Linear energy continues in the sweep of the tightly pleated hem emerging from under the right thigh, in the sinuous lotus stalks on each side, and in the fluttering ribbons of the elaborate crown. A profusion of details and varied textures creates an ornate effect—the lavish jewelry, the looped hair piled high and cascading over the shoulders, the ripe blossoms, the rich layers of the lotus seat. Though still friendly and human, the image is somewhat formalized. The features of the face, where we instinctively look for a human echo, are treated abstractly, and despite its reassuring smile, the statue's expression remains remote. Through richness of ornament and tension of line, this style expresses the heightened power of a perfected being.

With the fall of the Pala dynasty in the late twelfth century, the last centers of Buddhism in northern India collapsed, and the monks dispersed, mainly into Nepal and Tibet (SEE MAP 23–1). From that time, Tibet has remained the principal stronghold of Tantric Buddhist practice and its arts. The artistic style perfected under the Palas, however, became an influential international style throughout East and Southeast Asia.

Jain Art

The Jain religion traces its roots to a spiritual leader called Mahavira (c. 599–527 BCE), whom it regards as the final in a series of twenty-four saviors known as pathfinders, or *tirthankaras*. Devotees seek through purification to become worthy of rebirth in the heaven of the pathfinders, a zone of pure existence at the zenith of the universe. Jain monks live a life of austerity, and even laypersons avoid killing any living creature.

A MANUSCRIPT LEAF FROM THE *KALPA SUTRA*. As Islamic, or Muslim, territorial control over northern India expanded,

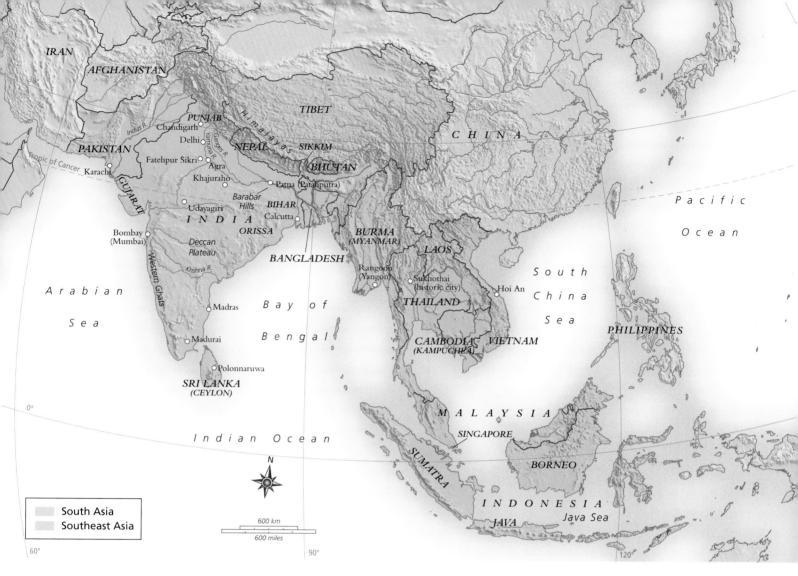

MAP 23–1 | **INDIA**

Throughout its history, the Indian subcontinent was subject to continual invasion that caused the borders of its kingdoms to contract and expand until the establishment of modern-day India in the mid-twentieth century.

non-Islamic religions resorted to more private forms of artistic expression, such as illustrating sacred texts, rather than public activities, such as building temples. In these circumstances, the Jains of western India, primarily in the region of Gujarat, created many illustrated manuscripts, such as this *Kalpa Sutra*, which explicates the lives of the pathfinders (FIG. 23–3). Produced during the late fourteenth century, it is one of the first Jain manuscripts on paper rather than palm leaf, the material which had previously been used for written documents.

With great economy, the illustration, inserted between blocks of Sanskrit text, depicts the birth of Mahavira. He is shown cradled in his mother's arms as she reclines in her bed under a canopy connoting royalty, attended by three ladies-in-waiting. Decorative pavilions and a shrine with peacocks on the roof suggest a luxurious palace setting. Everything appears two-dimensional against the brilliant red or blue

ground. Vibrant colors and crisp outlines impart an energy to the painting that suggests the arrival of the divine in the mundane world. Transparent garments with variegated designs reveal the swelling curves of the figures, whose alert postures and gestures convey a sense of the importance and excitement of the event. Strangely exaggerated features, such as the protruding eyes, contribute to the air of the extraordinary. With its angles and tense curves, the drawing is closely linked to the aesthetics of Sanskrit **calligraphy**, and the effect is as if the words themselves had suddenly flared into color and image.

Hindu Art

Hinduism became the dominant religious tradition of India. With the increasing popularity of Hindu sects came the rapid development of Hindu temples. Spurred by the ambitious building programs of wealthy rulers, well-formulated

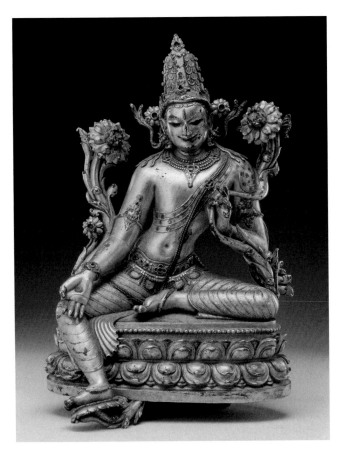

23-2 | **THE BODHISATTVA AVALOKITESHVARA**
Kurkihar, Bihar. Pala dynasty, 12th century. Gilt-bronze, height 10" (25.5 cm). Patna Museum, Patna.

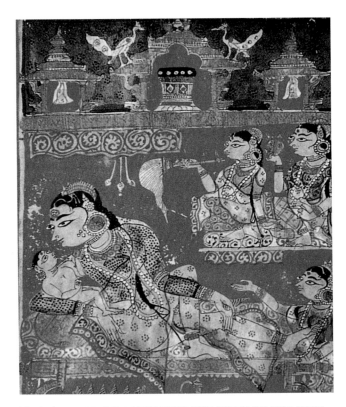

23-3 | **DETAIL OF A LEAF WITH THE BIRTH OF MAHAVIRA**
Kalpa Sutra. Western Indian school (probably Gujarat), c. 1375–1400. Gouache on paper, 3⅜ × 3" (8.5 × 7.6 cm). Prince of Wales Museum, Bombay.

regional styles had evolved by about 1000 CE. The most spectacular structures of the era were monumental, with a complexity and grandeur of proportion unequaled even in later Indian art.

Emphasis on monumental individual temples gave way to the building of vast temple complexes and more moderately scaled yet more richly ornamented individual temples. These developments took place largely in the south of India, for temple building in the north virtually ceased with the consolidation of Islamic rule there from the beginning of the thirteenth century. The mightiest of the southern Hindu kingdoms was Vijayanagar (c. 1336–1565), whose rulers successfully countered the southward progress of Islamic forces for more than 200 years. Viewing themselves as defenders and preservers of Hindu faith and culture, Vijayanagar kings lavished donations on sacred shrines. Under the patronage of the Vijayanagar and their successors, the Nayaks, the principal monuments of later Hindu architecture were created.

TEMPLE AT MADURAI. The enormous temple complex at Madurai, one of the capitals of the Nayaks, is an example of this fervent expression of Hindu faith. Founded around the thirteenth century, it is dedicated to the goddess Minakshi (the local name for Parvati, the consort of the god Shiva) and to Sundareshvara (the local name for Shiva himself). The temple complex stands in the center of the city and is the focus of Madurai life. At its heart are the two oldest shrines, one to Minakshi and the other to Sundareshvara. Successive additions over the centuries gradually expanded the complex around these small shrines and came to dominate the visual landscape of the city. The most dramatic features of this and similar "temple cities" of the south were the thousand-pillar halls, large ritual-bathing pools, and especially entrance gateways, called *gopuras*, which tower above the temple site and the surrounding city like modern skyscrapers (FIG. 23-4).

Gopuras proliferated as a temple city grew, necessitating new and bigger enclosing walls, and thus new gateways. Successive rulers, often seeking to outdo their predecessors, donated taller and taller *gopuras*. As a result, the tallest structures in temple cities are often at the periphery, rather than at the central temples, which are sometimes totally overwhelmed by the height of the surrounding structures. The temple complex at Madurai has eleven *gopuras*, the largest over 160 feet tall.

Formally, the *gopura* has its roots in the *vimana*, the pyramidal tower characteristic of the seventh-century southern temple style. As the *gopura* evolved, it took on the graceful concave silhouette shown here. The exterior is embellished with thousands of sculpted figures, evoking a teeming world of gods and goddesses. Inside, stairs lead to the top for an extraordinary view.

Myth and Religion
TANTRIC INFLUENCE IN THE ART OF NEPAL AND TIBET

The legacy of India's Tantric Buddhist art can be traced in the regions of Nepal and Tibet. Artistic expression of esoteric Buddhist ideals reached a high point in the seventeenth and eighteenth centuries. Indeed, even today, artists worldwide continue to explore aspects of this tradition.

Inlaid Devotional Sculpture. In Nepal, where Hinduism intermingled with Buddhism, sculptors developed a metalwork style in which a traditional artistic use of polished stones became prevalent in devotional sculptures as well. Inlaid gems and semiprecious stones often enlivened their copper or bronze sculptures, which were almost always brightly gilded. Complex representations of deities, often multiarmed and adorned with celestial attributes, predominated, but some themes from early Buddhism were revived. In one particularly fine eighteenth-century example, Maya, the Mother of Buddha, holds the legendary tree branch while the Buddha emerges from her side. The cast and chased details of the regal costume of Queen Maya, including fluttering scarves, elaborate jewelry, and a large crown, are studded with real jewels, pearls, and semiprecious stones. The tree, also, is richly inlaid, symbolizing the auspicious nature of the event. Both the tree and the figure rise from a pedestal shaped to suggest the blossoming lotus, a reference to

the appearance of the Buddha's purity in the muddy pond of the material world.

***Tangka* Painting.** Buddhism was established relatively late in Tibet but the region has since become almost wholly identified with the religion. With the rule of a lineage of Dalai Lamas established in the seventeenth century and continuing through to the twentieth century, and a related expansion of monasteries, the arts associated with Tantric Buddhism flourished. Wrathful manifestations of deities, mysterious and powerful, were evoked in sculpted and painted forms, with the scroll-like *tangka* emerging as a major format. A nineteenth-century painting of Achala, one of a group of wrathful deities associated with truth, resolve, and the overcoming of obstacles, exemplifies this major aspect of Tibetan art. The deity exudes brilliant red flames while brandishing a sword and posing as if to strike. Following traditional practice, the artist—or artists, as these may have employed highly specialized craftsmen—positions the terrifying figure on a lotus pedestal, establishing his ethereal nature. The background suggests the green hills and blue sky of the material world as well as the cosmic geometry envisioned in Tantric Buddhism. Repeated representations of the deity emphasize the efficacious function and conspicuous power of the image.

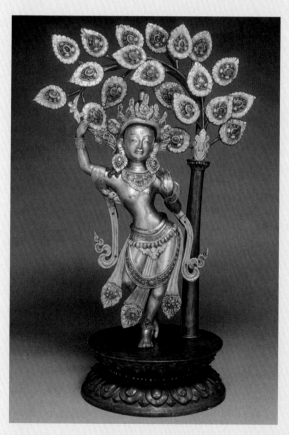

MAYA, MOTHER OF BUDDHA, HOLDING A TREE BRANCH
Nepal. 18th century. Gilt bronze with inlaid precious stones, height 22″ (56 cm). Musée Guimet, Paris.

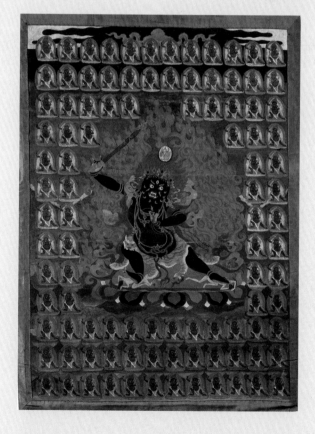

ACHALA
Tibet. 19th century. Gouache on cotton, 33½ × 23⅔″ (85 × 60 cm). Musée Guimet, Paris.
Photo Réunion des Musées Nationaux; Art Resource, New York

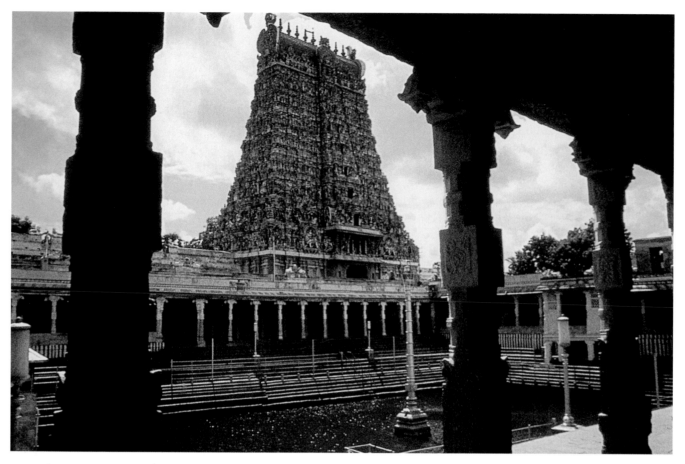

23–4 | **OUTER *GOPURA* OF THE MINAKSHI-SUNDARESHVARA TEMPLE**
Madurai, Tamil Nadu, South India. Nayak dynasty, mostly 13th to mid-17th century, with modern renovations.

THE BUDDHIST AND HINDU INHERITANCE IN SOUTHEAST ASIA

India's Buddhist and Hindu traditions influenced Southeast Asia (discussed in Chapter 9), where they were absorbed by newly rising kingdoms in the regions now comprising Burma (Myanmar), Thailand, Cambodia (Kampuchea), Vietnam, and Indonesia.

Theravada Buddhism in Burma and Thailand

In northern Burma, from the eleventh to the thirteenth century, rulers raised innumerable religious monuments—temples, monasteries, and stupas—in the Pagan plain, following the scriptures of Theravada Buddhism (or Hinayana Buddhism, see Chapter 9). To the south arose the port city

23–5 | **SHWE-DAGON STUPA (PAGODA)**
Terrace, 15th century. Construction at the site from at least the 14th century, with replastering and redecoration continuously to the present.

Art and Its Context
FOUNDATIONS OF INDIAN CULTURE

The earliest civilization on the Indian subcontinent flourished toward the end of the third millennium BCE along the Indus River in present-day Pakistan. Remains of its expertly engineered brick cities have been uncovered, together with works of art that intriguingly suggest spiritual practices and reveal artistic traits known in later Indian culture.

The decline of the Indus Valley civilization during the mid–second millennium BCE coincides with (and may be related to) the arrival from the northwest of a seminomadic warrior people known as the Indo-European Aryans. Over the next millennium they were influential in formulating the new civilization that gradually emerged. The most important Aryan contributions to this new civilization included the Sanskrit language and the sacred texts called the Vedas. The evolution of Vedic thought under the influence of indigenous Indian beliefs culminated in the mystical, philosophical texts called the Upanishads, which took shape sometime after 800 BCE.

The Upanishads teach that the material world is illusory; only Brahman, the universal soul, is real and eternal. We—that is, our individual souls—are trapped in this illusion in a relentless cycle of birth, death, and rebirth. The ultimate goal of religious life is to liberate ourselves from this cycle and to unite our individual soul with Brahman.

Buddhism and Jainism are two of the many religions that developed in the climate of Upanishadic thought. Buddhism (see "Buddhism" page 317) is based on the teachings of Shakyamuni Buddha, who lived in central India about 500 BCE; Jainism was shaped about the same time by the followers of the spiritual leader Mahavira. Both religions acknowledged the cyclical nature of existence and taught a means of liberation from it, but they rejected the authority, rituals, and social strictures of Vedic religion. Whereas the Vedic religion was in the hands of a hereditary priestly class, Buddhist and Jain communities welcomed all members of society, which gave them great appeal. The Vedic tradition eventually evolved into the many sects now collectively known as Hinduism (see "Hinduism" page 318).

Through most of its history India was a mosaic of regional dynastic kingdoms, but from time to time, empires emerged that unified large parts of the subcontinent. The first was the Maurya dynasty (c. 322-185 BCE), whose great king Ashoka patronized Buddhism. From this time Buddhist doctrines spread widely and its artistic traditions were established.

In the first century CE the Kushans, a Central Asian people, created an empire extending from present-day Afghanistan down into central India. Buddhism prospered under Kanishka, the most powerful Kushan king, and spread into Central Asia and to East Asia. At this time, under the evolving thought of Mahayana Buddhism, traditions first evolved for depicting the image of the Buddha in art.

Later, under the Gupta dynasty (c. 320-486 CE) in central India, Buddhist art and culture reached their high point. However, Gupta monarchs also patronized the Hindu religion, which from this time grew to become the dominant Indian religious tradition, with its emphasis on the great gods Vishnu (the Creator), Shiva (the Destroyer), and the Goddess—all with multiple forms.

After the tenth century, numerous regional dynasties prevailed, some quite powerful and long-lasting. During the early part of this period, to roughly 1200, Buddhism continued to decline as a cultural force, while artistic achievement under Hinduism soared. Hindu temples, in particular, developed monumental and complex forms that were rich in symbolism and ritual function, with each region of India producing its own variation.

of Rangoon (in Burmese Yangon, called Dagon in antiquity), now the nation's capital. Established by Mon rulers (SEE FIG. 9–29) at least by the eleventh century, Rangoon is site of the Shwe-dagon stupa (FIG. 23–5), which enshrines relics of the Buddha. The modern structures of Shwe-dagon (which means "Golden Dagon") rise from an ancient core—fourteenth century or earlier—and reflect centuries of continual restoration and enhancement. The site continues to be a center of Theravada devotion amid symbolic ornamentation—especially lotus elements symbolic of the Buddha's purity—and splendid decoration in gilding and precious stones supplied by pious contributions. Images of the Buddha, and sometimes his footprints alone, provide focal points for devotion.

In Thailand, the Sukhothai kingdom (mid-thirteenth to late fourteenth century) also embraced Theravada Buddhism, although Hindu shrines were constructed as well in its capital city called Sukhothai (ancient name Sukhodaya). Artisans working under royal patrons developed a classic statement of Theravada ideals in bronze sculptures of the Buddha. Notable was their development of a free-standing walking Buddha. The highest expression of the ascetic simplicity of Theravada Buddhism, however, may be found in their many renditions of the **BUDDHA CALLING THE EARTH TO WITNESS** (FIG. 23–6).

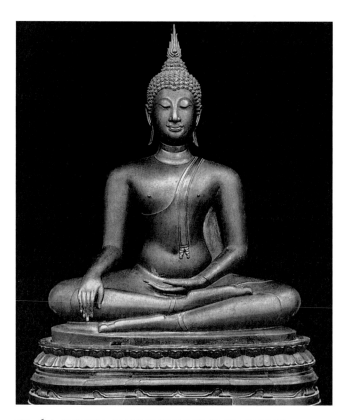

Inspired by devotional texts and poetry, and further refined through reference to models from Sri Lanka, the iconographical and stylistic elements reached a height of perfection. The Buddha's cranial protuberance is interpreted as a flame of divine knowledge, and details of his ecclesiastical costume are reduced to a few elegant lines. The *mudras* (see p. 325), or hand gestures, are quietly eloquent.

Vietnamese Ceramics

Both the Burmese and the Thai kingdoms produced ceramics, often inspired by the stonewares and porcelains from China. Sukhothai potters, for example, made green-glazed and brown-glazed wares, called Sawankhalok wares. Even more widespread were the wares of Vietnamese potters. For example, excavation of the Hoi An "hoard" (SEE FIG. 23–7), actually the contents of a sunken ship laden with ceramics for export, brought to light an impressive variety of ceramic forms made by Vietnamese potters of the late fifteenth to early sixteenth century. Painted in underglaze cobalt blue and further embellished with overglaze enamels, these wares were shipped throughout Southeast Asia and beyond, as far east as Japan and as far west as England and The Netherlands.

23–6 ⋮ **BUDDHA CALLING THE EARTH TO WITNESS**
Sukhothai style. Bronze. Height 37″ (94 cm). Collection of
H.R.H. Prince Chalermbol Yugala, Bangkok.

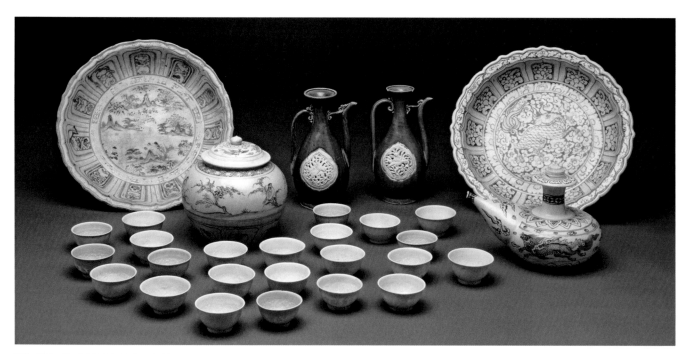

23–7 ⋮ **GROUP OF CERAMICS FROM THE HOI AN HOARD, VIETNAMESE**
Late 15th to early 16th century, porcelain with underglaze blue decoration, barbed-rim dishes:
(left) diam. 14″ (35.1 cm); (right) diam. 13¼″ (34.7 cm). Phoenix Art Museum, 2000.105–109.

More than 150,000 blue-and-white ceramics were found in the hold of a sunken ship excavated in the late 1990s under commission from the Vietnamese government, which later sent many of the retrieved items to public auction. Among the works shown here, the twenty-three small cups were found packed inside the jar.

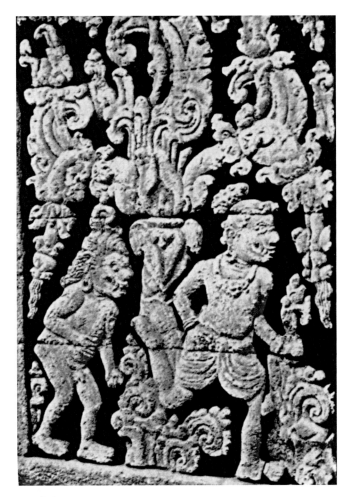

23–8 | **RAMAYANA SCENE**
Candi Panataran, Java. Stone relief, height 29½" (70 cm).
Early 14th century.

Indonesian Traditions

Indonesia experienced a Hindu revival in the centuries following its Buddhist period, which came to a close in the eighth or ninth century (see Chapter 9). As a consequence, it has maintained unique traditions that build upon the Hindu epics, especially the Ramayana. Javanese versions of these epics can be found illustrated in narrative reliefs from shrines of the fourteenth century (FIG. 23–8). Here modeling is reduced and rhythmic surface ornamentation increased. This style is often called the *wayang* style because of its similarities to the leather shadow puppets of Indonesia's *wayang* theater, still popular today. During the fifteenth century, Islam spread over Indonesia and subsequent religious monuments avoided figural representation. In their portrayal of botanical motifs and other ornaments, however, Indonesian sculptors preserved some elements of the relief style seen here.

MUGHAL PERIOD

Islam first touched the South Asian subcontinent in the eighth century, when Arab armies captured a small territory near the Indus River. Later, beginning around 1000, Turkic factions from Central Asia, relatively recent converts to Islam, began military campaigns into North India, at first purely for plunder, then seeking territorial control. From 1206, various Turkic dynasties ruled portions of the subcontinent from the northern city of Delhi. These sultanates, as they are known, constructed forts, **mausoleums**, monuments, and **mosques**. Although these early dynasties left their mark, it was the Mughal Dynasty that made the most inspired and lasting contribution to the art of India.

The Mughals, too, came from Central Asia. Muhammad Zahir-ud-Din, known as Babur ("Lion" or "Panther"), was the first Mughal emperor of India (ruled 1526–30). He emphasized his Turkic heritage, though he had equally impressive Mongol ancestry. After some initial conquests in Central Asia, he amassed an empire stretching from Afghanistan to Delhi, which he conquered in 1526. Akbar (ruled 1556–1605), the third ruler, extended Mughal control over most of North India, and under his two successors, Jahangir and Shah Jahan, northern India was generally unified by 1658. The Mughal Empire lasted until 1858, when the last Mughal emperor was deposed and exiled to Burma by the British.

Mughal Architecture

Mughal architects were heir to a 300-year-old tradition of Islamic building in India. The Delhi sultans who preceded them had great forts housing government and court buildings. Their architects had introduced two fundamental Islamic structures, the mosque and the tomb, along with construction based on the arch and the dome. (Earlier Indian architecture had been based primarily on post-and-lintel construction. They had also drawn freely on Indian architecture, borrowing both decorative and structural elements to create a variety of hybrid styles, and had especially benefited from the centuries-old Indian virtuosity in stone carving and masonry. The Mughals followed in this tradition, synthesizing Indian, Persian, and Central Asian elements for their forts, palaces, mosques, tombs, and **cenotaphs** (tombs or monuments to someone whose remains are actually somewhere else).

Akbar, an ambitious patron of architecture and city planning, constructed a new capital at a place he named *Fatehpur Sikri* ("City of Victory at Sikri"), celebrating his military conquests and the birth of his son Jahangir. The palatial and civic buildings, built primarily during Akbar's residence there from about 1572 to 1585, have drawn much admiration from modern and contemporary architects. Akbar's congregational mosque (Jami Masjid), completed about 1571–72, is one of

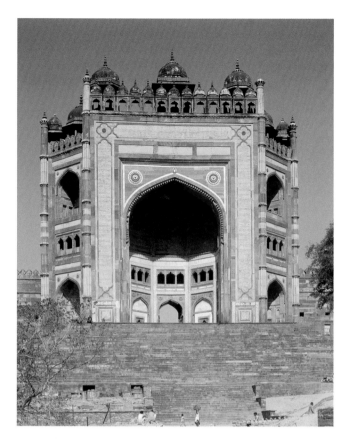

23–9 | **BULAND DARVAZA (THE LOFTY GATE)**
Fatehpur Sikri, approaching the Congregational Mosque (Jami Masjid), 1573-74.

the largest and most ornately finished mosques in India. Built on a high plinth, its vast central courtyard is approached from the south through the **BULAND DARVAZA (THE LOFTY GATE)**, as seen in FIGURE 23–9. This gateway is dignified in proportion but monumental in scale, rising more than 150 feet above the road below. An inscription dated 1601 cites Akbar's triumphant return from the Deccan; however, many scholars maintain a date in the 1570s or 1580s for the monumental gateway itself.

THE TAJ MAHAL. Perhaps the most famous of all Indian Islamic structures, the Taj Mahal is sited on the bank of the Yamuna River at Agra, in northern India. Built between 1631 and 1648, it was commissioned as a mausoleum for his wife by the emperor Shah Jahan (ruled 1628–58), who is believed to have taken a major part in overseeing its design and construction.

Visually, the Taj Mahal never fails to impress (SEE FIG. 23–1). As visitors enter through a monumental, hall-like gate, the tomb rises before them across a spacious garden set with long reflecting pools. Measuring some 1,000 by 1,900 feet, the enclosure is unobtrusively divided into quadrants planted with trees and flowers and framed by broad walkways and stone inlaid in geometric patterns. In Shah Jahan's time, fruit trees and cypresses—symbolic of life and death, respectively—lined the walkways, and fountains played in the shal-

low pools. One can imagine the melodies of court musicians that wafted through the garden. Truly, the senses were beguiled in this earthly evocation of paradise.

Set toward the rear of the garden, the tomb is flanked by two smaller structures not visible here, one a mosque and the other a hall designed in mirror image. They share a broad base with the tomb and serve visually as stabilizing elements. Like the entrance hall, they are made mostly of red sandstone, rendering even more startling the full glory of the tomb's white marble. The tomb is raised higher than these structures on its own marble platform. At each corner of the platform, a **minaret**, or slender tower, defines the surrounding space. The minarets' three levels correspond to those of the tomb, creating a bond between them. Crowning each minaret is a *chattri*, or pavilion. Traditional embellishments of Indian palaces, *chattris* quickly passed into the vocabulary of Indian Islamic architecture, where they appear prominently. Minarets occur in architecture throughout the Islamic world; from their heights, the faithful are called to prayer.

A lucid geometric symmetry pervades the tomb. It is basically square, but its **chamfered**, or sliced-off, corners create a subtle octagon. Measured to the base of the **finial** (the spire at the top), the tomb is almost exactly as tall as it is wide. Each façade is identical, with a central *iwan* flanked by two stories of smaller *iwans*. (A typical feature of eastern Islamic architecture, an *iwan* is a vaulted opening with an arched portal.) By creating voids in the façades, these *iwans* contribute markedly to the building's sense of weightlessness. On the roof, four octagonal *chattris*, one at each corner, create a visual transition to the lofty, bulbous dome, the crowning element that lends special power to this structure. Framed but not obscured by the *chattris*, the dome rises more gracefully and is lifted higher by its **drum** than in earlier Mughal tombs, allowing the swelling curves and lyrical lines of its beautifully proportioned, surprisingly large form to emerge with perfect clarity.

By the seventeenth century, India was well known for exquisite craftsmanship and luxurious decorative arts (see "Luxury Arts," page 827). The pristine surfaces of the **TAJ MAHAL** are embellished with utmost subtlety (FIG. 23–10). Even the sides of the platform on which the Taj Mahal stands are carved in relief with a **blind arcade** motif and carved relief panels of flowers. The portals are framed with verses from the Qur'an inlaid in black marble, while the **spandrels** are decorated with floral **arabesques** inlaid in colored semiprecious stones, a technique known by its Italian name, *pietra dura*. Not strong enough to detract from the overall purity of the white marble, the embellishments enliven the surfaces of this impressive yet delicate masterpiece.

Mughal Painting

Probably no one had more control over the solidification of the Mughal Empire and the creation of Mughal art than the emperor Akbar. A dynamic, humane, and just leader, Akbar

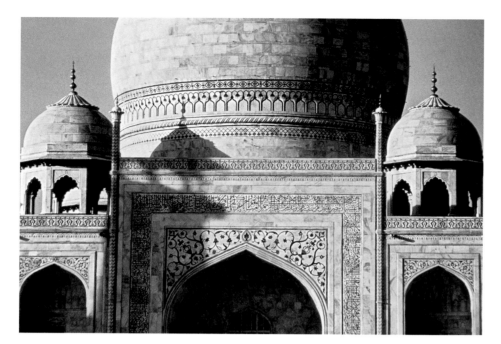

23–10 | **TAJ MAHAL**
Agra, India. Mughal period, reign of Shah Jahan, c. 1631–48.

enjoyed religious discourse and loved the arts, especially painting. He created an imperial **atelier** (workshop) of painters, which he placed under the direction of two artists from the Persian court. Learning from these two masters, the Indian painters of the atelier soon transformed Persian styles into the more vigorous, naturalistic styles that mark the Mughal school (see "Indian Painting on Paper," page 820). At Akbar's cosmopolitan court, pictorial sources from Europe also became inspiration for Mughal artists.

PAINTING IN THE COURT OF AKBAR. Akbar's court painters also produced paintings documenting Akbar's own life and accomplishments in the *Akbarnama*. Among the most fascinating in the series are those which record Akbar's supervision of the construction of Fatehpur Sikri. One painting (**FIG. 23–11**) documents Akbar's inspection of the stone masons and other craftsmen, and includes an ambitious rendering of the Buland Darwaza (The Lofty Gate), shown above in FIGURE 23–9.

One of the most famous and extraordinary works produced in Akbar's atelier is an illustrated manuscript of the *Hamzanama*, a Persian classic about the adventures of Hamza, uncle of the Prophet Muhammad. Painted on cotton cloth, each illustration is more than 2½ feet high. The entire project gathered 1,400 illustrations into twelve volumes and took fifteen years to complete.

One illustration shows Hamza's spies scaling a fortress wall and surprising some men as they sleep (**FIG. 23–12**). One man climbs a rope; another has already beheaded a figure in yellow and lifts his head aloft—realistic details are not avoided in paintings from the Mughal atelier. The receding lines of the architecture, viewed from a slightly elevated vantage point, provide a reasonably three-dimensional setting. Yet the

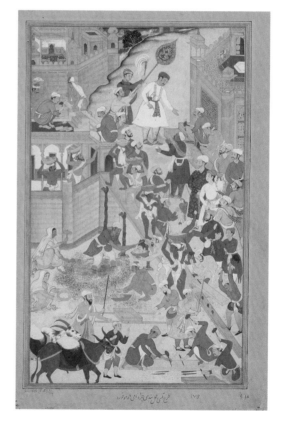

23–11 | **AKBAR INSPECTING THE CONSTRUCTION OF FATEHPUR SIKRI**
Akbarnama, c. 1590. Opaque watercolor on paper, 14¾ × 10″ (37.5 × 25 cm). Victoria & Albert Museum, London. (I.S.2-1896 91/117)

Many of the painters in the Mughal imperial workshops are recorded in texts of the period. Based on those records and on signatures that occur on some paintings, scholars have attributed the design of this work to Tulsi Kalan (Tulsi the Elder), the painting to Bandi, and the portraits to Madhu Kalan (Madhu the Elder) or Madhu Khurd (Madhu the Younger).

Technique
INDIAN PAINTING ON PAPER

Before the fourteenth century most painting in India had been on walls or palm leaves. With the introduction of paper, Indian artists adapted painting techniques from Persia and over the ensuing centuries produced jewel-toned works of surpassing beauty on paper.

Painters usually began their training early. As young apprentices, they learned to make brushes and grind pigments. Brushes were made from the curved hairs of a squirrel's tail, arranged to taper from a thick base to a single hair at the tip. Paint came from pigments of vegetables and minerals—lapis lazuli to make blue, malachite for pale green—that were ground to a paste with water, then bound with a solution of gum from the acacia plant. Paper was made by crushing fibers of cotton and jute to a pulp, pouring the mixture onto a woven mat, drying, and then burnishing with a smooth piece of agate, often achieving a glossy finish.

Artists frequently worked from a collection of sketches belonging to a master painter's atelier. Sometimes, to transfer the drawing to a blank sheet beneath, sketches were pricked with small, closely spaced holes that were then daubed with wet color. The resulting dots were connected into outlines, and the process of painting began.

First, the painter applied a thin wash of a chalk-based white, which sealed the surface of the paper while allowing the underlying sketch to show through. Next, outlines were filled with thick washes of brilliant, opaque, unmodulated color. When the colors were dry, the painting was laid facedown on a smooth marble surface and burnished with a rounded agate stone, rubbing first up and down, then side to side. The indirect pressure against the marble polished the pigments to a high luster. Then outlines, details, and modeling—depending on the style—were added with a fine brush.

Sometimes certain details were purposely left for last, such as the eyes, which were said to bring the painting to life. Gold and raised details were applied when the painting was nearly finished. Gold paint, made from pulverized, 24-karat gold leaf bound with acacia gum, was applied with a brush and burnished to a high shine. Raised details such as the pearls of a necklace were made with thick, white, chalk-based paint, with each pearl a single droplet hardened into a tiny raised mound.

sense of depth is boldly undercut by the richly variegated geometric patterns of the tilework, which are painted as though they had been set flat on the page. Contrasting with the flat geometric patterns are the large human figures, whose rounded forms and softened contours create a convincing sense of volume. The energy exuded by the figures is also characteristic of painting under Akbar—even the sleepers seem active. This robust, naturalistic figure style is quite different from the linear style seen earlier in Jain manuscripts (SEE FIG. 23–3) and even from the Persian styles that inspired Mughal paintings.

Nearly as prominent as the architectural setting with its vivid human adventure is the sensuous landscape in the foreground, where monkeys, foxes, and birds inhabit a grove of trees that shimmer and glow against the darkened background like precious gems. The treatment of the gold-edged leaves at first calls to mind the patterned geometry of the tilework, yet a closer look reveals a skillful naturalism born of careful observation. Each tree species is carefully distinguished—by the way its trunk grows, the way its branches twist, the shape and veining of its leaves, the silhouette of its overall form. Pink and blue rocks with lumpy, softly outlined forms add still further interest to this painting, whose every inch is full of intriguing elements.

PAINTING IN THE COURT OF JAHANGIR. Painting from the reign of Jahangir (ruled 1605–27) presents a different tone. Like his father, Jahangir admired painting and, if anything, paid even more attention to his atelier. Indeed, he boasted that he could recognize the hand of each of his artists even in collaborative paintings, which were common. Unlike Akbar, however, Jahangir preferred the courtly life to the adventurous one, and paintings produced for him reflect his subdued and refined tastes and his admiration for realistic detail.

One such painting is **JAHANGIR IN DARBAR (FIG. 23–13)**. The work, probably part of a series on Jahangir's reign, shows the emperor holding an audience, or *darbar*, at court. Jahangir himself is depicted at top center, seated on a balcony under a canopy. Members of his court, including his son, the future emperor Shah Jahan, stand somewhat stiffly to each side. The audience, too, is divided along the central axis, with figures lined up in profile or three-quarter view. In the foreground, an elephant and a horse complete the symmetrical format.

Jahangir insisted on fidelity in portraiture, including his own in old age. The figures in the audience are a medley of portraits, possibly taken from albums meticulously kept by the court artists. Some represent people known to have died before Jahangir's reign, so the painting may represent a symbolic gathering rather than an actual event. Standing out amid the bright array of garments is the black robe of a Jesuit priest from Europe. Both Akbar and Jahangir were known for their interest in things foreign, and many foreigners flocked to the courts of these open-minded rulers.

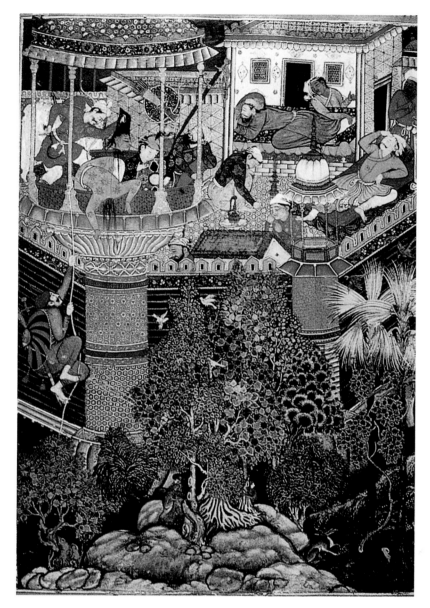

23–12 | **HAMZA'S SPIES SCALE THE FORTRESS**
Hamzanama, North India. Mughal period, Mughal, reign of Akbar, c. 1567-82.
Gouache on cotton, 30 × 24″ (76 × 61 cm). Museum of Applied Arts, Vienna.

The scene is formal, the composition static, and the treatment generally two-dimensional. Nevertheless, the sensitively rendered portraits and the fresh colors, with their varied range of pastel tones, provide the aura of a keenly observed, exquisitely idealized reality that marks the finest paintings of Jahangir's time.

Rajput Painting

Outside of the Mughal strongholds at Delhi and Agra, much of northern India was governed regionally by local Hindu princes, descendants of the so-called Rajput warrior clans, who were allowed to keep their lands in return for allegiance to the Mughals. Like the Mughals, Rajput princes frequently supported painters at their courts, and in these settings, a variety of strong, indigenous Indian painting styles were perpetu-

ated. Rajput painting, more abstract and poetic than the Mughal style, included subjects like those treated by Mughal painters, royal portraits and court scenes, as well as indigenous subjects such as Hindu myths, love poetry, and the Ragamala (illustrations relating to musical modes).

The Hindu devotional movement known as *bhakti*, which had done much to spread the faith in the south from around the seventh century, now experienced a revival in the north. As it had earlier in the south, *bhakti* inspired an outpouring of poetic literature, this time devoted especially to Krishna, the popular human incarnation of the god Vishnu. Most renowned is the *Gita Govinda*, a cycle of rhapsodic poems about the love between God and humans expressed metaphorically through the love between the young Krishna and the cowherd Radha.

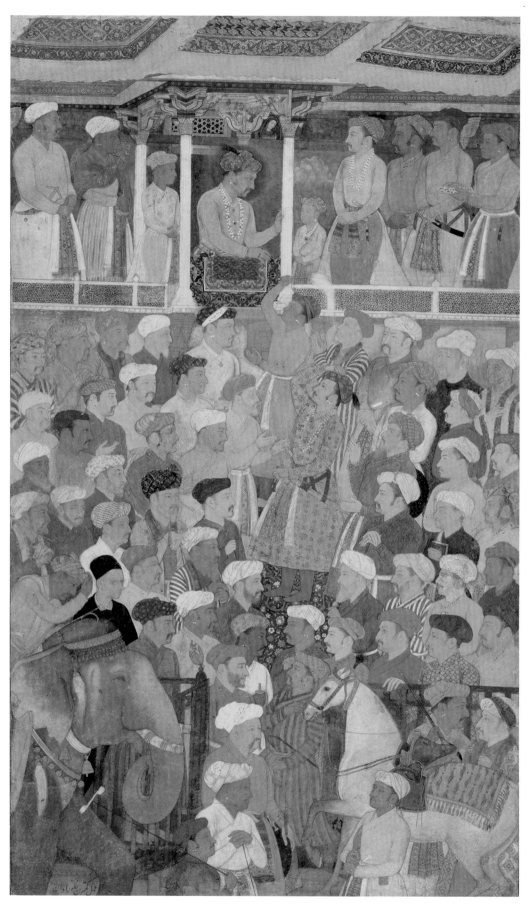

23–13 | Abul Hasan and Manohar **JAHANGIR IN DARBAR**
Jahangirnama. North India. Mughal period, Mughal, reign of Jahangir, c. 1620. Gouache on paper, 13¾ × 7⅞" (35 × 20 cm). Museum of Fine Arts, Boston.

Frances Bartlett Donation of 1912 and Picture Fund (14, 654)

The illustration here is from a manuscript of the *Gita Govinda* produced in the region of Rajasthan about 1525–50. The blue god Krishna sits in dalliance with a group of cowherd women. Standing with her maid and consumed with love for Krishna, Radha peers through the trees, overcome by jealousy. Her feelings are indicated by the cool blue color behind her, while the crimson red behind the Krishna grouping suggests passion **(FIG. 23–14)**. The curving stalks and bold patterns of the flowering vines and trees express not only the exuberance of springtime, when the story unfolds, but also the heightened emotional tensions of the scene. Birds, trees, and flowers are brilliant as fireworks against the black, hilly landscape edged in an undulating white line. As in the Jain manuscript earlier (SEE FIG. 23–3), all the figures are of a single type, with plump faces in profile and oversized eyes. Yet the resilient line of the drawing gives them life, and the variety of textile patterns provides some individuality. The intensity and resolute flatness of the scene seem to thrust all of its energy outward, irrevocably engaging the viewer in the drama.

Quite a different mood pervades **HOUR OF COWDUST**, a work from the Kangra school in the Punjab Hills, foothills of the Himalayas north of Delhi **(FIG. 23–15)**. Painted around 1790, some 250 years later than the previous work, it shows the influence of Mughal naturalism on the later schools of Indian painting. The theme is again Krishna.

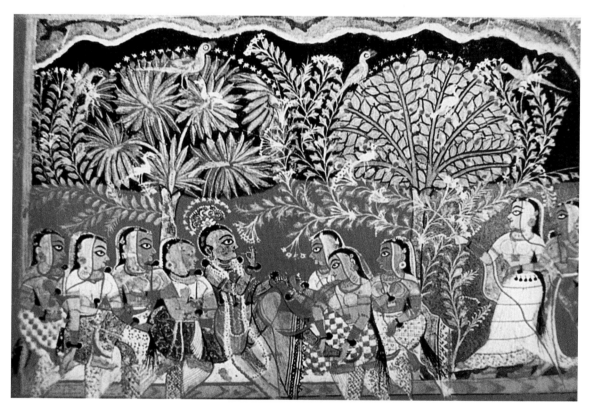

23–14 KRISHNA AND THE GOPIS
From the *Gita Govinda*, Rajasthan, India. Mughal period, Rajput, c. 1525–50. Gouache on paper, 4⅞ × 7½" (12.3 × 19 cm). Prince of Wales Museum, Bombay.

The lyrical poem *Gita Govinda*, by the poet-saint Jayadeva, was probably written in eastern India during the latter half of the twelfth century. The episode illustrated here occurs early in the relationship of Radha and Krishna, which in the poem is a metaphor for the connection between humans and god. The poem traces the progress of their love through separation, reconciliation, and fulfillment. Intensely sensuous imagery characterizes the entire poem, as in the final song, when Krishna welcomes Radha to his bed. (Narayana is the name of Vishnu in his role as cosmic creator.)

> Leave lotus footprints on my bed of tender shoots, loving Radha!
> Let my place be ravaged by your tender feet!
>   Narayana is faithful now. Love me Radhika!
> I stroke your feet with my lotus hand—you have come far.
> Set your golden anklet on my bed like the sun.
>   Narayana is faithful now. Love me Radhika!
> Consent to my love. Let elixir pour from your face!
> To end our separation I bare my chest of the silk that bars your breast.
>   Narayana is faithful now. Love me Radhika!
>
>   (Translated by Barbara Stoler Miller)

Wearing his peacock crown, garland of flowers, and yellow garment—all traditional iconography of Krishna-Vishnu—he returns to the village with his fellow cowherds and their cattle. All eyes are upon him as he plays his flute, said to enchant all who hear it. Women with water jugs on their heads turn to look; others lean from windows to watch and call out to him. We are drawn into this charming village scene by the diagonal movements of the cows as they surge through the gate and into the courtyard beyond. Pastel houses and walls create a sense of space, and in the distance we glimpse other villagers going about their work or peacefully sitting in their houses. A rim of dark trees softens the horizon, and an atmospheric sky completes the aura of enchanted naturalism. Again, all the figures are similar in

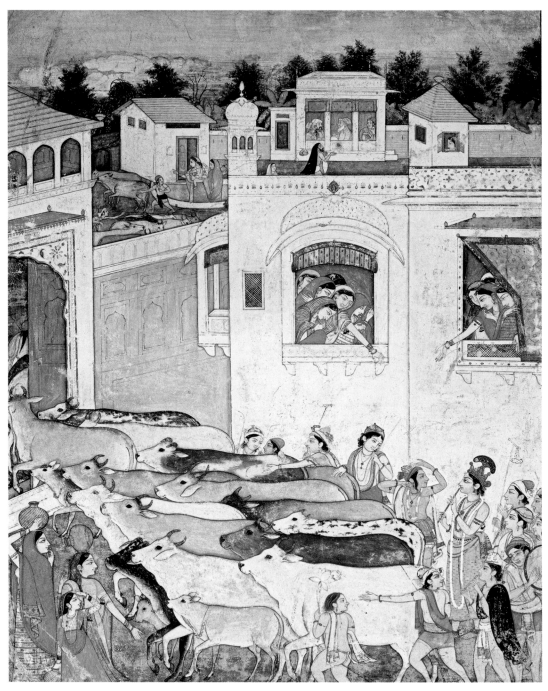

23–15 | **HOUR OF COWDUST**
From Punjab Hills, India. Mughal period, Rajput, Kangra school, c. 1790. Gouache on paper, 14¹⁵⁄₁₆ × 12³⁄₁₆″ (36 × 31.9 cm). Museum of Fine Arts, Boston.
Denman W. Ross Collection (22.683)

type, this time with a perfection of proportion and a gentle, lyrical movement that complement the idealism of the setting. The scene embodies the sublime purity and grace of the divine, which, as in so much Indian art, is evoked into our human world to coexist with us as one.

INDIA'S ENGAGEMENT WITH THE WEST

By the time *Hour of Cowdust* was painted, India's regional princes had reasserted themselves, and the vast Mughal Empire had shrunk to a small area around Delhi. At the same time, however, a new power, Britain, was making itself felt, inaugurating a markedly different period in Indian history.

British Colonial Period

First under the mercantile interests of the British East India Company in the seventeenth and eighteenth centuries, and then under the direct control of the British government as a part of the British Empire in the nineteenth century, India was brought forcefully into contact with the West and its culture. The political concerns of the British Empire extended even to the arts, especially architecture. Over the course of the nineteenth century, the great cities of India, such as Calcutta, Madras, and Bombay (now Mumbai), took on a European aspect as British architects built in the revivalist styles favored in England.

NEW DELHI.   In 1911 the British announced their intention to move the seat of government from Calcutta to a newly constructed Western-style capital city to be built at New Delhi. Two years later, Sir Edwin Lutyens (1869–1944) was appointed joint architect for New Delhi (with Herbert Baker), and was charged with laying out the new city and designing the Viceroy's House (now Rashtrapati Bhavan or President's House). Drawing inspiration from Classical antiquity—as well as from more recent urban models, such as Washington, D.C.—Lutyens sited the Viceroy's House as a focal point along with the triumphal arch that he designed as the All India War Memorial, now called the **INDIA GATE** (FIG. 23–16). In these works Lutyens sought to maintain the tradition of Classical architecture— he developed a "Delhi order" based on the Roman Doric—while incorporating massing, detail, and ornamentation derived from Indian architecture as well. The new capital was inaugurated in 1931.

MOTHER INDIA.   Far prior to Britain's consolidation of imperial power in New Delhi a new spirit asserting Indian independence and pan-Asiatic solidarity was awakening. For example, working near Calcutta, the painter Abanindranath Tagore (1871–1951)—nephew of the poet Rabindranath Tagore (1861–1941), who went on to win the Nobel Prize for Litera-

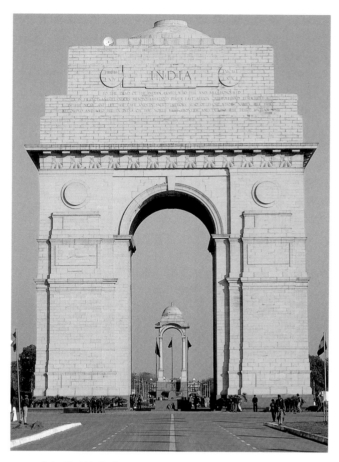

23–16 | Sir Edwin Lutyens **INDIA GATE**
(Originally the All India War Memorial), New Delhi. British Colonial Period, 20th century.

ture in 1913—deliberately rejected the medium of oil painting and the academic realism of Western art. Like the Nihonga artists of Japan (SEE FIG. 25–16) with whom he was in contact, Tagore strove to create a style that reflected his ethnic origins. In **BHARAT MATA (MOTHER INDIA)** he invents a nationalistic icon by using Hindu symbols while also drawing upon the format and techniques of Mughal painting (FIG. 23–17).

The Modern Period

In the wake of World War II, the imperial powers of Europe began to shed their colonial domains. The attainment of self-rule had been five long decades in the making, when finally—chastened by the non-violent example of Mahatma Gandhi (1869–1948)—the British Empire relinquished its "Jewel in the Crown," which was partitioned to form two modern nations: India and Pakistan.

MODERNISM AT CHANDIGARH.   After Indian independence in 1947, a modern, internationalist approach was welcomed by the exuberant young nation. One example of this new spirit is the **GANDHI BHAVAN** at Punjab University in Chandigarh, in North India (FIG. 23–18). Used for both lectures and prayer, the hall was designed in the late 1950s by Indian architect B. P. Mathur in collaboration with Pierre Jeanneret, cousin of the French Modernist architect Le Corbusier (Chapter 31), who had drawn plans for the new city at Chandigarh and whose version of the International Style had become influential in India.

The Gandhi Bhavan's three-part, pinwheel plan and abstract sculptural qualities reflect the modern vision of the International Style. Yet other factors speak to India's heritage. Its robust combinations of angles and curves recall ancient Sanskrit letterforms, while the pools surrounding the building evoke Mughal tombs, as well as the ritual-bathing pools of Hindu temples. Yet the abstract style is free of specific religious associations.

A MODERN INDIAN PAINTER. Artists working after Indian independence have continued to study and work abroad, but often draw upon India's distinctive literary and religious traditions as well as regional and folk art traditions. One example is Manjit Bawa (born 1941), who worked in Britain as a silkscreen artist before returning to India to settle in New Delhi. His distinctive canvases, painted meticulously in oil, juxtapose illusionistically modeled figures and animals against brilliantly colored backgrounds of flat, unmodulated color. The composite result, for example in **DHARMA AND THE GOD** (FIG. 23–19), brings a strikingly new interpretation to the heroic figures of Indian tradition.

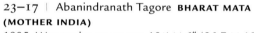

23–17 | Abanindranath Tagore **BHARAT MATA (MOTHER INDIA)**
1905. Watercolor on paper, 10½ × 6″ (26.7 × 15.3 cm). Rabindra Bharati Society, Calcutta.

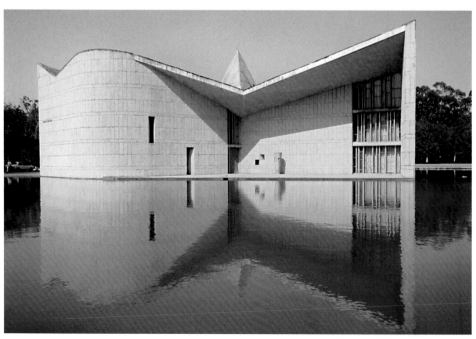

23–18 | B. P. Mathur and Pierre Jeanneret **GANDHI BHAVAN** Punjab University, Chandigarh, North India. Modern period, 1959–61.

THE ◉BJECT SPEAKS

LUXURY ARTS

The decorative arts of India represent the height of opulent luxury. Ornament embellishes even the invisible backs of pendants and bottoms of containers. Technically superb and crafted from precious materials, tableware, jewelry, furniture, and containers enhance the prestige of their owners and give visual pleasure as well. Metalwork and work in rock crystal, agate, and jade, carving in ivory, and intricate jewelry are all characteristic Indian arts. Because of the intrinsic value of their materials, however, pieces have been disassembled, melted down, and reworked, making the study of Indian luxury arts very difficult. Many pieces, like the carved ivory panel illustrated here, have no date or records of manufacture or ownership. And, like it, many such panels have been removed from a larger container or piece of furniture.

Frozen in timeless delight, carved in ivory against a golden ground, where openwork, stylized vines with spiky leaves, weave an elegant arabesque; loving couples dally under the arcades of a palace courtyard, the thin columns and cusped arches of which resemble the arcades of the palace of Tirumala Nayak (reigned 1623–59) in Madurai (Tamil Nadu). Their huge eyes under heavy brows suggest the intensity of their gaze, and the artist's choice of the profile view shows off their long noses and sensuously thick lips. Their hair is tightly controlled; the men have huge buns and the women, long braids hanging down their backs. Are they divine lovers? After all, Krishna lived and loved on earth among the cowherd maidens. Or are we observing scenes of courtly romance?

The rich jewelry and well-fed look of the couples indicate a high station in life. Men as well as women have voluptuous figures—rounded buttocks and thighs, abdomens hanging over jeweled belts, and sharply indented slim waists that emphasize seductive breasts. Their smooth flesh contrasts with the diaphanous fabrics that swath their plump legs, and their long arms and elegant gestures seem designed to show off their rich jewelry—bracelets, armbands, necklaces, huge earrings, and ribbons. Such amorous couples symbolize harmony as well as fertility.

The erotic imagery suggests that the panel illustrated here might have adorned a container for personal belongings such as jewelry, perfume, or cosmetics. In any event, the ivory relief is a brilliant example of South Indian secular arts.

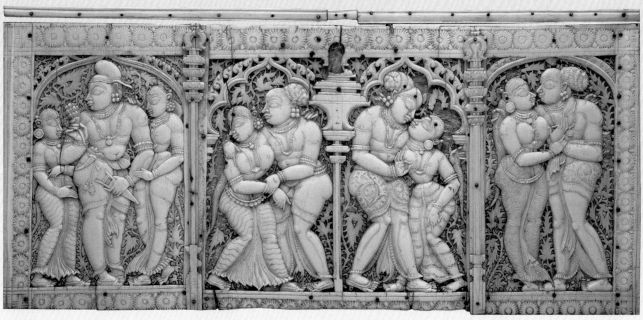

PANEL FROM A BOX
Nayak dynasty, Tamil Nadu, South India. Late 17th–18th century. Ivory backed with gilded paper, 6 × 12⅜ × ⅛″ (15.2 × 31.4 × 0.3 cm). Virginia Museum of Fine Arts.
The Arthur and Margaret Glasgow Fund. 80.171

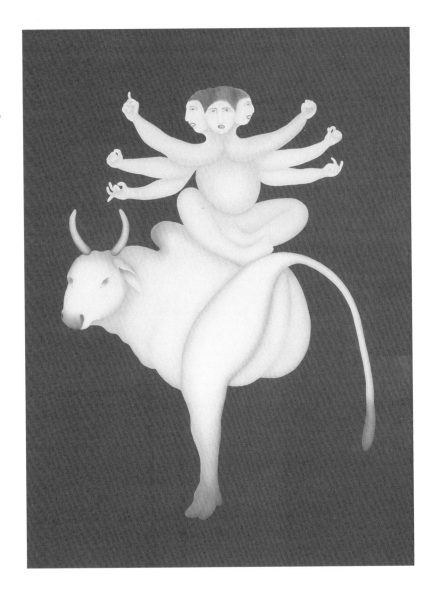

23—19 | Manjit Bawa **DHARMA AND THE GOD**
1984. Oil on canvas, 216 x 185.4 cm. Peabody
Essex Museum. Salem, Massachusetts.
The Davida and Chester Hervitz Collection

IN PERSPECTIVE

India's voluptuous figurative art, together with her rich religious traditions, had already reached a high point when the Mughals gained control of North India in the sixteenth century, and these traditions continued to thrive under regional patrons throughout the subcontinent. Within the Mughal empire, however, styles introduced from Persia mingled with these sensibilities, and Islamic ideals imparted a new emphasis to nonfigural art forms.

Under their Mughal patrons, architects developed vast building programs based on symmetrical plans and proportionate elevations. The pointed arches and complex vaults in their interiors were matched by the corresponding shapes of their open pavilions and exterior elements, thus providing graceful notes of repetition throughout the imperial complexes. Craftsmen embellished the surfaces of these buildings with intricate inlays of colored, hard stones portraying floral motifs inspired by nature's rhythms, thus perfecting the architectural whole to the pinnacle of refinement.

In the nineteenth century, as the British imposed their rule throughout India, Western academic painting attracted followers in the major cities. Gradually, British architects found opportunity in the construction of civic buildings in India, first in Calcutta and Bombay, and later culminating in the design of the modern capital at New Delhi.

Simultaneously, however, a move for independence from Britain, together with a search for modernity, led artists first to embrace Western artistic ideals and then to modify them, all the while aiming to identify and develop a tradition drawn from India's own history. As elsewhere in Asia, this search for a modern identity occasionally required the conscientious rejection of Western influences. On the one hand, modern Indian artists have drawn inspiration from sources in their "folk art," admired for its directness and the variety of its local characteristics. At the same time, India's sophisticated literary and religious traditions continue to inspire its art at the highest level.

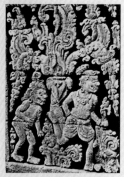

RAMAYANA SCENE,
CANDI PANATARAN
EARLY 14TH CENTURY

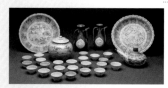

CERAMICS FROM THE HOI AN HOARD
LATE 15TH–EARLY 16TH CENTURY

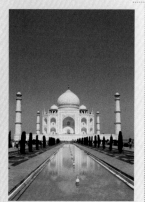

TAJ MAHAL
c. 1631–48

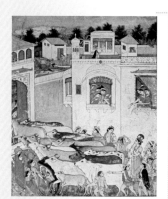

HOUR OF COWDUST
c. 1790

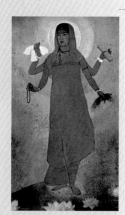

TAGORE
BHARAT MATA (MOTHER INDIA)
1905

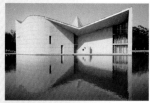

MATHUR AND JEANNERET
GANDHI BHAVAN
1959–61

ART OF SOUTH AND SOUTHEAST ASIA AFTER 1200

◄ **Fall of Pala Dynasty** c. 1199

◄ **Turkic Dynasties Begin to Rule Portions of Indian Subcontinent** c. 1206

◄ **Sukhothai Kingdom, Thailand** Mid 13th–late 14th century

◄ **Vijayanagar Dynasties** c. 1336–1565

◄ **Babur, First Mughal Emperor, Begins Rule** 1526

◄ **British East India Company Begins Activity in India** c. 1600

◄ **Unfied Mughal Empire in Northern India** c.1658

◄ **End of Mughal Empire** 1858
◄ **Peak of British Imperial Power in India** 1858–1947

◄ **Independent India** 1947

1200
1300
1400
1500
1600
1700
1800
1900
2000

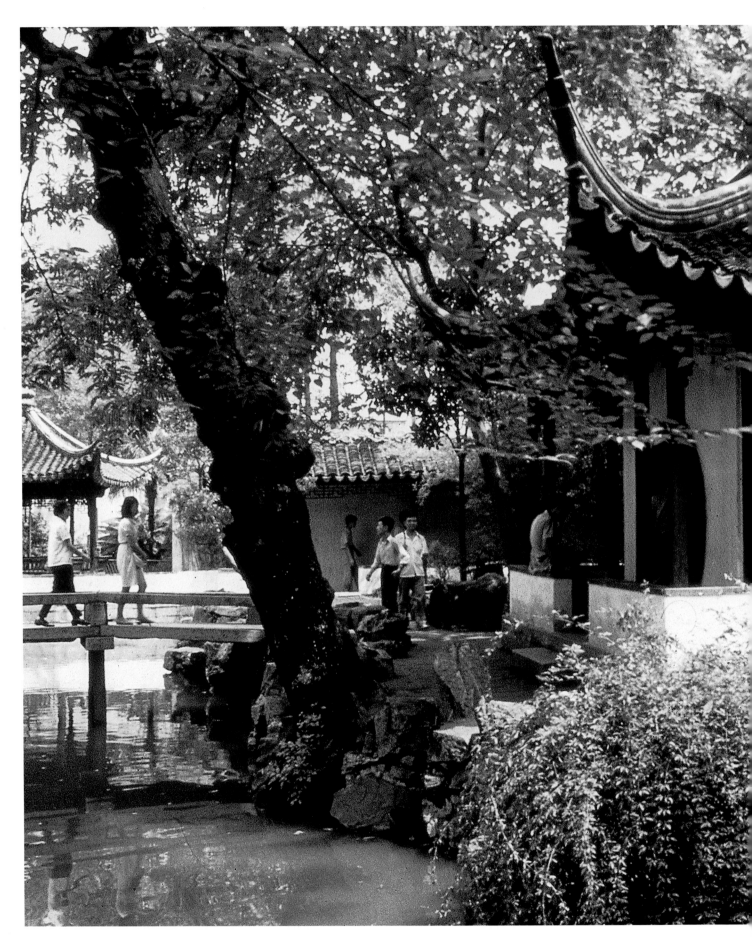

24–1 | **GARDEN OF THE CESSATION OF OFFICIAL LIFE** (also known as the Humble Administrator's Garden) Suzhou, Jiangsu. Ming dynasty, early 16th century.

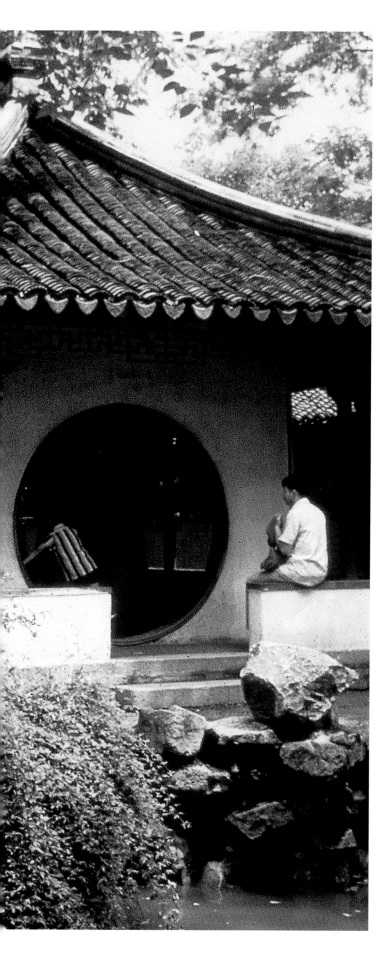

CHAPTER TWENTY-FOUR

CHINESE AND KOREAN ART AFTER 1279

24 Early in the sixteenth century, an official in Beijing, frustrated after serving in the capital for many years without promotion, returned to his home near Shanghai. Taking an ancient poem, "The Song of Leisurely Living," for his model, he began to build a garden. He called his retreat the Garden of the Cessation of Official Life (FIG. 24–1) to indicate that he had exchanged his career as a bureaucrat for a life of leisure. By leisure, he meant that he could now dedicate himself to calligraphy, poetry, and painting, the three arts dear to scholars in China.

The scholar class of imperial China was a phenomenon unique in the world, the product of an examination system designed to recruit the finest minds in the country for government service. Instituted during the Tang dynasty (618–907) and based on even earlier traditions, the civil service examinations were excruciatingly difficult, but for the tiny percentage that passed at the highest level, the rewards were prestige, position, power, and wealth. During the Song dynasty (960–1279) the examinations were expanded and regularized, and more than half of all government positions came to be filled by scholars.

Steeped in the classic texts of philosophy, literature, and history, China's scholars—often called *wenren* or literati—shared a common bond in education and outlook. Their lives typically moved between the philosophical poles of Confucianism and Daoism (see "Foundations of Chinese Culture," page 834). Following Confucianism, they became officials to fulfill their obligation to the world; pulled by Daoism, they retreated from society in order to come to terms with nature and the universe: to create a garden, to write poetry, to paint.

Under a series of remarkably cultivated emperors, the literati reached the height of their influence during the Song dynasty. Their world was about to change dramatically, however, with lasting results for Chinese art.

THE MONGOL INVASIONS

At the beginning of the thirteenth century the Mongols, a nomadic people from the steppes north of China, began to amass an empire. Led first by Jenghiz Khan (c. 1162–1227), then by his sons and grandsons, they swept westward into central Europe and overran Islamic lands from Central Asia through present-day Iraq. To the east, they quickly captured northern China, and in 1279, led by Kublai Khan, they conquered southern China as well. Grandson of the mighty Jenghiz, Kublai proclaimed himself emperor of China and founder of the Yuan dynasty (1279–1368).

The Mongol invasions were traumatic, and their effect on China was long lasting. During the Song dynasty, China had grown increasingly introspective. Rejecting foreign ideas and influences, intellectuals had focused on defining the qualities that constituted true "Chinese-ness." They drew a clear distinction between their own people, whom they characterized as gentle, erudite, and sophisticated, and the "barbarians" outside China's borders, whom they regarded as crude, wild, and uncivilized. Now, faced with the reality of barbarian occupation, China's inward gaze intensified in spiritual resistance. For centuries to come, long after the Mongols had gone, leading scholars continued to seek intellectually more challenging, philosophically more profound, and artistically more subtle expressions of all that could be identified as authentically Chinese.

YUAN DYNASTY

The Mongols established their capital in the northern city now known as Beijing (MAP 24–1). The cultural centers of China, however, remained the great cities of the south, where the Song court had been located for the previous 150 years. Combined with the tensions of Yuan rule, this separation of China's political and cultural centers created a new situation dynamic in the arts.

Throughout most of Chinese history, the imperial court had set the tone for artistic taste; artisans attached to the court produced architecture, paintings, gardens, and objects of jade, lacquer, ceramics, and silk especially for imperial use. Over the centuries, painters and calligraphers gradually moved higher up the social scale, for these "arts of the brush" were often practiced by scholars and even emperors, whose high status reflected positively on whatever interested them. With the establishment of an imperial painting academy during the Song dynasty, painters finally achieved a status equal to that of court officials. For the literati, painting came to be grouped with **calligraphy** and poetry as the trio of accomplishments suited to members of the cultural elite.

But while the literati elevated the status of painting by virtue of practicing it, they also began to develop their own ideas of what painting should be. Not needing to earn an income from their art, they cultivated an amateur ideal in which personal expression counted for more than "mere" professional skill. They created for themselves a status as artists totally separate from and superior to professional painters, whose art they felt was inherently compromised, since it was done to please others, and impure, since it was tainted by money.

The conditions of Yuan rule now encouraged a clear distinction between court taste, ministered to by professional artists and artisans, and literati taste. The Yuan dynasty continued the imperial role as patron of the arts, commissioning buildings, murals, gardens, paintings, and decorative arts. Western visitors such as the Italian Marco Polo were impressed by the magnificence of the Yuan court (see "Marco Polo," page 836). But scholars, profoundly alienated from the new government, took little notice of these accomplishments, and thus wrote nothing about them. Nor

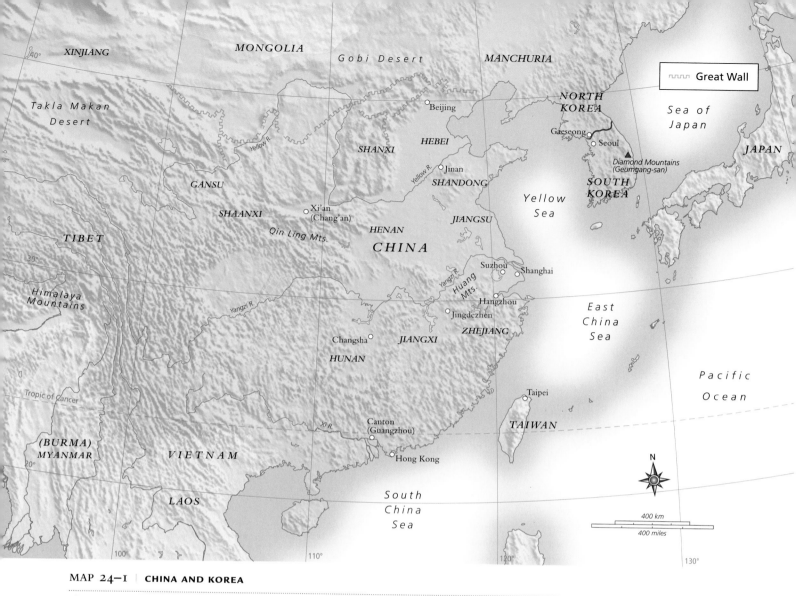

MAP 24–1 | **CHINA AND KOREA**

The Qinling Mountains divide China into northern and southern regions with distinctively different climates and cultures.

did Yuan rulers have much use for scholars, especially those from the south. The civil service examinations were abolished, and the highest government positions were bestowed, instead, on Mongols and their foreign allies. Scholars now tended to turn inward, to search for solutions of their own and to try to express themselves in personal and symbolic terms.

ZHAO MENGFU. Typical of this trend was Zhao Mengfu (1254–1322), a descendant of the imperial line of Song. Unlike many scholars of his time, he eventually chose to serve the Yuan government and was made a high official. A painter, calligrapher, and poet, all of the first rank, Zhao was especially known for his carefully rendered paintings of horses. But he also cultivated another manner, most famous in his landmark painting **AUTUMN COLORS ON THE QIAO AND HUA MOUNTAINS** (FIG. 24–2).

Zhao painted this work for a friend whose ancestors came from Jinan, the present-day capital of Shandong province, and the painting supposedly depicts the landscape there. Yet the mountains and trees are not painted in the accomplished naturalism of Zhao's own time but rather in the archaic yet oddly elegant manner of the earlier Tang dynasty (618–907). The Tang dynasty was a great era in Chinese history, when the country was both militarily strong and culturally vibrant. Through his painting Zhao evoked a nostalgia not only for his friend's distant homeland but also for China's past.

This educated taste for the "spirit of antiquity" became an important aspect of **literati painting** in later periods. Also typical of literati taste are the unassuming brushwork, the subtle colors sparingly used (many literati paintings forgo color altogether), the use of landscape to convey personal meaning, and even the intended audience—a close friend. The literati did not paint for public display but for each other. They favored small formats such as **handscrolls, hanging scrolls,** or **album leaves** (book pages), which could easily be shown to friends or shared at small gatherings (see "Formats of Chinese Painting," page 837).

Art and Its Context
FOUNDATIONS OF CHINESE CULTURE

Chinese culture is distinguished by its long and continuous development. Between 6000 and 2000 BCE a variety of Neolithic cultures flourished across China. Through long interaction these cultures became increasingly similar and they eventually gave rise to the three Bronze Age dynastic states with which Chinese history traditionally begins: the Xia, the Shang (c. 1700–1100 BCE), and the Zhou (1100–221 BCE).

The Shang developed traditions of casting ritual vessels in bronze, working jade in ceremonial shapes, and writing consistently in scripts that directly evolved into the modern Chinese written language. Society was stratified, and the ruling group maintained its authority in part by claiming power as intermediaries between the human and spirit worlds. Under the Zhou a feudal society developed, with nobles related to the king ruling over numerous small states.

During the latter part of the Zhou dynasty, states began to vie for supremacy through intrigue and increasingly ruthless warfare. The collapse of social order profoundly influenced China's first philosophers, who largely concerned themselves with the pragmatic question of how to bring about a stable society.

In 221 BCE, rulers of the state of Qin triumphed over the remaining states, unifying China as an empire for the first time. The Qin created the mechanisms of China's centralized bureaucracy, but their rule was harsh and the dynasty was quickly overthrown. During the ensuing Han dynasty (206 BCE–220 CE), China at last knew peace and prosperity. Confucianism was made the official state ideology, in the process assuming the form and force of a religion. Developed from the thought of Confucius (551–479 BCE), one of the many philosophers of the Zhou, Confucianism is an ethical system for the management of society based on establishing correct relationships among people. Providing a counterweight was Daoism, which also came into its own during the Han dynasty. Based on the thought of Laozi, a possibly legendary contemporary of Confucius, and the

philosopher Zhuangzi (369–286 BCE), Daoism is a view of life that seeks to harmonize the individual with the *Dao*, or Way, the process of the universe. Confucianism and Daoism have remained central to Chinese thought—the one addressing the public realm of duty and conformity, the other the private world of individualism and creativity.

Following the collapse of the Han dynasty, China experienced a centuries-long period of disunity (220–589 CE). Invaders from the north and west established numerous kingdoms and dynasties, while a series of six precarious Chinese dynasties held sway in the south. Buddhism, which had begun to filter over trade routes from India during the Han dynasty, now spread widely. The period also witnessed the economic and cultural development of the south (all previous dynasties had ruled from the north).

China was reunited under the Sui dynasty (581–618 CE), which quickly fell to the Tang (618–907 CE), one of the most successful dynasties in Chinese history. Strong and confident, Tang China fascinated and, in turn, was fascinated by the cultures around it. Caravans streamed across Central Asia to the capital, Chang'an, then the largest city in the world. Japan and Korea sent thousands of students to study Chinese culture, and Buddhism reached the height of its influence before a period of persecution signaled the start of its decline.

The mood of the Song dynasty (960–1279 CE) was quite different. The martial vigor of the Tang gave way to a culture of increasing refinement and sophistication, and Tang openness to foreign influences was replaced by a conscious cultivation of China's own traditions. In art, landscape painting emerged as the most esteemed genre, capable of expressing both philosophical and personal concerns. With the fall of the north to invaders in 1126, the Song court set up a new capital in the south, which became the cultural and economic center of the country.

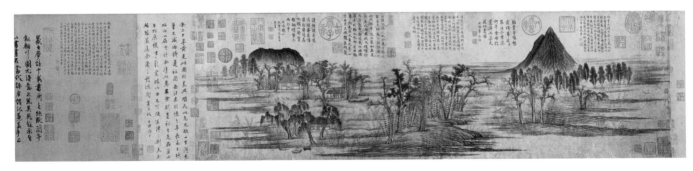

24–2 | Zhao Mengfu **AUTUMN COLORS ON THE QIAO AND HUA MOUNTAINS**
Yuan dynasty, 1296. Handscroll, ink and color on paper, 11¼ × 36¾" (28.6 × 9.3 cm).
National Palace Museum, Taipei, Republic of China.

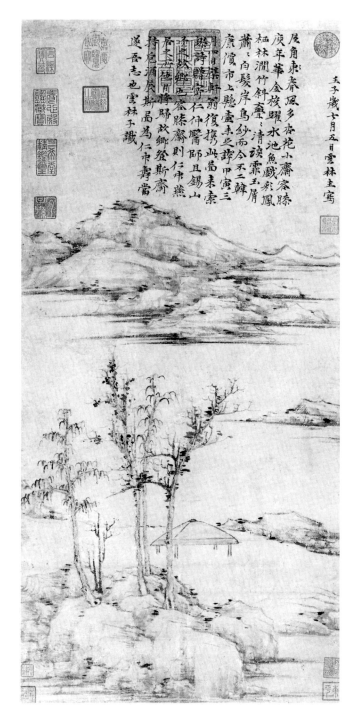

24–3 | Ni Zan **THE RONGXI STUDIO**
Yuan dynasty, 1372. Hanging scroll, ink on paper, height 29⅜″ (74.6 cm). National Palace Museum, Taipei, Republic of China.

The idea that a painting is not done to capture a likeness or to satisfy others but is executed freely and carelessly for the artist's own amusement is at the heart of the literati aesthetic. Ni Zan once wrote this comment on a painting: "What I call painting does not exceed the joy of careless sketching with a brush. I do not seek formal likeness but do it simply for my own amusement. Recently I was rambling about and came to a town. The people asked for my pictures, but wanted them exactly according to their own desires and to represent a specific occasion. [When I could not satisfy them,] they went away insulting, scolding, and cursing in every possible way. What a shame! But how can one scold a eunuch for not growing a beard?" (cited in Bush and Shih, page 266).

Sequencing Events
CHINESE DYNASTIES AFTER 1279

1279–1368	Yuan Dynasty
1368–1644	Ming Dynasty
1644–1911	Qing Dynasty
1911–Present	Modern Period

NI ZAN. Of the considerable number of Yuan painters who took up Zhao's ideas, several became models for later generations. One such was Ni Zan (1301–74), whose most famous surviving painting is **THE RONGXI STUDIO** (FIG. 24–3). Done entirely in ink, the painting depicts the lake region in Ni's home district. Mountains, rocks, trees, and a pavilion are sketched with a minimum of detail using a dry brush technique—a technique in which the brush is not fully loaded with ink but rather about to run out, so that white paper "breathes" through the ragged strokes. The result is a painting with a light touch and a sense of simplicity and purity. Literati styles were believed to reflect the painter's personality. Ni's spare, dry style became associated with a noble spirit, and many later painters adopted it or paid homage to it.

Ni Zan was one of those eccentrics whose behavior has become legendary in the history of Chinese art. In his early years he was one of the richest men in the region, the owner of a large estate. His pride and his aloofness from daily affairs often got him into trouble with the authorities. His cleanliness was notorious. In addition to washing himself several times daily, he also ordered his servants to wash the trees in his garden and to clean the furniture after his guests had left. He was said to be so unworldly that late in life he gave away most of his possessions and lived as a hermit in a boat, wandering on rivers and lakes.

Whether these stories are true or not, they were important elements of Ni's legacy to later painters, for Ni's life as well as his art served as a model. The painting of the literati was bound up with certain views about what constituted an appropriate life. The ideal, as embodied by Ni Zan and others, was of a brilliantly gifted scholar whose spirit was too refined for the dusty world of government service and who thus preferred to live as a recluse, or as one who had retired after having become frustrated by a brief stint as an official.

MING DYNASTY

The founder of the next dynasty, the Ming (1368–1644), came from a family of poor uneducated peasants. As he rose through the ranks in the army, he enlisted the help of scholars to gain

China under Kublai Khan was one of four Mongol khanates that together extended west into present-day Iraq and through Russia to the borders of Poland and Hungary. For roughly a century, travelers moved freely across this vast expanse, making the era one of unprecedented cross-cultural exchange. Diplomats, missionaries, merchants, and adventurers flocked to the Yuan court, and Chinese envoys were dispatched to the West. The most celebrated European traveler of the time was a Venetian named Marco Polo (c. 1254-1324), whose descriptions of his travels were for several centuries the only firsthand account of China available in Europe.

Marco Polo was still in his teens when he set out for China in 1271. He traveled with his uncle and father, both merchants, bearing letters for Kublai Khan from Pope Gre-

gory X. After a four-year journey the Polos arrived at last in Beijing. Marco became a favorite of the emperor and spent the next seventeen years in his service, during which time he traveled extensively throughout China. He eventually returned home in 1295.

Imprisoned later during a war between Venice and Genoa, rival Italian city-states, Marco Polo passed the time by dictating an account of his experiences to a fellow prisoner. The resulting book, *A Description of the World*, has fascinated generations of readers with its depiction of prosperous and sophisticated lands in the East. Translated into almost every European language, it was an important influence in stimulating further exploration. When Columbus set sail across the Atlantic in 1492, one of the places he hoped to find was a country Marco Polo called Zipangu—Japan.

power and solidify his following. Once he had driven the Mongols from Beijing and firmly established himself as emperor, however, he grew to distrust intellectuals. His rule was despotic, even ruthless. Throughout the nearly 300 years of Ming rule, most emperors shared his attitude, so although the civil service examinations were reinstated, scholars remained alienated from the government they were trained to serve.

Court and Professional Painting

The contrast between the luxurious world of the court and the austere ideals of the literati continued through the Ming dynasty.

A typical example of Ming court taste is **HUNDREDS OF BIRDS ADMIRING THE PEACOCKS**, a large painting on silk by Yin Hong, an artist active during the late fifteenth and early sixteenth centuries (**FIG. 24–4**). A pupil of some well-known courtiers, Yin most probably served in the court at Beijing. The painting is an example of the birds-and-flowers **genre**, which had been popular with artists of the Song academy. Here the subject takes on symbolic meaning, with the homage of the birds to the peacocks representing the homage of court officials to the emperor. The style goes back to Song academy models, although the large format and multiplication of details are traits of the Ming.

A related, yet bolder and less constrained, landscape style was also popular during this period. Sometimes called the Zhe style since its roots were in Hangzhou, Zhejiang province, where the Southern Song court had been located, this manner especially influenced painters in Korea and Japan. A major

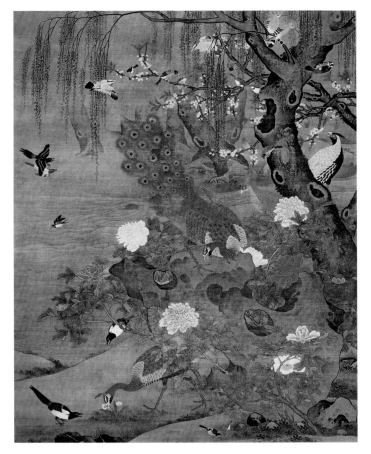

24–4 | Yin Hong **HUNDREDS OF BIRDS ADMIRING THE PEACOCKS**
Ming dynasty, late 15th–early 16th century. Hanging scroll, ink and color on silk, 7'10½" × 6'5" (2.4 × 1.96 m). The Cleveland Museum of Art.
Purchase from the J. H. Wade Fund, 74.31

Technique
FORMATS OF CHINESE PAINTING

With the exception of large wall paintings that typically decorated palaces, temples, and tombs, most Chinese paintings were done in ink and water-based colors on silk or paper. Finished works were generally mounted as **handscrolls, hanging scrolls**, or leaves in an **album**.

An album comprises a set of paintings of identical size mounted in a book. (A single painting from an album is called an **album leaf**.) The paintings in an album are usually related in subject, such as various views of a famous site or a series of scenes glimpsed on one trip.

Album-sized paintings might also be mounted as a handscroll, a horizontal format generally about 12 inches high and anywhere from a few feet to dozens of feet long. More typically, however, a handscroll would be a single continuous painting. Handscrolls were not meant to be displayed all at once, the way they are commonly presented today in museums. Rather, they were unrolled only occasionally, to be savored in much the same spirit as we might view a favorite film. Placing the scroll on a flat surface such as a table, a viewer would unroll it a foot or two at a time, moving gradually through the entire scroll from right to left, lingering over favorite details. The scroll was then rolled up and returned to its box until the next viewing.

Like handscrolls, hanging scrolls were not displayed permanently but were taken out for a limited time—a day, a week, a season. Unlike a handscroll, however, the painting on a hanging scroll was viewed as a whole, unrolled and put up on a wall,

with the roller at the lower end acting as a weight to help the scroll hang flat. Although some hanging scrolls are quite large, they are still fundamentally intimate works, not intended for display in a public place.

Creating a scroll was a time-consuming and exacting process accomplished by a professional mounter. The painting was first backed with paper to strengthen it. Next, strips of paper-backed silk were pasted to the top, bottom, and sides, framing the painting on all four sides. Additional silk pieces were added to extend the scroll horizontally or vertically, depending on the format. The assembled scroll was then backed again with paper and fitted with a half-round dowel, or wooden rod, at the top of a hanging scroll or on the right end of a handscroll, with ribbons for hanging and tying, and with a wooden roller at the other end. Hanging scrolls were often fashioned from several patterns of silk, and a variety of piecing formats were developed and codified. On a handscroll, a painting was generally preceded by a panel giving the work's title and often followed by a long panel bearing **colophons**—inscriptions related to the work, such as poems in its praise or comments by its owners over the centuries. A scroll would be remounted periodically to better preserve it, and colophons and inscriptions would be preserved in each remounting. **Seals** added another layer of interest. A treasured scroll often bears not only the seal of its maker but also those of collectors and admirers through the centuries.

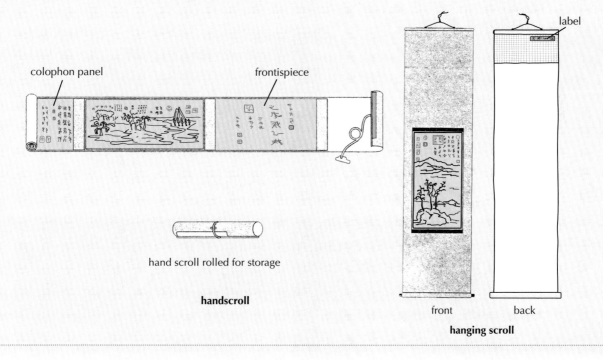

colophon panel

frontispiece

label

hand scroll rolled for storage

handscroll

front   back

hanging scroll

example is **RETURNING HOME LATE FROM A SPRING OUTING** (**FIG. 24–5**), unsigned but attributed to Dai Jin (1388–1462). This work reflects the Chinese sources for such artists as An Gyeon (SEE FIG. 24–17) and Sesshu (SEE FIG. 25–3).

QIU YING. The preeminent professional painter in the Ming period was Qiu Ying (1494–1552), who lived in Suzhou, a prosperous southern city. He inspired generations of imitators with exceptional works, such as a long handscroll

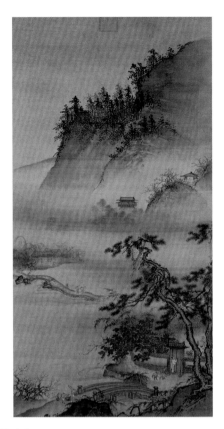

24–5 | Dai Jin **RETURNING HOME LATE FROM A SPRING OUTING**
Ming dynasty. Hanging scroll, ink on silk, 167.9 × 83.1 cm. National Palace Museum, Taipei, Republic of China.

known as **SPRING DAWN IN THE HAN PALACE** (FIGS. 24–6, 24–7). The painting is based on Tang-dynasty depictions of women in the court of the Han dynasty (206 BCE–220 CE). While in the service of a well-known collector, Qiu Ying had the opportunity to study many Tang paintings, whose artists usually concentrated on the figures, leaving out the background entirely. Qiu's graceful and elegant figures—although modeled after those in Tang works—are portrayed in a setting of palace buildings, engaging in such pastimes as chess, music, calligraphy, and painting. With its antique subject matter, refined technique, and flawless taste in color and composition, *Spring Dawn in the Han Palace* brought professional painting to a new high point.

Decorative Arts

Qiu Ying painted to satisfy his patrons in Suzhou. The cities of the south were becoming wealthy, and newly rich merchants collected paintings, antiques, and art objects. The court, too, was prosperous and patronized the arts on a lavish scale. In such a setting, the decorative arts thrived.

MING BLUE-AND-WHITE WARES. The Ming became famous the world over for its exquisite ceramics, especially **porcelain** (see "The Secret of Porcelain," page 840). The imperial **kilns** in Jingdezhen, in Jiangxi province, became the most renowned center for porcelain not only in all of China, but in all the world. Particularly noteworthy are the blue-and-white wares

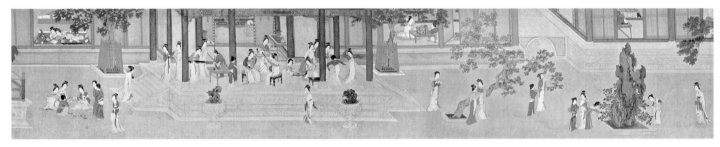

24–6 | Qiu Ying **SECTION OF SPRING DAWN IN THE HAN PALACE**
Ming dynasty, first half of the 16th century. Handscroll, ink and color on silk, 1′ × 18′13⁄16″ (0.30 × 5.7 m). National Palace Museum, Taipei, Republic of China.

24–7 | **DETAIL OF SECTION OF SPRING DAWN IN THE HAN PALACE**

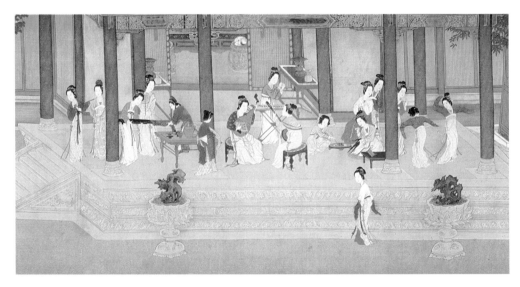

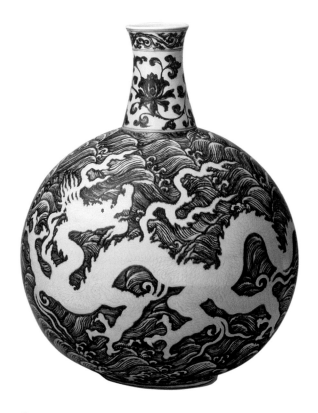

24—8 | FLASK
Ming dynasty, 1426–35. Porcelain with decoration painted in underglaze cobalt blue. Collection of the Palace Museum, Beijing.

Dragons have featured prominently in Chinese folklore from earliest times—Neolithic examples have been found painted on pottery and carved in jade. In Bronze Age China, dragons came to be associated with powerful and sudden manifestations of nature, such as wind, thunder, and lightning. At the same time, dragons became associated with superior beings such as virtuous rulers and sages. With the emergence of China's first firmly established empire during the Han dynasty, the dragon was appropriated as an imperial symbol, and it remained so throughout Chinese history. Dragon sightings were duly recorded and considered auspicious. Yet even the Son of Heaven could not monopolize the dragon. During the Tang and Song dynasties the practice arose of painting pictures of dragons to pray for rain, and for Chan (Zen) Buddhists, the dragon was a symbol of sudden enlightenment.

produced there during the ten-year reign of the ruler known as the Xuande Emperor (ruled 1426–35), such as the flask in FIGURE 24–8. The subtle shape, the refined yet vigorous decoration of dragons writhing above the sea, and the flawless **glazing** embody the high achievement of Ming artisans.

Architecture and City Planning

Centuries of warfare and destruction have left very few Chinese architectural monuments intact. The most important remaining example of traditional Chinese architecture is the Forbidden City, the imperial palace compound in Beijing, whose principal buildings were constructed during the Ming dynasty (FIG. 24–9).

THE FORBIDDEN CITY. The basic plan of Beijing was the work of the Mongols, who laid out their capital city accord-

ing to traditional Chinese principles. City planning began early in China—in the seventh century, in the case of Chang'an (present-day Xi'an), the capital of the Sui and Tang emperors. The walled city of Chang'an was laid out on a rectangular grid, with evenly spaced streets that ran north-south and east-west. At the northern end stood a walled imperial complex.

Beijing, too, was developed as a walled, rectangular city with streets laid out in a grid. The palace enclosure occupied the center of the northern part of the city, which was reserved for the Mongols. Chinese lived in the southern third of the city. Later, Ming and Qing emperors preserved this division, with officials living in the northern or Inner City and commoners living in the southern or Outer City. Under the third Ming emperor, Yongle (ruled 1403–24), the Forbidden City was rebuilt as we see it today.

The approach to the Forbidden City was impressive. Visitors entered through the Meridian Gate, a monumental gate with side wings (at the center in FIG. 24–9). Inside the Meridian Gate a broad courtyard is crossed by a bow-shaped waterway that is spanned by five arched marble bridges. At the opposite end of the courtyard is the Gate of Supreme Harmony, opening onto an even larger courtyard that houses three ceremonial halls raised on a broad platform. First is the Hall of Supreme Harmony, where, on the most important state occasions, the emperor was seated on his throne, facing south. Beyond is the smaller Hall of Central Harmony, then the Hall of Protecting Harmony. Behind these vast ceremonial spaces, still on the central axis, is the inner court, again with a progression of three buildings, this time more intimate in scale. In its balance and symmetry the plan of the Forbidden City reflects ancient Chinese beliefs about the harmony of the universe, and it emphasizes the emperor's role as the Son of Heaven, whose duty was to maintain the cosmic order from his throne in the middle of the world.

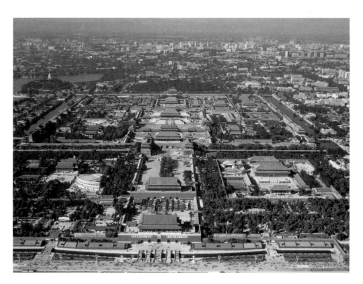

24—9 | THE FORBIDDEN CITY
Now the Palace Museum, Beijing
Mostly Ming dynasty. View from the southwest.

Technique
THE SECRET OF PORCELAIN

Marco Polo, it is said, was the one who named a new type of ceramic he found in China. Its translucent purity reminded him of the smooth whiteness of the cowry shell, *porcellana* in Italian. **Porcelain** is made from kaolin, an extremely refined white clay, and petuntse, a variety of the mineral feldspar. When properly combined and fired at a sufficiently high temperature, the two materials fuse into a glasslike, translucent ceramic that is far stronger than it looks.

Porcelaneous stoneware, fired at lower temperatures, was known in China by the seventh century, but true porcelain was perfected during the Song dynasty. To create blue-and-white porcelain such as the flask in FIGURE 24-8, blue pigment was made from cobalt oxide, finely ground and mixed with water. The decoration was painted directly onto the unfired porcelain vessel, then a layer of clear glaze was applied over it. (In this technique, known as *underglaze painting,* the pattern is painted beneath the glaze.) After firing, the piece emerged from the kiln with a clear blue design set sharply against a snowy white background.

Entranced with the exquisite properties of porcelain, European potters tried for centuries to duplicate it. The technique was finally discovered in 1709 by Johann Friedrich Böttger in Dresden, Germany, who tried—but failed—to keep it a secret.

The Literati Aesthetic

In the south, particularly in the district of Suzhou, literati painting, associated with the educated men who served the court as government officials, remained the dominant trend. One of the major literati figures from the Ming period is Shen Zhou (1427–1509), who had no desire to enter government service and spent most of his life in Suzhou. He studied the Yuan painters avidly and tried to recapture their spirit in such works as *Poet on a Mountaintop* (see "Poet on a Mountaintop," page 842). Although the style of the painting recalls the freedom and simplicity of Ni Zan (SEE FIG. 24–3), the motif of a poet surveying the landscape from a mountain plateau is Shen's creation.

LITERATI INFLUENCE ON FURNITURE, ARCHITECTURE, AND GARDEN DESIGN. The taste of the literati came to influence furniture and architecture, and especially the design of gardens. Chinese furniture made for domestic use reached the height of its development in the sixteenth and seventeenth centuries. Characteristic of Chinese furniture, the chair in FIGURE 24–10 is constructed without the use of glue or nails. Instead, pieces fit together based on the principle of the **mortise-and-tenon joint**, in which a projecting element (tenon) on one piece fits snugly into a cavity (mortise) on another. Each piece of the chair is carved, as opposed to being bent or twisted, and the joints are crafted with great precision. The patterns of the wood grain provide subtle interest unmarred by any painting or other embellishment. The style, like that of Chinese architecture, is one of simplicity, clarity, symmetry, and balance. The effect is formal and dignified but natural and simple—virtues central to the Chinese view of proper human conduct as well.

The art of landscape gardening also reached a high point during the Ming dynasty, as many literati surrounded their homes with gardens. The most famous gardens were created in the southern cities of the Yangzi River (Chang Jiang) delta, especially in Suzhou. The largest surviving garden of the era is the Garden of the Cessation of Official Life, with which this chapter opened (SEE FIG. 24–1). Although modified and reconstructed many times through the centuries, it still reflects many of the basic ideas of the original Ming owner. About a third of the garden is devoted to water through artificially created brooks and ponds. The landscape is dotted with pavilions, kiosks, libraries, studios, and corridors. Many

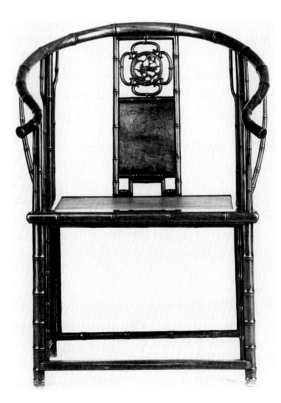

24–10 ARMCHAIR
Ming dynasty, 16th–17th century. Huanghuali wood (hardwood), 39⅜ × 27¼ x 20″ (100 × 69.2 x 50.8 cm). The Nelson-Atkins Museum of Art, Kansas City, Missouri.
Purchase, Nelson Trust (46-78/1)

of the buildings have poetic names, such as Rain Listening Pavilion and Bridge of the Small Flying Rainbow.

DONG QICHANG, LITERATI THEORIST.   The ideas underlying literati painting found their most influential expression in the writings of Dong Qichang (1555–1636). A high official in the late Ming period, Dong Qichang embodied the literati tradition as poet, calligrapher, and painter. He developed a view of Chinese art history that divided painters into two opposing schools, northern and southern. The names have nothing to do with geography—a painter from the south might well be classed as northern—but reflect a parallel Dong drew to the northern and southern schools of Chan (Zen) Buddhism in China. The southern school of Chan, founded by the eccentric monk Huineng (638–713), was unorthodox, radical, and innovative; the northern school was traditional and conservative. Similarly, Dong's two schools of painters represented progressive and conservative traditions. In Dong's view the conservative northern school was dominated by professional painters whose academic, often decorative, style emphasized technical skill. In contrast, the progressive southern school preferred ink to color and free brushwork to meticulous detail. Its painters aimed for poetry and personal expression. In promoting this theory, Dong gave his unlimited sanction to literati painting, which he positioned as the culmination of the southern school, and he fundamentally influenced the way the Chinese viewed their own tradition.

Dong Qichang summarized his views on the proper training for literati painters in the famous statement "Read ten thousand books and walk ten thousand miles." By this he meant that one must first study the works of the great masters, then follow "heaven and earth," the world of nature. These studies prepared the way for greater self-expression through brush and ink, the goal of literati painting. Dong's views rested on an awareness that a painting of scenery and the actual scenery are two very different things. The excellence of a painting does not lie in its degree of resemblance to reality—that gap can never be bridged—but in its expressive power. The expressive language of painting is inherently abstract and lies in its nature as a construction of brushstrokes. For example, in a painting of a rock, the rock itself is not expressive; rather, the brushstrokes that add up to a "rock" are expressive.

With such thinking Dong brought painting close to the realm of calligraphy, which had long been considered the highest form of artistic expression in China. More than a thousand years before Dong's time, a body of critical terms and theories had evolved to discuss calligraphy in light of the formal and expressive properties of brushwork and composition. Dong introduced some of these terms—ideas such as opening and closing, rising and falling, and void and solid—to the criticism of painting.

Sequencing Works of Art

1617	**Dong Qichang.** *The Qingbian Mountains,* Chinese
1693	**Wang Hui:** *A Thousand Peaks and Myriad Ravines,* Chinese
c. 1700	**Shitao.** *Landscape,* Chinese
1734	**Jeong Seon.** *Panoramic View of the Diamond Mountains (Geumgang-san),* Korean
Late 18th century	**Sin Yunbok.** *Picnic at the Lotus Pond,* Korean

Dong's theories are fully embodied in his painting **THE QINGBIAN MOUNTAINS (FIG. 24–11)**. According to Dong's own inscription, the painting was based on a work by the tenth-century artist Dong Yuan. Dong Qichang's style, however, is quite different from the master's he admired. Although there is some indication of foreground, middle ground, and distant

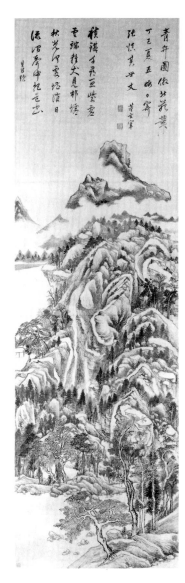

24–11 | Dong Qichang
THE QINGBIAN MOUNTAINS
Ming dynasty, 1617. Hanging scroll, ink on paper, 21′8″ × 7′4⅜″ (6.72 × 2.25 m). The Cleveland Museum of Art.
Leonard C. Hanna, Jr., Fund (1980.10)

POET ON A MOUNTAINTOP

In earlier landscape paintings, human figures were typically shown dwarfed by the grandeur of nature. Travelers might be seen scuttling along a narrow path by a stream, while overhead towered mountains whose peaks conversed with the clouds and whose heights were inaccessible. Here, the poet has climbed the mountain and dominates the landscape. Even the clouds are beneath him. Before his gaze, a poem hangs in the air, as though he were projecting his thoughts.

The poem, composed by Shen Zhou himself, and written in his distinctive hand, reads:

White clouds like a scarf enfold the mountain's waist;
Stone steps hang in space—a long, narrow path.
Alone, leaning on my cane, I gaze intently at the scene,
And feel like answering the murmuring brook with the music of my flute.

(Translation by Jonathan Chaves, *The Chinese Painter as Poet*, New York, 2000, page 46.)

Shen Zhou composed the poem and wrote the inscription at the time he painted the album. The style of the calligraphy, like the style of the painting, is informal, relaxed, and straightforward—qualities that were believed to reflect the artist's character and personality.

The painting reflects Ming philosophy, which held that the mind, not the physical world, was the basis for reality. With its perfect synthesis of poetry, calligraphy, and painting, and with its harmony of mind and landscape, *Poet on a Mountaintop* represents the essence of Ming literati painting.

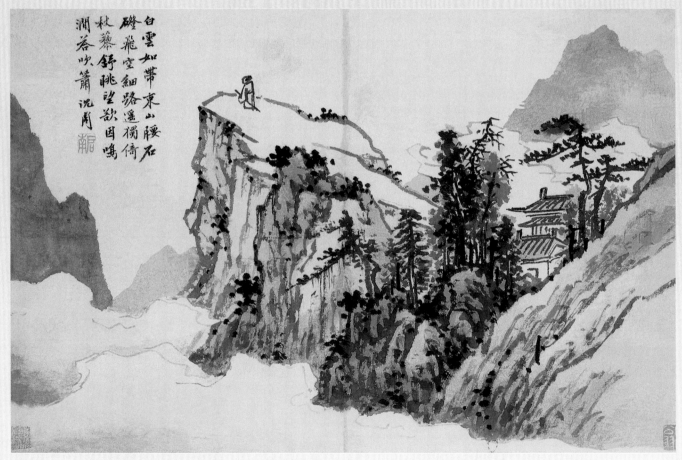

Shen Zhou **POET ON A MOUNTAINTOP**
Leaf from an album of landscapes; painting mounted as part of a handscroll. Ming dynasty, c. 1500. Ink and color on paper, 15¼ × 23¾" (40 × 60.2 cm).
The Nelson-Atkins Museum of Art, Kansas City, Missouri.
Purchase, Nelson Trust (46-51/2)

mountains, the space is ambiguous, as if all the elements were compressed to the surface of the picture. With this flattening of space, the trees, rocks, and mountains become more readily legible in a second way, as semiabstract forms made of brushstrokes.

Six trees arranged diagonally define the extreme foreground and announce themes that the rest of the painting repeats, varies, and develops. The tree on the left, with its outstretched branches and full foliage, is echoed first in the shape of another tree just across the river and again in a tree farther up and toward the left. The tallest tree of the foreground grouping anticipates the high peak that towers in the distance almost directly above it. The forms of the smaller foreground trees, especially the one with dark leaves, are repeated in numerous variations across the painting. At the same time, the simple and ordinary-looking boulder in the foreground is transformed in the conglomeration of rocks, ridges, hills, and mountains above. This double reading, both abstract and representational, parallels the work's double nature as a painting of a landscape and an interpretation of a traditional landscape painting.

The influence of Dong Qichang on the development of Chinese painting of later periods cannot be overstated. Indeed, nearly all Chinese painters since the early seventeenth century have reflected his ideas in one way or another.

QING DYNASTY

In 1644, when the armies of the Manchu people to the northeast of China marched into Beijing, many Chinese reacted as though their civilization had come to an end. Yet, the Manchus had already adopted many Chinese customs and institutions before their conquest. After gaining control of all of China, a process that took decades, they showed great respect for Chinese tradition. In art, all the major trends of the late Ming dynasty eventually continued into the Manchu, or Qing, dynasty (1644–1911).

Orthodox Painting

Literati painting was by now established as the dominant tradition; it had become orthodox. Scholars followed Dong Qichang's recommendation and based their approach on the study of past masters, and they painted large numbers of works in the manner of Song and Yuan artists as a way of expressing their learning, technique, and taste.

WANG HUI. The grand, symphonic composition **A THOU-SAND PEAKS AND MYRIAD RAVINES** (**FIG. 24–12**), painted by Wang Hui (1632–1717) in 1693, exemplifies all the basic elements of Chinese landscape painting: mountains, rivers, waterfalls, trees, rocks, temples, pavilions, houses, bridges, boats, wandering scholars, fishers—the familiar and much-loved cast of actors from a tradition now many centuries old. At the upper right corner, the artist has written:

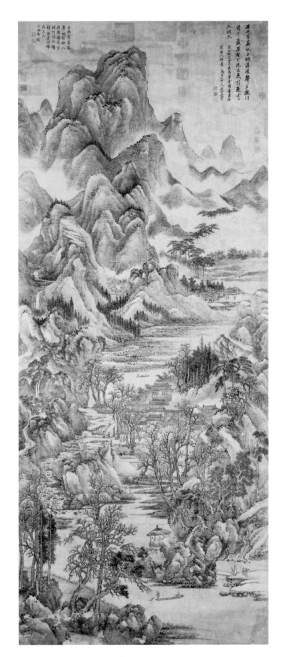

24–12 | Wang Hui **A THOUSAND PEAKS AND MYRIAD RAVINES**
Qing dynasty, 1693. Hanging scroll, ink on paper, 8'2½" × 3'4½" (2.54 × 1.03 m). National Palace Museum, Taipei, Republic of China.

> Moss and weeds cover the rocks and mist hovers over the water.
> The sound of dripping water is heard in front of the temple gate.
> Through a thousand peaks and myriad ravines the spring flows,
> And brings the flying flowers into the sacred caves.
> In the fourth month of the year 1693, in an inn in the capital, I painted this based on a Tang-dynasty poem in the manner of [the painters] Dong [Yuan] and Ju[ran].
>
> (Translated by Chu-tsing Li)

This inscription shares Wang Hui's complex thoughts as he painted this work. In his mind were both the lines of a Tang-dynasty poem, which offered the subject, and the paintings of the tenth-century masters Dong Yuan and Juran, which inspired his style. The temple the poem asks us to imagine is nestled on the right bank in the middle distance, but the painting shows us the scene from afar, as when a camera pulls slowly away from some small human drama until its actors can barely be distinguished from the great flow of nature. Giving viewers the experience of dissolving their individual identity in the cosmic flow had been a goal of Chinese landscape painting since its first era of greatness during the Song dynasty.

The Qing emperors of the late seventeenth and eighteenth centuries were painters themselves. They collected literati painting, and their taste was shaped mainly by artists such as Wang Hui. Thus literati painting, long associated with reclusive scholars, ultimately became an academic style practiced at court.

Individualist Painting

The first few decades of Qing rule had been both traumatic and dangerous for those who were loyal—or worse, related—to the Ming. Some committed suicide, while others sought refuge in monasteries or wandered the countryside. Among them were several painters who expressed their anger, defiance, frustration, and melancholy in their art. They took Dong Qichang's idea of painting as an expression of the artist's personal feelings very seriously and cultivated highly original styles. These painters have become known as the *individualists*.

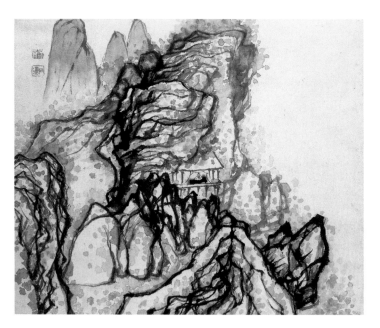

24–13 Shitao **LANDSCAPE**
One leaf from *An Album of Landscapes*. Qing dynasty, c. 1700. Ink and color on paper, 9½ × 11″ (24.1 × 28 cm).
Collection C. C. Wang family

SHITAO. One of the individualists was Shitao (1642–1707), who was descended from the first Ming emperor and who took refuge in Buddhist temples when the dynasty fell. In his later life he brought his painting to the brink of abstraction in such works as **LANDSCAPE** (FIG. 24–13). A monk sits in a small hut, looking out onto mountains that seem to be in turmoil. Dots, used for centuries to indicate vegetation on rocks, here seem to have taken on a life of their own. The rocks also seem alive—about to swallow up the monk and his hut. Throughout his life Shitao continued to identify himself with the fallen Ming, and he felt that his secure world had turned to chaos with the Manchu conquest.

THE MODERN PERIOD

In the mid- and late nineteenth century, China was shaken from centuries of complacency by a series of humiliating military defeats at the hands of Western powers and Japan. Only then did the government finally realize that these new rivals were not like the Mongols of the thirteenth century. China was no longer at the center of the world, a civilized country surrounded by "barbarians." Spiritual resistance was no longer sufficient to solve the problems brought on by change. New ideas from Japan and the West began to filter in, and the demand arose for political and cultural reforms. In 1911 the Qing dynasty was overthrown, ending 2,000 years of imperial rule, and China was reconceived as a republic.

During the first decades of the twentieth century Chinese artists traveled to Japan and Europe to study Western art. Returning to China, many sought to introduce the ideas and techniques they had learned, and they explored ways to synthesize the Chinese and the Western traditions. After the establishment of the present-day Communist government in 1949, individual artistic freedom was curtailed as the arts were pressed into the service of the state and its vision of a new social order. After 1979, however, cultural attitudes began to relax, and Chinese painters again pursued their own paths.

WU GUANZHONG. One artist who emerged during the 1980s as a leader in Chinese painting is Wu Guanzhong (b. 1919). Combining his French artistic training and Chinese background, Wu Guanzhong has developed a semiabstract style to depict scenes from the Chinese landscape. His usual method is to make preliminary sketches on site, then, back in his studio, he develops these sketches into free interpretations based on his feeling and vision. An example of his work, **PINE SPIRIT**, depicts a scene in the Huang (Yellow) Mountains (FIG. 24–14). The technique, with its sweeping gestures of paint, is clearly linked to Abstract Expressionism, an influential Western movement of the post–World War II years (Chapter 32); yet the painting also claims a place in the long tradition of Chinese landscape as exemplified by such masters as Shitao.

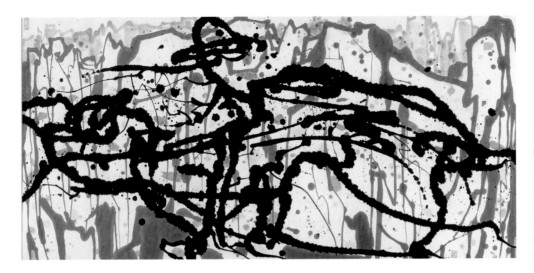

24–14 | Wu Guanzhong
PINE SPIRIT
1984. Ink and color on paper,
2'3⅝" × 5'3½"
(0.70 × 1.61 m). Spencer
Museum of Art, The University
of Kansas, Lawrence.
Gift of the E. Rhodes and Leonard B.
Carpenter Foundation

Like all aspects of Chinese society, Chinese art has felt the strong impact of Western influence, and the question remains whether Chinese artists will absorb Western ideas without losing their traditional identity. Interestingly, landscape remains an important subject, as it has been for more than a thousand years, and calligraphy continues to play a vital role. Using the techniques and methods of the West, some of China's artists have joined an international avant-garde (see, for example, Wenda Gu in Chapter 32) while other painters still seek communion with nature through their ink brushstrokes as a means to come to terms with human life and the world.

ARTS OF KOREA: THE JOSEON DYNASTY TO THE MODERN ERA

In 1392, General Yi Seonggye (1335–1408) overthrew the the Goryeo dynasty (918–1392), establishing the Joseon dynasty (1392–1910), sometimes called the Yi dynasty. He first maintained his capital at Gaeseong, the old Goreyo capital, but moved it to Seoul in 1394, where it remained through the end of the dynasty. The Joseon regime rejected Buddhism, espousing Neo-Confucianism as the state philosophy. Taking Ming-dynasty China as its model, the new government patterned its bureaucracy on that of the Ming emperors, even adopting as its own such outward symbols of Ming imperial authority as blue-and-white porcelain. The early Joseon era was a period of cultural refinement and scientific achievement, during which Koreans invented Han'geul (the Korean alphabet) and moveable type, not to mention the rain gauge, astrolabe, celestial globe, sundial, and water clock.

Joseon Ceramics

Like their Silla and Goryeo forebears, Joseon potters excelled in the manufacture of ceramics, taking their cue from contemporaneous Chinese wares, but seldom copying them directly.

BUNCHEONG CERAMICS. Descended from Goryeo celadons, Joseon-dynasty stonewares, known as *buncheong* wares, enjoyed widespread usage throughout the peninsula. Their decorative effect relies on the use of white slip that makes the humble stoneware resemble more expensive white porcelain. In fifteenth-century examples, the slip is often seen inlaid into repeating design elements stamped into the body.

Sixteenth-century *buncheong* wares are characteristically embellished with wonderfully fluid, calligraphic brushwork painted in iron-brown slip on a white slip ground. Most painted *buncheong* wares have stylized floral décor, but rare pieces, such as the charming wine bottle in FIGURE 24–15, feature pictorial decoration. In fresh, lively brushstrokes, a bird with outstretched wings grasps a fish that it has just caught in its talons; waves roll below, while two giant lotus blossoms frame the scene.

Japanese armies repeatedly invaded the Korean peninsula between 1592 and 1597, destroying many of the *buncheong* kilns, and essentially bringing the ware's production to a halt. Tradition holds that the Japanese took many *buncheong* potters

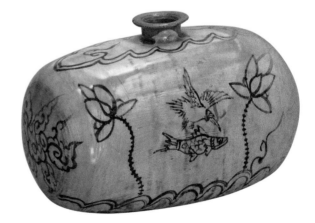

24–15 | **HORIZONTAL WINE BOTTLE WITH DECORATION OF A BIRD CARRYING A NEWLY CAUGHT FISH**
Korean. Joseon dynasty, 16th century. *Buncheong* ware: light gray stoneware with decoration painted in iron-brown slip on a white slip ground. 6⅒ × 9½" (15.5 × 24.1 cm). Museum of Oriental Ceramics, Osaka, Japan.
Gift of the Sumitomo Group [20773]

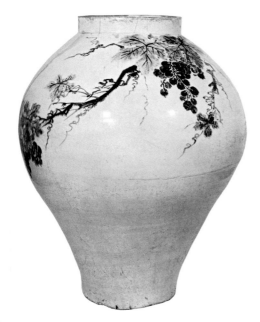

24–16 | BROAD-SHOULDERED JAR
With Decoration of a Fruiting Grapevine. Korean. Joseon dynasty, 17th century. Porcelain with decoration painted in underglaze iron-brown slip. Height 22⅛″ (53.8 cm). Ehwa Women's University Museum, Seoul, Republic of Korea.

Chinese potters invented porcelain during the Tang dynasty, probably in the eighth century. Generally fired in the range of 1300° to 1400° centigrade, porcelain is a high-fired, white-bodied ceramic ware. Its unique feature is its translucency. Korean potters learned to make porcelain during the Goryeo dynasty, probably as early as the eleventh or twelfth century, though few Goryeo examples remain today. For many centuries, the Chinese and Koreans were the only peoples able to produce porcelains.

home with them to produce *buncheong*-style wares, which were greatly admired by connoisseurs of the tea ceremony. In fact, the spontaneity of Korean *buncheong* pottery has inspired Japanese ceramics to this day.

PAINTED PORCELAIN. Korean potters produced porcelains with designs painted in underglaze cobalt blue as early as the fifteenth century, inspired by Chinese porcelains of the early Ming period (SEE FIG. 24–8). The Korean court dispatched artists from the royal painting academy to the porcelain kilns—located some thirty miles southeast of Seoul—to train porcelain decorators. As a result, from the fifteenth century onward, the painting on the best Korean porcelains closely approximated that on paper and silk, unlike in China, where ceramic decoration followed a path of its own with but scant reference to painting traditions.

In another unique development, Korean porcelains from the sixteenth and seventeenth centuries often feature designs painted in underglaze iron-brown rather than the cobalt blue customary in Ming porcelain. Also uniquely Korean are porcelain jars with bulging shoulders, slender bases and short, vertical necks, which appeared by the seventeenth century and came to be the most characteristic ceramic shapes in the later Joseon period. Painted in underglaze iron-brown, the seventeenth-century jar shown here depicts a fruiting grape branch around its shoulder (FIG. 24–16). In typical Korean fashion, the design spreads over a surface unconstrained by borders, resulting in a balanced but asymmetrical design that incorporates the Korean taste for unornamented spaces.

Joseon Painting

Korean secular painting came into its own during the Joseon dynasty. Continuing Goryeo traditions, early Joseon examples employ Chinese styles and formats, their range of subjects expanding from botanical motifs to include landscapes, figures, and a variety of animals.

Painted in 1447 by An Gyeon (b. 1418), **DREAM JOURNEY TO THE PEACH BLOSSOM LAND** (FIG. 24–17) is the earliest extant and dated Joseon secular painting. It illustrates a fanciful tale by China's revered nature poet Tao Qian (365–427) and recounts a dream about chancing upon a utopia secluded from the world for centuries while meandering among the peach blossoms of spring.

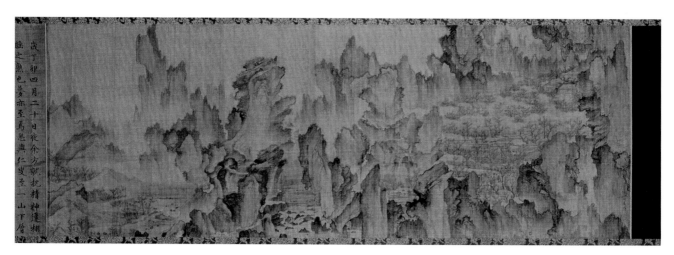

24–17 | An Gyeon DREAM JOURNEY TO THE PEACH BLOSSOM LAND
Korean. Joseon dynasty, 1447. Handscroll, ink and light colors on silk, 15¼ × 41⅞″ (38.7 × 106.1 cm). Central Library, Tenri University, Tenri (near Nara), Japan.

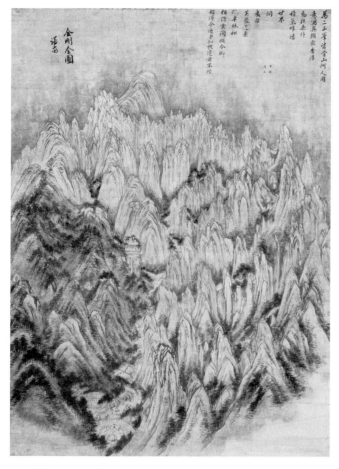

24–18 | Jeong Seon **PANORAMIC VIEW OF THE DIAMOND MOUNTAINS (GEUMGANG-SAN)**
Korean. Joseon dynasty, 1734. Hanging scroll, ink and colors on paper, 40⅝ × 37″ (130.1 × 94.0 cm). Lee'um, Samsung Museum, Seoul, Republic of Korea.

The monumental mountains and vast, panoramic vistas of such fifteenth-century Korean paintings, as with their Goryeo forebears, echo Northern Song painting styles. Chinese paintings of the Southern Song (1127–1279) and Ming periods (1368–1644) also influenced Korean painting of the fifteenth, sixteenth, and seventeenth centuries, though these styles never completely supplanted the imprint of the Northern Song masters.

THE SILHAK MOVEMENT. In the eighteenth century, a truly Korean style emerged, inspired by the *silhak,* or "practical learning," movement, which emphasized the study of things Korean in addition to the Chinese classics. The impact of the *silhak* movement is exemplified by the painter Jeong Seon (1676–1759), who chose well-known Korean vistas as the subjects of his paintings, rather than the Chinese themes favored by earlier artists. Among Jeong Seon's paintings are numerous representations of the Diamond Mountains (Geumgang-san), a celebrated range of craggy peaks along Korea's east coast. Painted in 1734, the scroll reproduced here aptly captures the Diamond Mountains' needlelike peaks (**FIG. 24–18**). The subject is Korean, and so is the energetic spirit and the intensely personal style, with its crystalline mountains, distant clouds of delicate ink wash, and individualistic brushwork.

Among figure painters, Sin Yunbok (b. 1758) is an important exemplar of the *silhak* attitude. Active in the late eighteenth and early nineteenth centuries, Sin typically depicted aristocratic figures in native Korean garb. Entitled **PICNIC AT THE LOTUS POND,** the album leaf illustrated here (**FIG. 24–19**) represents a group of Korean gentlemen enjoying themselves in the countryside on an autumn day in the

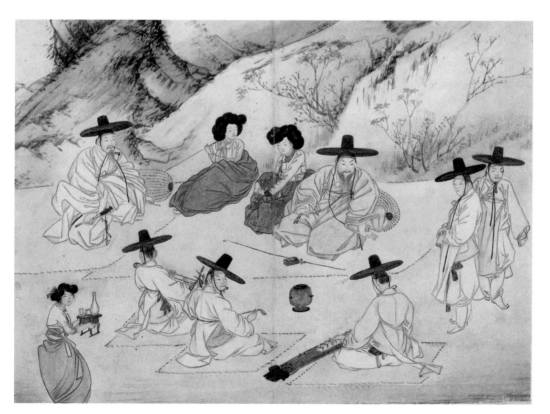

24–19 | Sin Yunbok **PICNIC AT THE LOTUS POND**
From an *Album of Genre Scenes.* Korean. Joseon dynasty, late 18th century. Leaf from an album of thirty leaves; ink and colors on paper, 11⅛ × 13⅞″ (28.3 × 35.2 cm). Kansong Museum of Art, Seoul, Republic of Korea.

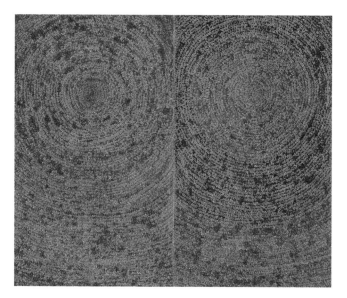

24–20 | Gim Hwangi **5-IV-71**,
Korean. 1971. Oil on canvas, 39½ × 39½″
(100 × 100 cm). Whanki Museum.

company of several *gisaeng,* or female entertainers. The figures are recognizably Korean—the women with their full coiffures, short jackets, and generous skirts, and the men with their beards, white robes, and wide-brimmed hats woven of horse hair and coated with black lacquer. The stringed instrument played by the gentleman seated in the lower right corner is a *gayageum,* or Korean zither, the most hallowed of all Korean musical instruments.

Modern Korea

Long known as "the Hermit Kingdom," the Joseon dynasty pursued a policy of isolationism, closing its borders to most of the world, except China, until 1876. Japan's annexation of Korea in 1910 brought the Joseon dynasty to a close, but effectively prolonged Korea's seclusion from the outside world. The legacy of self-imposed isolation compounded by colonial occupation (1910–45)—not to mention the harsh circumstances imposed by World War II (1939–45), followed by the even worse conditions of the Korean War (1950–53)—impeded Korea's artistic and cultural development during the first half of the twentieth century.

A MODERNIST PAINTER FROM KOREA. Despite these privations, some modern influences did reach Korea indirectly via China and Japan, and beginning in the 1920s and 1930s a few Korean artists experimented with contemporary Western styles, typically painting in the manner of Cézanne or Gauguin, but sometimes trying abstract, nonrepresentational styles. Among these, Gim Hwangi (1913–1974) was influenced by Constructivism and geometric abstraction and would become one of twentieth-century Korea's influential painters. Like many Korean artists after the Korean War, Gim wanted to examine Western modernism at its source. He visited Paris in

1956 and then, from 1964 to 1974, lived and worked in New York, where he produced his best-known works. His painting **5-IV-71** presents a large pair of circular radiating patterns composed of small dots and squares in tones of blue, black, and gray (FIG. 24–20). While appearing wholly Western in style, medium, concept, and even title—Gim Hwangi typically adopted the date of a work's creation as its title—*5-IV-71* also seems related to Asia's venerable tradition of monochrome ink painting, while suggesting a transcendence that seems Daoist or Buddhist in feeling. Given that the artist was Korean, that he learned the Chinese classics in his youth, that he studied art in Paris, and that he then worked in New York, it is possible that his painting embodies all of the above. Gim's painting illustrates the paradox that the modern artist faces while finding a distinctive, personal style: whether to paint in an updated version of a traditional style, in a wholly international style, in an international style with a distinctive local twist, or in an eclectic, hybrid style that incorporates both native and naturalized elements from diverse traditions. By addressing these questions, Gim Hwangi blazed a trail for subsequent Korean-born artists, such as the renowned video artist Nam June Paik (1932–2006), whose work can be seen in figure 32–86.

IN PERSPECTIVE

Invading from the steppes of Asia, the Mongols conquered China and established there the Yuan dynasty. While maintaining their foreign connections, Mongol leaders also adopted the values of Chinese dynastic rule, becoming patrons and collectors of art. Scholars educated for government service preserved and further developed the literati ideals that had coalesced during the earlier Song dynasty.

When the Yuan period of foreign rule came to an end, the new Ming ruling house revived the court traditions of the Song, including Southern Song court painting styles, and they commissioned decorated porcelains of exquisite quality. The Ming also became the model for the rulers of Korea's Joseon dynasty, under whose patronage these styles achieved a distinctive and austere beauty.

In the Qing era, China was again ruled by an outside group, this time the Manchus. While maintaining their traditional connections to Tibet and inner Asia through their patronage of Tibetan Buddhism, the Manchu rulers also embraced Chinese ideals, especially those of the literati. Practicing painting and calligraphy, composing poetry in Chinese, and collecting esteemed Chinese works of art, these rulers amassed the great palace collections that can now be seen in Beijing and Taipei.

By the twentieth century, China gradually embraced modern international trends. Chinese artists, and those in neighboring Korea, strove to choose among ideals of Western art, attracted first to its documentary qualities and then to its increasing abstraction, all the while maintaining ties to their own traditions.

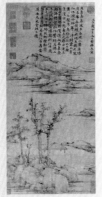

NI ZAN
THE RONGXI STUDIO
1372

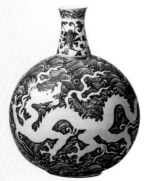

MING FLASK
1426–35

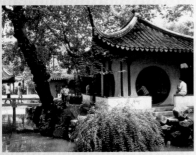

**GARDEN OF CESSATION OF
OFFICIAL LIFE**
EARLY 16TH CENTURY

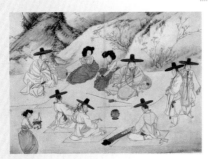

SIN YUNBOK
LATE 18TH CENTURY

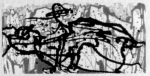

WU GUANZHONG
PINE SPIRIT
1984

CHINESE AND KOREAN ART AFTER 1279

1300

◀ **Yuan Dynasty** 1279–1368

◀ **Ming Dynasty** 1368–1644

◀ **Joseon Dynasty, Korea** 1392–1910

1400

1500

1600

◀ **Qing Dynasty** 1644–1911

1700

1800

1900

◀ **Korea a Japanese Colony** 1910–1945
◀ **Republic of China: Mainland**
  1912–1949
◀ **South Korea** 1945–Present
◀ **North Korea** 1945–Present
◀ **Republic of China: Taiwan**
  1949–Present
◀ **People's Republic of China**
  1949–Present
◀ **Korean War** 1950–1953

2000

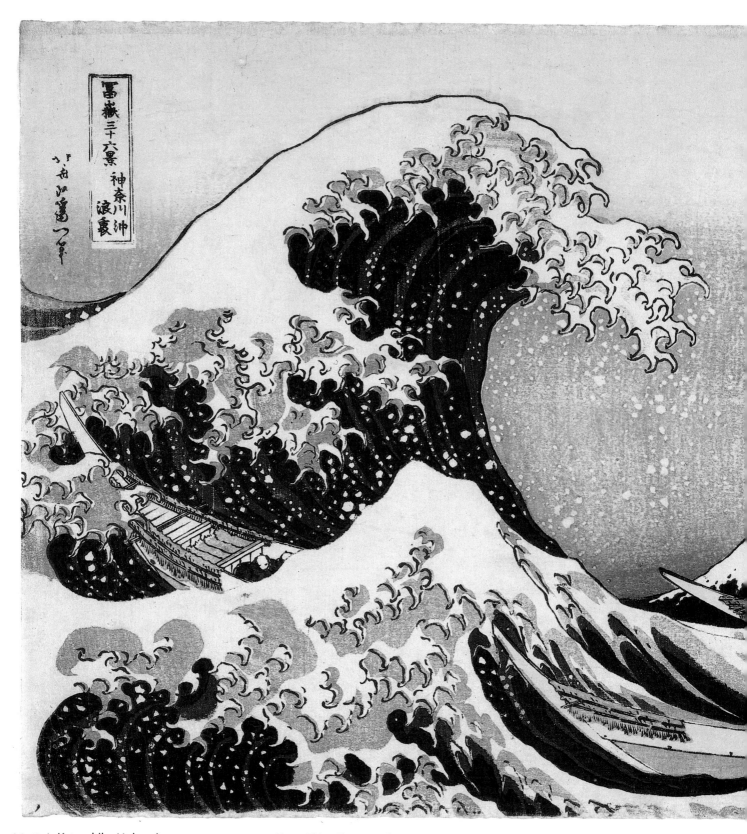

25–1 | Katsushika Hokusai **THE GREAT WAVE** From *Thirty-Six Views of Mt. Fuji*. Edo period, c. 1831. Polychrome woodblock print on paper, 9 ⅞ × 14 ⅝″ (25 × 37.1 cm). Honolulu Academy of Arts, Honolulu, Hawaii.
James A. Michener Collection (HAA 13, 695)

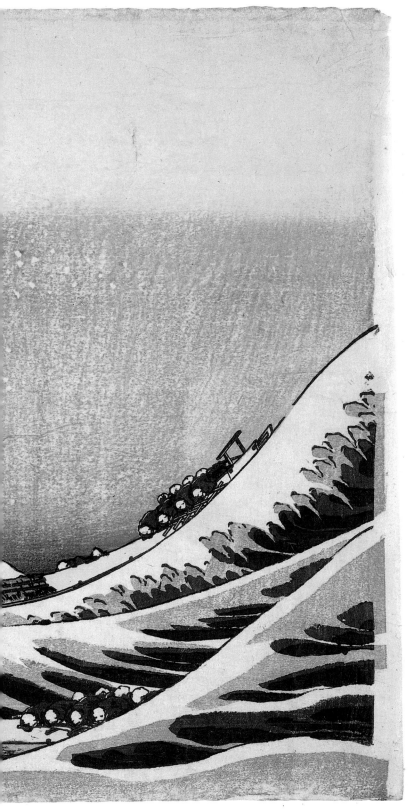

CHAPTER TWENTY-FIVE

JAPANESE ART AFTER 1392

25

The great wave rears up like a dragon with claws of foam, ready to crash down on the figures huddled in the boat below. Exactly at the point of imminent disaster, but far in the distance, rises Japan's most sacred peak, Mount Fuji, whose slopes, we suddenly realize, swing up like waves and whose snowy crown is like foam—comparisons the artist makes clear in the wave nearest us, caught just at the moment of greatest resemblance. This woodblock print (FIG. 25–1), known as **THE GREAT WAVE**—from a series called *Thirty-Six Views of Mt. Fuji* by Katsushika Hokusai (1760–1849)—has inspired countless imitations and witty parodies, yet its forceful composition remains ever fresh.

Today, Japanese color woodblock prints of the eighteenth and nineteenth centuries are collected avidly around the world, but in their own day they were barely considered art. Commercially produced by the hundreds for ordinary people to buy, they were the fleeting secular souvenirs of their era—an era that was one of the most fascinating in Japanese history. When seen in Europe and America, these and other Japanese prints were immediately acclaimed, and they strongly influenced late nineteenth- and early twentieth-century Western art (Chapter 30). **Japonisme**, or *japonism*, became the vogue, and Hokusai and Hiroshige (1797–1858) became as famous in the West as in Japan. Indeed, their art was taken more seriously in the West; the first book on Hokusai was published in France, and according to one estimate, by the early twentieth century more than 90 percent of Japanese prints had been sold to Western collectors.

MUROMACHI PERIOD

By the year 1392, Japanese art had already developed a long and rich history (see "Foundations of Japanese Culture," page 854). Beginning with prehistoric pottery and tomb art, then expanding through cultural influences from China and Korea, Japanese visual expression reached high levels of sophistication in both religious and secular arts. Very early in the tradition, a particularly Japanese aesthetic emerged, including a love of natural materials, a taste for asymmetry, a sense of humor, and a tolerance for qualities that may seem paradoxical or contradictory—characteristics that continue to distinguish Japanese art, appearing and reappearing in ever-changing guises.

By the end of the twelfth century, the political and cultural dominance of the emperor and his court had given way to rule by warriors, or samurai, under the leadership of the shogun, the general-in-chief. In 1338 the Ashikaga family gained control of the shogunate and moved its headquarters to the Muromachi district in Kyoto. In 1392 they reunited northern and southern Japan and retained their grasp on the office for more than 150 years. The Muromachi period after the reunion (1392–1573) is also known as the Ashikaga era.

The Muromachi period is especially marked by the ascendance of Zen Buddhism, whose austere ideals particularly appealed to the highly disciplined samurai. While Pure Land Buddhism, which had spread widely during the latter part of the Heian period (794–1185), remained popular, Zen, patronized by the samurai, became the dominant cultural force in Japan.

Ink Painting

Several forms of visual art flourished during the Muromachi period, but **ink painting**—monochrome painting in black ink and its diluted grays—reigned supreme. Muromachi ink painting was heavily influenced by the aesthetics of Zen, yet it also marked a shift away from the earlier Zen painting tradition. As Zen moved from an "outsider" sect to the chosen sect of the ruling group, the fierce intensity of earlier masters gave way to a more subtle and refined approach. And whereas earlier Zen artists had concentrated on rough-hewn depictions of Zen figures such as monks and teachers, now Chinese-style ink landscapes became the most important theme. Traditionally, the monk-artist Shubun (active c. 1418–63) is regarded as Japan's first great master of the ink landscape. Unfortunately, no works survive that can be proven to be his. Two landscapes by Shubun's pupil Bunsei (active c. 1450–60) have survived, however. In the one shown here **(FIG. 25–2),**

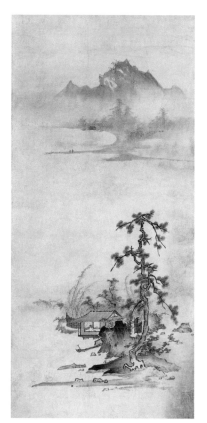

25–2 | **Bunsei**
LANDSCAPE
Muromachi period, mid-15th century. Hanging scroll, ink, and light colors on paper, 28 ¾ × 13″ (73.2 × 33 cm). Museum of Fine Arts, Boston.

Special Chinese and Japanese Fund (05.203)

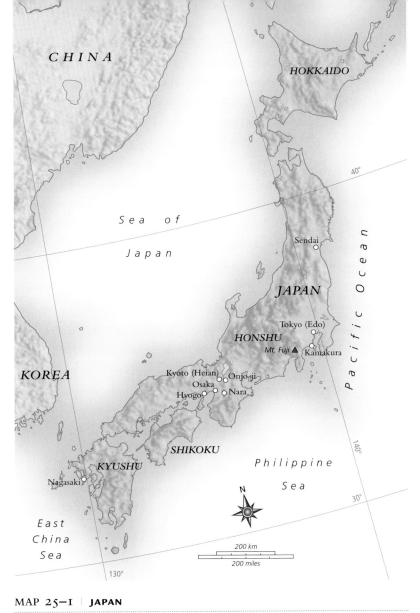

MAP 25–1 | **JAPAN**

Ideas and artistic influences from the Asian continent flowed to Japan before and after the island nation's self-imposed isolation from the 17th to the 19th century.

the foreground reveals a spit of rocky land with an overlapping series of motifs—a spiky pine tree, a craggy rock, a poet seated in a hermitage, and a brushwood fence holding back a small garden of trees and bamboo. In the middle ground is space—emptiness, the void.

We are expected to "read" the empty paper as representing water, for subtle tones of gray ink suggest the presence of a few people fishing from their boats near the distant shore. The two parts of the painting seem to echo each other across a vast expanse. A depiction of nature echoing the human spirit, the painting illustrates well the pure, lonely, and ultimately serene spirit of the Zen-influenced poetic landscape tradition.

SESSHU. Ink painting soon took on a different spirit. Zen monks painted—just as their Western counterparts illuminated manuscripts—but gave away their artworks. By the turn of the sixteenth century, temples were being asked for so many paintings that they formed ateliers staffed by monks

who specialized in art rather than religious ritual or teaching. Some painters even found they could survive on their own as professional artists. Nevertheless, many of the leading masters remained monks, at least in name, including the most famous of them all, Sesshu (1420–1506). Although he lived his entire life as a monk, Sesshu devoted himself primarily to painting. Like Bunsei, he learned from the tradition of Shubun, but he also had the opportunity to visit China in 1467. Sesshu traveled extensively there, viewing the scenery, stopping at Zen monasteries, and seeing whatever Chinese paintings he could. He does not seem to have had access to works by contemporary **literati** masters such as Shen Zhou (see Chapter 24), but saw instead the works of professional painters. Sesshu later claimed that he learned nothing from Chinese artists, but only from the mountains and rivers he had seen. When Sesshu returned from China, he found his homeland rent by the Onin Wars, which devastated the capital of Kyoto. Japan was to be torn apart by further civil warfare for the next hundred years. The refined art patronized by a secure society in

Art and Its Context
FOUNDATIONS OF JAPANESE CULTURE

With the end of the last Ice Age roughly 15,000 years ago, rising sea levels submerged the lowlands connecting Japan to the Asian landmass, creating the chain of islands we know today as Japan (SEE MAP 25–1). Not long afterward, early Paleolithic cultures gave way to a Neolithic culture known as Jomon (c. 11,000–400 BCE), after its characteristic cord-marked pottery. During the Jomon period, a sophisticated hunter-gatherer culture developed. Agriculture supplemented hunting and gathering by around 5000 BCE, and rice cultivation began some 4,000 years later.

A fully settled agricultural society emerged during the Yayoi period (c. 400 BCE–300 CE), accompanied by hierarchical social organization and more centralized forms of government. As people learned to manufacture bronze and iron, use of those metals became widespread. Yayoi architecture, with its unpainted wood and thatched roofs, already showed the Japanese affinity for natural materials and clean lines, and the style of Yayoi granaries in particular persisted in the design of shrines in later centuries. The trend toward centralization continued during the Kofun period (c. 300–552 CE), an era characterized by the construction of large royal tombs, following the Korean practice. Veneration of leaders grew into the beginnings of the imperial system that has lasted to the present day.

The Asuka era (552–645 CE) began with a century of profound change as elements of Chinese civilization flooded into Japan, initially through the intermediary of Korea. The three most significant Chinese contributions to the developing Japanese culture were Buddhism (with its attendant art and architecture), a system of writing, and the structures of a centralized bureaucracy. The earliest extant Buddhist temple compound in Japan—the oldest currently existing wooden building in the world—dates from this period.

The arrival of Buddhism also prompted some formalization of Shinto, the loose collection of indigenous Japanese beliefs and practices. Shinto is a shamanistic religion that emphasizes cere-

monial purification. Its rituals include the invocation and appeasement of spirits, including those of the recently dead. Many Shinto deities are thought to inhabit various aspects of nature, such as particularly magnificent trees, rocks, and waterfalls, and living creatures such as deer. Shinto and Buddhism have in common an intense awareness of the transience of life, and as their goals are complementary—purification in the case of Shinto, enlightenment in the case of Buddhism—they have generally existed comfortably alongside each other to the present day.

The Nara period (645–794 CE) takes its name from Japan's first permanently established imperial capital. During this time the founding works of Japanese literature were compiled, among them an important collection of poetry called the *Manyoshu*. Buddhism advanced to become the most important force in Japanese culture. Its influence at court grew so great as to become worrisome, and in 794 the emperor moved the capital from Nara to Heian-kyo (present-day Kyoto), far from powerful monasteries.

During the Heian period (794–1185) an extremely refined court culture thrived, embodied today in an exquisite legacy of poetry, calligraphy, and painting. An efficient method for writing the Japanese language was developed, and with it a woman at the court wrote the world's first novel, *The Tale of Genji*. Esoteric Buddhism, as hierarchical and intricate as the aristocratic world of the court, became popular.

The end of the Heian period was marked by civil warfare as regional warrior (samurai) clans were drawn into the factional conflicts at court. Pure Land Buddhism, with its simple message of salvation, offered consolation to many in troubled times. In 1185 the Minamoto clan defeated their arch rivals, the Taira, and their leader, Minamoto Yoritomo, assumed the position of shogun (general-in-chief). While paying respects to the emperor, Minamoto Yoritomo kept actual military and political power to himself, setting up his own capital in Kamakura. The Kamakura era (1185–1333) began a tradition of rule by shogun that lasted in various forms until 1868.

---

peacetime was no longer possible. Instead, the violent spirit of the times sounded its disturbing note, even in the world of landscape painting.

This new spirit is evident in Sesshu's **WINTER LAND-SCAPE,** which makes full use of the forceful style that he developed (FIG. 25–3). A cliff descending from the mist seems to cut the composition in two. Sharp, jagged brushstrokes delineate a series of rocky hills, where a lone figure makes his way to a Zen monastery. Instead of a gradual recession into space, flat overlapping planes fracture the composition into crystalline facets. The white of the paper is left to indicate snow, while the sky is suggested by tones of gray. A few trees cling desperately to the rocky land, and the harsh chill of winter is boldly expressed.

IKKYU. A third important artist of the Muromachi period was a monk named Ikkyu (1394–1481). A genuine eccentric and one of the most famous Zen masters in Japanese history, Ikkyu derided the Zen of his day, writing, "The temples are rich but Zen is declining, there are only false teachers, no true teachers." Ikkyu recognized that success was distorting the spirit of Zen. Originally, Zen had been a form of counterculture for those who were not satisfied with prevailing ways. Now, however, Zen monks acted as government advisers, teachers, and even leaders of merchant missions to China. Although true Zen masters were able to withstand all outside pressures, many monks became involved with political matters, with factional disputes among the temples, or with their reputations as poets or artists. Ikkyu did not hesitate to mock what he regarded as "false Zen." He even paraded through the streets with a wooden sword, claiming that his sword would be as much use to a samurai as false Zen to a monk.

Ikkyu's **calligraphy**, which is especially admired, has a spirit of spontaneity. To write out the classic Buddhist couplet "Abjure evil, practice only the good," he created a pair of single-line scrolls (**FIG. 25–4**). At the top of each scroll—first the right scroll and then the left—Ikkyu began with standard script, in which each stroke of a character is separate and distinct. As his brush moved down a scroll, he grew more excited and wrote in increasingly cursive script, until finally his frenzied brush did not leave the paper at all. This calligraphy displays the intensity that is the hallmark of Zen.

The Zen Dry Garden

Elegant simplicity—profound and personal—was the result of disciplined meditation coupled with manual labor, as practiced in the Zen Buddhism introduced into Japan in the late twelfth century. Zen monasteries aimed at self-sufficiency. Monks were expected to be responsible for their physical as well as spiritual needs. Consequently, the performance of

simple tasks—weeding the garden, cooking meals, mending garments—became occasions for meditation in the search for enlightenment. Zen monks turned to their gardens not as the focus of detached viewing and meditation but as the objects of constant vigilance and work—pulling weeds, tweaking unruly shoots, and raking the gravel of the dry gardens. This philosophy profoundly influenced Japanese art.

The dry landscape gardens of Japan, *karesansui* (literally "dried-up mountains and water"), exist in perfect harmony with Zen Buddhism. The dry garden in front of the abbot's quarters in the Zen temple of Ryoan-ji is one of the most

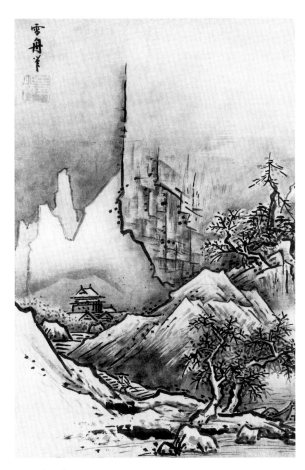

25–3 | Sesshu **WINTER LANDSCAPE**
Muromachi period, c. 1470s. Ink on paper, 18 ¼ × 11 ½″ (46.3 × 29.3 cm). Collection of the Tokyo National Museum.

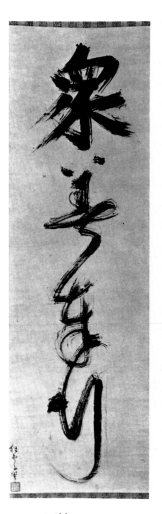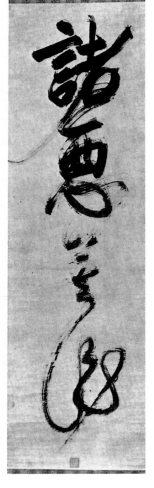

25–4 | Ikkyu **CALLIGRAPHY COUPLET**
Daitoku-ji, Kyoto. Muromachi period, c. mid-15th century. Ink on paper, each 10′2 ⅞″ × 1′4 ½″ (3.12 × 0.42 m).

renowned Zen creations in Japan (FIG. 25–5). A flat rectangle of raked gravel, about 29 by 70 feet, surrounds fifteen stones of different sizes in islands of moss. The stones are set in asymmetrical groups of two, three, and five. Low, plaster-covered walls establish the garden's boundaries, but beyond the perimeter wall, maple, pine, and cherry trees add color and texture to the scene. Called "borrowed scenery," these elements are a considered part of the design even though they grow outside the garden. The garden is celebrated for its severity and emptiness.

Dry gardens began to be built in the fifteenth and sixteenth centuries in Japan. By the sixteenth century, Chinese landscape painting influenced the gardens' composition, and miniature clipped plants and beautiful stones were arranged to resemble famous paintings. Especially fine and unusual stones were coveted and even carried off as war booty, such was the cultural value of these seemingly mundane objects.

The Ryoan-ji garden's design, as we see it today, probably dates from the mid-seventeenth century, since earlier written sources refer only to cherry trees, not to a garden. By the time this garden was created, such stone and gravel gardens had become highly intellectualized, abstract reflections of nature. This garden has been interpreted as representing islands in the sea, or mountain peaks rising above the clouds, perhaps even a swimming tigress with her cubs, or constellations of stars and planets. All or none of these interpretations may be equally satisfying—or irrelevant—to a monk seeking clarity of mind through contemplation. The austere beauty of the naked gravel has led many people to meditation.

MOMOYAMA PERIOD

The civil wars sweeping Japan laid bare the basic flaw in the Ashikaga system, which was that samurai were primarily loyal to their own feudal lord, or *daimyo*, rather than to the central government. Battles between feudal clans grew more frequent, and it became clear that only a *daimyo* powerful and bold enough to unite the entire country could control Japan. As the Muromachi period drew to a close, three leaders emerged who would change the course of Japanese history.

The first of these leaders was Oda Nobunaga (1534–82), who marched his army into Kyoto in 1568, signaling the end of the Ashikaga family as a major force in Japanese politics. A ruthless warrior, Nobunaga went so far as to destroy a Buddhist monastery because the monks refused to join his forces. Yet he was also a patron of the most rarefied and refined arts. Assassinated in the midst of one of his military campaigns, Nobunaga was succeeded by the military commander Toyotomi Hideyoshi (1537–98), who soon gained complete power in Japan. He, too, patronized the arts when not leading his army, and he considered culture a vital adjunct to his rule. Hideyoshi, however, was overly ambitious. He believed that he could conquer both Korea and China, and he wasted much of his resources on two ill-fated invasions. A stable government finally emerged in 1600 with the triumph of a third leader, Tokugawa Ieyasu (1543–1616), who established his shogunate in 1603. But despite its turbulence, the era of Nobunaga and Hideyoshi, known as the Momoyama period (1568–1615), was one of the most creative eras in Japanese history.

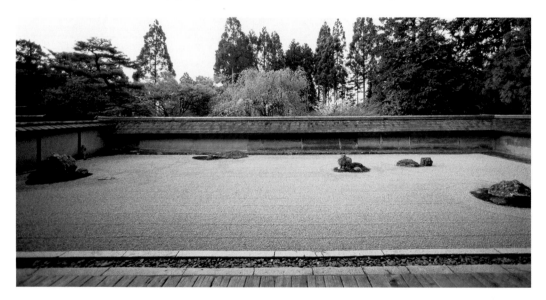

25–5 | **ROCK GARDEN, RYOAN-JI, KYOTO**
Photographed spring 1993. Muromachi period, c. 1480.
Photograph by Michael S. Yamashita

The American composer John Cage once exclaimed that every stone at Ryoan-ji was in just the right place. He then said, "And every other place would also be just right." His remark is thoroughly Zen in spirit. There are many ways to experience Ryoan-ji. For example, we can imagine the rocks as having different visual "pulls" that relate them to one another. Yet there is also enough space between them to give each one a sense of self-sufficiency and permanence.

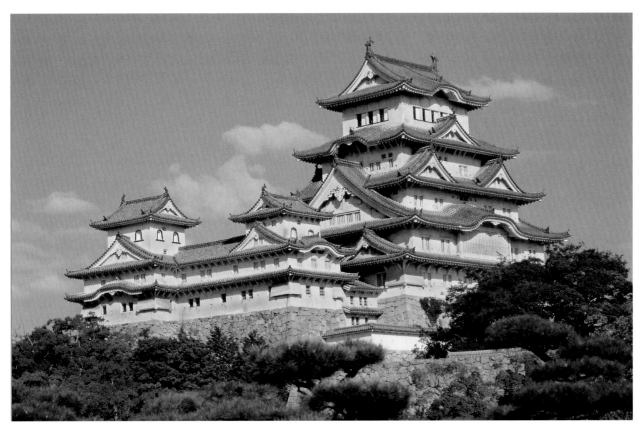

25–6 | **HIMEJI CASTLE**
Hyogo, near Osaka. Momoyama period, 1601–09.

Architecture

Today the very word *Momoyama* conjures up images of bold warriors, luxurious palaces, screens shimmering with **gold leaf**, and magnificent ceramics. The Momoyama period was also the era when Europeans first made an impact in Japan. A few Portuguese explorers had arrived at the end of the Muromachi era in 1543, and traders and missionaries were quick to follow. It was only with the rise of Nobunaga, however, that Westerners were able to extend their activities beyond the ports of Kyushu, Japan's southernmost island. Nobunaga welcomed foreign traders, who brought him various products, the most important of which were firearms.

European muskets and cannons soon changed the nature of Japanese warfare and influenced Japanese architecture. In response to the new weapons, monumental fortified castles were built in the late sixteenth century. Some were eventually lost to warfare or torn down by victorious enemies, and others have been extensively altered over the years. One of the most beautiful of the surviving castles is Himeji, not far from the city of Osaka (FIG. 25–6). Rising high on a hill above the plains, Himeji has been given the name White Heron. To reach the upper fortress, visitors must follow angular paths beneath steep walls, climbing from one area to the next past stone ramparts and through narrow fortified gates, all the while feeling as though lost in a maze, with no sense of direction or progress. At the main building, a further climb up a series of narrow ladders leads to the uppermost chamber.

There, the footsore visitor is rewarded with a stunning 360-degree view of the surrounding countryside. The sense of power is overwhelming.

Kano School Decorative Painting

Castles such as Himeji were sumptuously decorated, offering artists unprecedented opportunities to work on a grand scale. Large murals on **fusuma**—paper-covered sliding doors—were particular features of Momoyama design, as were folding screens with gold-leaf backgrounds, whose glistening surfaces not only conveyed light within the castle rooms but also displayed the wealth of the warrior leaders. Temples, too, commissioned large-scale paintings for their rebuilding projects after the devastation of the civil wars.

The Momoyama period produced a number of artists who were equally adept at decorative golden screens and broadly brushed *fusuma* paintings. Daitoku-ji, a celebrated Zen monastery in Kyoto, has a number of subtemples that are treasure troves of Japanese art. One, the Juko-in, possesses *fusuma* by Kano Eitoku (1543–90), one of the most brilliant painters from the professional school of artists founded by the Kano family and patronized by government leaders for several centuries. Founded in the Muromachi period, the Kano school combined training in the ink-painting tradition with new skills in decorative subjects and styles. The illustration here shows two of the three walls of *fusuma* panels painted when the artist was in his mid-twenties (FIG. 25–7). To the

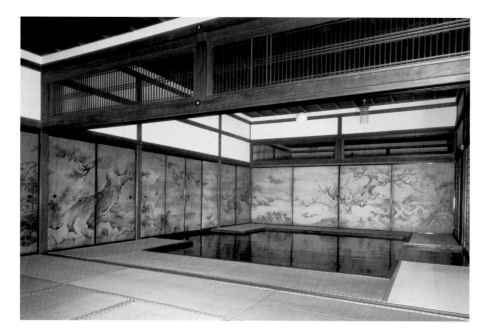

25–7 | Kano Eitoku **FUSUMA**
Depicting pine and cranes (left) and plum tree (right) from the central room of the Juko-in, Daitoku-ji, Kyoto. Momoyama period, c. 1563–73. Ink and gold on paper, height 5′9 ⅛″ (1.76 m).

left, the subject is the familiar Kano school theme of cranes and pines, both symbols of long life; to the right is a great gnarled plum tree, symbol of spring. The trees are so massive they seem to extend far beyond the panels. An island rounding both walls of the far corner provides a focus for the out-reaching trees. Ingeniously, it belongs to both compositions at the same time, thus uniting them into an organic whole. Eitoku's vigorous use of brush and ink, his powerfully jagged outlines, and his dramatic compositions all hark back to the style of Sesshu, but the bold new sense of scale in his works is a leading characteristic of the Momoyama period.

The Tea Ceremony

Japanese art is never one-sided. Along with castles, golden screens, and massive *fusuma* paintings there was an equal interest during the Momoyama period in the quiet, the restrained, and the natural. This was expressed primarily through the tea ceremony.

The term "tea ceremony," a phrase now in common use, does not convey the full meaning of *cha no yu*, the Japanese ritual drinking of tea, which has no counterpart in Western culture. Tea itself had been introduced to Japan from the Asian continent hundreds of years earlier. At first, tea was molded into cakes and boiled. However, the advent of Zen in the late Kamakura period (1185–1392) brought to Japan a different way of preparing tea, with the leaves crushed into powder and then whisked in bowls with hot water. Zen monks used such tea as a mild stimulant to aid meditation, and it also was considered a form of medicine.

SEN NO RIKYU. The most famous tea master in Japanese history was Sen no Rikyu (1522–91). He conceived of the tea ceremony as an intimate gathering in which a few people would enter a small rustic room, drink tea carefully prepared in front of them by their host, and quietly discuss the tea utensils or a Zen scroll hanging on the wall. He did a great

deal to establish the aesthetic of modesty, refinement, and rusticity that permitted the tearoom to serve as a respite from the busy and sometimes violent world outside. A traditional tearoom is quite small and simple. It is made of natural materials such as bamboo and wood, with mud walls, paper windows, and a floor covered with tatami—mats of woven straw. One tearoom that preserves Rikyu's design is named Tai-an (FIG. 25–8). Built in 1582, it is distinguished by its tiny door (guests must crawl to enter) and its alcove, or **tokonoma,** where a Zen scroll or a simple flower arrangement may be

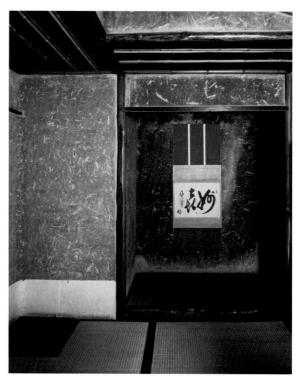

25–8 | Sen no Rikyu **TAI-AN TEAROOM**
Myoki-an Temple, Kyoto. Momoyama period, 1582.

displayed. At first glance, the room seems symmetrical. But the disposition of the *tatami* does not match the spacing of the *tokonoma*, providing a subtle undercurrent of irregularity. A longer look reveals a blend of simple elegance and rusticity. The walls seem scratched and worn with age, but the tatami are replaced frequently to keep them clean and fresh. The mood is quiet; the light is muted and diffused through three small paper windows. Above all, there is a sense of spatial clarity. All nonessentials have been eliminated, so there is nothing to distract from focused attention. The tearoom aesthetic became an important element in Japanese culture, influencing secular architecture through its simple and evocative style (see "Shoin Design," page 860).

EDO PERIOD

Three years after Tokugawa Ieyasu gained control of Japan, he proclaimed himself shogun. His family's control of the shogunate was to last more than 250 years, a span of time known as the Edo period (1615–1868) or the Tokugawa era.

Under the rule of the Tokugawa family, peace and prosperity came to Japan at the price of an increasingly rigid and often repressive form of government. The problem of potentially rebellious *daimyo* was solved by ordering all feudal lords to spend either half of each year or every other year in the new capital of Edo (present-day Tokyo), where their wives and children were sometimes required to live permanently. Zen Buddhism was supplanted as the prevailing intellectual force by a form of neo-Confucianism, a philosophy formulated in Song-dynasty China that emphasized loyalty to the state. More drastically, Japan was soon closed off from the rest of the world by its suspicious government. Japanese were forbidden to travel abroad, and with the exception of small Chinese and Dutch trading communities on an island off the southern port of Nagasaki, foreigners were not permitted in Japan.

Edo society was officially divided into four classes. Samurai officials constituted the highest class, followed by farmers, artisans, and finally merchants. As time went on, however, merchants began to control the money supply, and in Japan's increasingly mercantile economy they soon reached a high, if unofficial, position. Reading and writing became widespread at all levels of society. Many segments of the population—samurai, merchants, intellectuals, and even townspeople—were now able to patronize artists, and a pluralistic cultural atmosphere developed unlike anything Japan had experienced before.

The Tea Ceremony

The rebuilding of temples continued during the first decades of the Edo period, and for this purpose government officials, monks, and wealthy merchants needed to cooperate. The tea ceremony was one way that people of different classes could come together for intimate conversations. Every utensil connected with tea, including the waterpot, the kettle, the bam-

boo spoon, the whisk, the tea caddy, and, above all, the teabowl, came to be appreciated for their aesthetic qualities, and many works of art were created for use in *cha no yu*.

The age-old Japanese admiration for the natural and the asymmetrical found full expression in tea ceramics. Korean-style rice bowls made for peasants were suddenly considered the epitome of refined taste, and tea masters urged potters to mimic their imperfect shapes. But not every misshapen bowl would be admired. An extremely rarified appreciation of beauty developed that took into consideration such factors as how well a teabowl fit into the hands, how subtly the shape and texture of the bowl appealed to the eye, and who had previously used and admired it. For this purpose, the inscribed box became almost as important as the ceramic that fit within it, and if a bowl had been given a name by a leading tea master, it was especially treasured by later generations.

One of the finest teabowls extant is named **MOUNT FUJI** after Japan's most sacred peak (**FIG. 25–9**). (Mount Fuji is

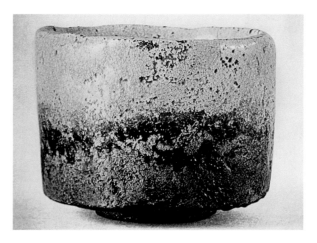

25–9 | Hon'ami Koetsu **TEABOWL, CALLED MOUNT FUJI**
Edo period, early 17th century. Raku ware, height 3 ⅜"
(8.5 cm). Sakai Collection, Tokyo.

Connoisseurs developed a subtle vocabulary to discuss the aesthetics of tea. A favorite term was *sabi* (literally, "loneliness"), which refers to the tranquility found when feeling alone. Other virtues were *wabi* (literally, "poverty"), which suggests the artlessness of humble simplicity, and *shibui*, (literally, "bitter" or "astringent"), meaning elegant restraint, and said to be exemplified by the color of the inside of an old teapot.

Elements of Architecture
SHOIN DESIGN

Of the many expressions of Japanese taste that reached great refinement in the Momoyama period, **shoin** architecture has had perhaps the most enduring influence. *Shoin* are upper-class residences that combine a number of traditional features in more-or-less standard ways, always asymmetrically. These features include wide verandas, wood posts as framing and defining decorative elements, woven straw **tatami** mats as floor and ceiling covering, several shallow alcoves for prescribed purposes, **fusuma** (sliding doors) as fields for painting or textured surfaces, and **shoji** screens—wood frames covered with translucent rice paper. The *shoin* illustrated here was built in 1601 as a guest hall, called Kojo-in, at the great Onjo-ji monastery. *Tatami, shoji*, alcoves, asymmetry, and other features of *shoin* are still seen in Japanese interiors today.

In the original *shoin*, one of the alcoves would contain a hanging scroll, an arrangement of flowers, or a large painted screen. Seated in front of that alcove, called a **tokonoma**, the owner of the house would receive guests, who could contemplate the object above the head of their host. Another alcove contained staggered shelves, often for writing instruments. A writing space fitted with a low writing desk was on the veranda side of the room, with *shoji* that could open to the outside.

The architectural harmony of *shoin* was based on the proportionate disposition of basic units, or **modules**. In Japanese carpentry, the common module of design and construction is the **bay**, reckoned as the distance from the center of one post to the center of another, which is governed in turn by the standard size of *tatami* floor mats. Although varying slightly from region to region, the size of a single *tatami* is about 3 by 6 feet. Room area in Japan is still expressed in terms of the number of *tatami* mats, so that, for example, a room may be described as an eight-mat room.

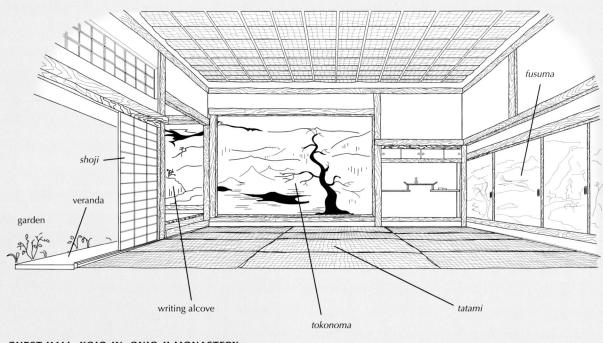

GUEST HALL, KOJO-IN, ONJO-JI MONASTERY
Shiga prefecture. Momoyama period. 1601.

depicted in FIGURE 25–1.) An example of **raku** ware—a hand-built, low-fired ceramic developed especially for use in the tea ceremony—the bowl was crafted by Hon'ami Koetsu (1558–1637), a leading cultural figure of the early Edo period. Koetsu was most famous as a calligrapher, but he was also a painter, lacquer designer, poet, landscape gardener, connoisseur of swords, and potter. With its small foot, straight sides, slightly irregular shape, and crackled texture, this bowl exemplifies tea taste. In its rough exterior we sense directly the two elements of earth and fire that create pottery. Merely looking at it suggests the feeling one would get from holding it, warm with tea, cupped in one's hands.

Rimpa School Painting

One of Koetsu's friends was the painter Tawaraya Sotatsu (active c. 1600–40), with whom he collaborated on several magnificent handscrolls. Sotatsu is considered the first great painter of the Rimpa school, a grouping of artists with similar tastes rather than a formal school, such as the Kano school. Rimpa masters excelled in decorative designs of strong expressive force, and they frequently worked in several mediums.

Sotatsu painted some of the finest golden screens that have survived. The splendid pair here depict the celebrated islands of Matsushima near the northern city of Sendai (FIG. 25–10). Working in a boldly decorative style, the artist has created asymmetrical and almost abstract patterns of waves, pines, and island forms. On the right screen (shown here on top), mountainous islands echo the swing and sweep of the waves, with stylized gold clouds in the upper left. The left screen continues the gold clouds until they become a sand spit from which twisted pines grow. Their branches seem to lean toward a strange island in the lower left, composed of an

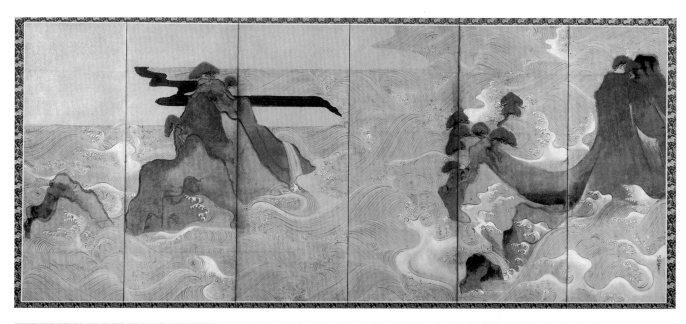

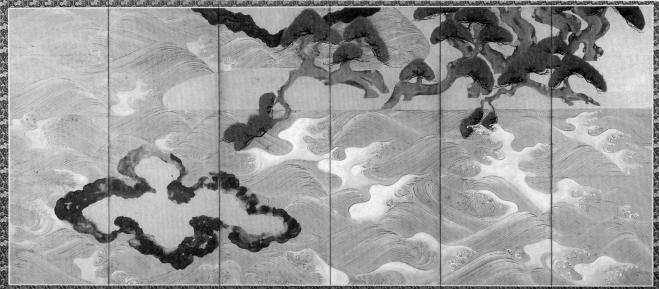

25–10 | Tawaraya Sotatsu **PAIR OF SIX-PANEL SCREENS, KNOWN AS THE MATSUSHIMA SCREENS**
Edo period, 17th century. Ink, mineral colors, and gold leaf on paper; each screen 4′9 ⅞″ × 11′8 ½″ (1.52 × 3.56 m).
Freer Gallery of Art, Smithsonian Institution, Washington, D.C.
Gift of Charles Lang Freer (F1906.231 & 232)

The six-panel screen format was a triumph of scale and practicality. Each panel consisted of a light wood frame surrounding a latticework interior covered with several layers of paper. Over this foundation was pasted a high-quality paper, silk, or gold-leaf ground, ready to be painted by the finest artists. Held together with ingenious paper hinges, a screen could be folded for storage or transportation, resulting in a mural-size painting light enough to be carried by a single person, ready to be displayed as needed.

THE ◉BJECT SPEAKS

LACQUER BOX FOR WRITING IMPLEMENTS

Ogata Korin (1658–1716), another great master of the Rimpa school, originated many remarkable works, including colorful golden screens, monochrome scrolls, and paintings in glaze on his brother Kenzan's pottery. He also designed some highly prized works in **lacquer**. His writing box is a lidded container designed to hold tools and materials for calligraphy. Korin's design for this black lacquer box sets a motif of irises and a plank bridge in a dramatic combination of mother-of-pearl, silver, lead, and gold lacquer. For Japanese viewers the decoration immediately recalls a famous passage from the tenth-century *Tales of Ise*, a classic of Japanese literature. A nobleman poet, having left his wife in the capital, pauses at a place called Eight Bridges, where a river branches into eight streams, each covered with a plank bridge. Irises are in full bloom, and his traveling companions urge the poet to write a *tanka*—a five-line, thirty-one-syllable poem—beginning each line with a syllable from the word for "iris": *Kakitsubata* (*ka-ki-tsu-ba-ta*). The poet responds (substituting *ha* for *ba*):

> **Ka**ragoromo
> **ki**tsutsu narenishi
> **tsu**ma shi areba
> **ha**rubaru kinuru
> **ta**bi o shi zo omou.

When I remember
my wife, fond and familiar
as my courtly robe,
I feel how far and distant
my travels have taken me.

(Translated by Stephen Addiss)

The poem brought tears to all their eyes, and the scene became so famous that any painting of a group of irises, with or without a plank bridge, immediately calls it to mind.

Lacquer is derived in Asia from the sap of the lacquer tree, *Rhus Verniciflua*. The tree is indigenous to China, where examples of lacquerware have been found dating back to the Neolithic period. Knowledge of lacquer spread early to Korea and Japan, and the tree came to be grown commercially throughout East Asia.

Gathered by tapping into a tree and letting the sap flow into a container, lacquer is then strained to remove impurities and heated to evaporate excess moisture. The thickened sap can be colored with vegetable or mineral dyes and lasts for several years if carefully stored. Applied in thin coats to a surface such as wood or leather, lacquer hardens into a smooth, glasslike, protective coating that is waterproof, heat- and acid-resistant, and airtight. Lacquer's practical qualities made it ideal for storage containers and vessels for food and drink. In Japan the leather scales

of samurai armor were coated in lacquer, as were leather saddles. The decorative potential of lacquer was developed in the manufacture of expensive luxury items.

The creation of a piece of lacquer is a painstaking process that can take a sequence of specialized artisans several years. First, the item is fashioned of wood and sanded smooth. Next, layers of lacquer are built up. In order to dry properly, lacquer must be applied in extremely thin coats. (If the lacquer is applied too thickly, the exterior surface dries first, forming an airtight seal that prevents the lacquer below from drying.) Optimal temperature and humidity are also essential to drying, and artisans quickly learned to control them artificially. Up to thirty coats of lacquer, each dried and polished before the next is brushed on, are required.

In China, lacquer was often applied to a thickness of up to 300 coats, then elaborately carved. In Japan and Korea, inlay with mother-of-pearl and precious metals was brought to a high point of refinement. Japanese artisans also perfected a variety of methods known collectively as *maki-e* ("sprinkled design"), in which flaked or powdered gold or silver was embedded in a still-damp coat of lacquer.

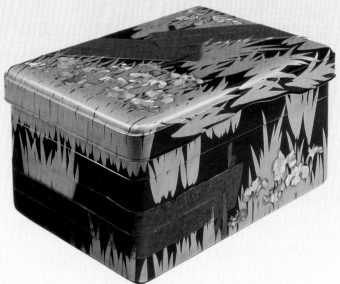

Ogata Korin LACQUER BOX FOR WRITING IMPLEMENTS
Edo period, late 17th–early 18th century. Lacquer, lead, silver, and mother-of-pearl, 5 ⅝ × 10 ¾ × 7 ¾"
(14.2 × 27.4 × 19.7 cm). Tokyo National Museum, Tokyo.

organic, amoebalike form in gold surrounded by mottled ink. This mottled effect was a specialty of Rimpa school painters.

As one of the "three famous beautiful views of Japan," Matsushima was often depicted in art. Most painters, however, emphasized the large number of pine-covered islands that make the area famous. Sotatsu's genius was to simplify and dramatize the scene, as though the viewer were passing the islands in a boat on the roiling waters. Strong, basic mineral colors dominate, and the sparkling two-dimensional richness of the gold leaf contrasts dramatically with the three-dimensional movement of the waves.

Nanga School Painting

Rimpa artists such as Sotatsu and Korin are considered quintessentially Japanese in spirit, both in the expressive power of their art and in their use of poetic themes from Japan's past. Other painters, however, responded to the new Confucian atmosphere by taking up some of the ideas of the literati painters of China. These painters are grouped together as the Nanga ("Southern") school. Nanga was not a school in the sense of a professional workshop or a family tradition. Rather, it took its name from the southern school of amateur artists described by the Chinese literati theorist Dong

Qichang (Chapter 24). Educated in the Confucian mold, Nanga masters were individualists, creating their own variations of literati painting from unique blendings of Chinese models, Japanese aesthetics, and personal brushwork. They were often experts at calligraphy and poetry as well as painting, but one, Uragami Gyokudo (1745–1820), was even more famous as a musician, an expert on the seven-string Chinese zither called the *qin*. Most instruments are played for entertainment or ceremonial purposes, but the *qin* has so deep and soft a sound that it is played only for oneself or a close friend. Its music becomes a kind of meditation, and for Gyokudo it opened a way to commune with nature and his own inner spirit.

Gyokudo was a hereditary samurai official, but midway through his life he resigned from his position and spent seventeen years wandering through Japan, absorbing the beauty of its scenery, writing poems, playing music, and beginning to paint. During his later years Gyokudo produced many of the strongest and most individualistic paintings in Japanese history, although they were not appreciated by people during his lifetime. **GEESE ASLANT IN THE HIGH WIND** is a leaf from an album Gyokudo painted in 1817, three years before his death (**FIG. 25–11**). The creative power in this painting is remarkable. The wind seems to have the force of a hurricane, sweeping the tree branches and the geese into swirls of action. The greatest force comes from within the land itself, which mushrooms out and bursts forth in peaks and plateaus as though an inner volcano were erupting.

Zen Painting

Deprived of the support of the government and samurai officials, who now favored neo-Confucianism, Zen initially went into something of a decline during the Edo period. In the early eighteenth century, however, it was revived by a monk named Hakuin Ekaku (1685–1769), who had been born in a small village not far from Mount Fuji and who resolved to become a monk after hearing a fire-and-brimstone sermon in his youth. For years he traveled around Japan seeking out the strictest Zen teachers. After a series of enlightenment experiences, he eventually became an important teacher himself.

In his later years Hakuin turned more and more to painting and calligraphy as forms of Zen expression and teaching. Since the government no longer sponsored Zen, Hakuin reached out to ordinary people, and many of his paintings portray everyday subjects that would be easily understood by farmers and merchants. The paintings from his sixties have great charm and humor, and by his eighties he was creating works of astonishing force. Hakuin's favorite subject was Daruma (Bodhidharma), the semilegendary Indian monk who had begun the Zen tradition in China

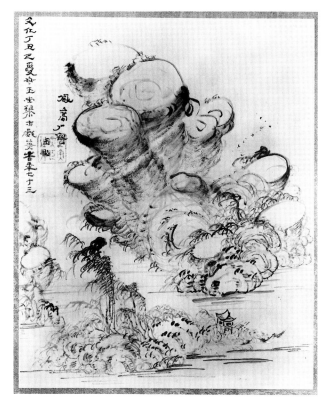

25–11 | Uragami Gyokudo **GEESE ASLANT IN THE HIGH WIND**
Edo period, 1817. Ink and light colors on paper, 12 3/16 × 9 7/8″ (31 × 25 cm). Takemoto Collection, Aichi.

Technique
INSIDE A WRITING BOX

The interior of a writing box is fitted with compartments for holding an ink stick, an ink stone, brushes, and paper—tools and materials not only for writing but also for **ink painting**.

Ink sticks are made by burning wood or oil inside a container. Soot deposited by the smoke then is collected, bound into a paste with resin, heated for several hours, kneaded and pounded, and finally pressed into small stick-shaped or cake-shaped molds to harden. Molds are often carved to produce an ink stick (or ink cake) decorated in low relief. The tools of writing and painting are also beautiful objects in their own right.

Fresh ink is made for each writing or painting session by grinding the hard, dry ink stick in water against a fine-grained stone. A typical ink stone has a shallow well at one end sloping up to a grinding surface at the other. The artist fills the well with water from a waterpot. The ink stick, held vertically, is dipped into the well to pick up a small amount of water, then is rubbed in a circular motion firmly on the grinding surface. The process is repeated until enough ink has been prepared. Grinding ink is viewed as a meditative task, time for collecting one's thoughts and concentrating on the painting or calligraphy ahead.

Brushes are made from animal hair set in simple bamboo or hollow-reed handles. Brushes taper to a fine point that responds with great sensitivity to any shift in pressure. Although great painters and calligraphers do eventually develop their own styles of holding and using the brush, all begin by learning the basic position for writing. The brush is held vertically, grasped firmly between the thumb and first two fingers, with the fourth and fifth fingers often resting against the handle for more subtle control.

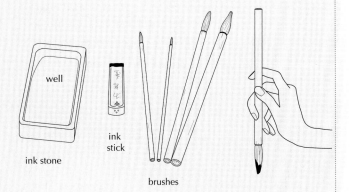

well

ink stone

ink stick

brushes

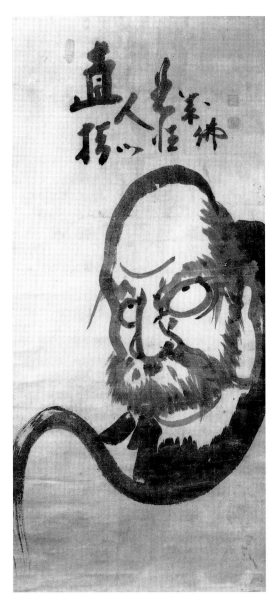

25–12 | Hakuin Ekaku **BODHIDHARMA MEDITATING** Edo period, 18th century. Ink on paper, 49 ½ × 21 ¾″ (125.7 × 55.3 cm). On extended loan to the Spencer Museum of Art, The University of Kansas, Lawrence.

Hakuin had his first enlightenment experience while meditating upon the *koan* (mysterious Zen riddle) about *mu*. One day a monk asked a Chinese Zen master, "Does a dog have the *buddha* nature?" Although Buddhist doctrine teaches that all living beings have *buddha* nature, the master answered, "*Mu*," meaning "has not" or "nothingness." The riddle of this answer became a problem that Zen masters gave their students as a focus for meditation. With no logical answer possible, monks were forced to go beyond the rational mind and penetrate more deeply into their own being. Hakuin, after months of meditation, reached a point where he felt "as though frozen in a sheet of ice." He then happened to hear the sound of the temple bell, and "it was as though the sheet of ice had been smashed." Later, as a teacher, Hakuin invented a *koan* of his own that has since become famous: "What is the sound of one hand clapping?"

(**FIG. 25–12**). Here he has portrayed the wide-eyed Daruma during his nine years of meditation in front of a temple wall in China. Intensity, concentration, and spiritual depth are conveyed by broad and forceful brushstrokes. The inscription is the ultimate Zen message, attributed to Daruma himself: "Pointing directly to the human heart, see your own nature and become Buddha."

Hakuin's pupils followed his lead in communicating their vision through brushwork. The Zen figure once again became the primary subject of Zen painting, and the painters were again Zen masters rather than primarily artists.

Maruyama-Shijo School Painting

Zen paintings were given away to all those who wished them, including poor farmers as well as artisans, merchants, and samurai. Many merchants, however, were more concerned with displaying their increasing wealth than with spiritual matters, and their aspirations fueled a steady demand for golden screens and other decorative works of art.

MARUYAMA OKYO. One school that arose to satisfy this demand was the Maruyama-Shijo school, formed in Kyoto by Maruyama Okyo (1733–95). Okyo had studied Western-style "perspective pictures" in his youth, and he was able in his mature works to incorporate shading and perspective into a decorative style, creating a sense of volume that was new to East Asian painting. Okyo's new style proved very popular in Kyoto, and it soon spread to Osaka and Edo (present-day Tokyo) as well. The subjects of Maruyama-Shijo painting were seldom difficult to understand. Instead of legendary Chinese themes, Maruyama-Shijo painters portrayed the birds, animals, hills, trees (**FIG. 25–13**), farmers, and townsfolk of Japan. Although highly educated people might make a point of preferring Nanga painting, Maruyama-Shijo works suited the tastes of the emerging upper middle class.

NAGASAWA ROSETSU. The leading pupil of Okyo was Nagasawa Rosetsu (1754–99), a painter of great natural talent who added his own boldness and humor to the Maruyama-Shijo tradition. Rosetsu delighted in surprising his viewers with odd juxtapositions and unusual compositions. One of his finest works is a pair of screens, the left one depicting a bull and a puppy (**FIG. 25–14**). The bull is so immense that it fills almost the entire six panels of the screen and still cannot be contained at the top, left, and bottom. The puppy, white

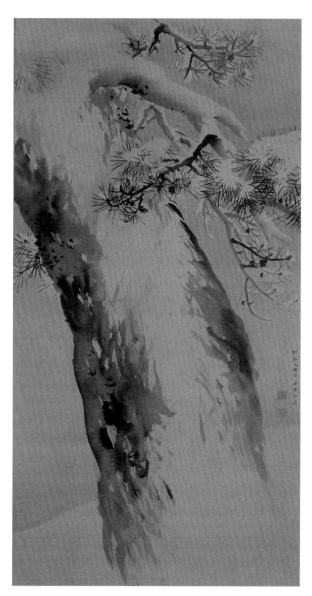

25–13 Maruyama Okyo **PINE TREE IN SNOW**
Edo period, 1765. Hanging scroll, ink and color on silk,
48 ½ × 28 ¼″ (123 × 71.75 cm). Tokyo National Museum.

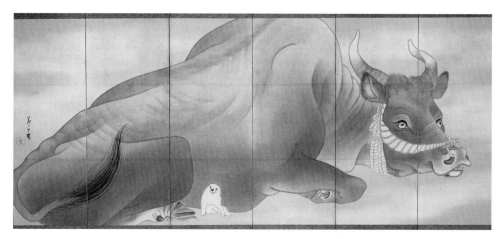

25–14 Nagasawa Rosetsu **BULL AND PUPPY**
Edo period, 18th century. One of a pair of six-panel screens, ink and gold wash on paper,
5′7 ¼ × 12′3″ (1.70 × 3.75 m). Los Angeles County Museum of Art, California.
Joe and Etsuko Price Collection (L.83.45.3a)

against the dark gray of the bull, helps to emphasize the huge size of the bull by its own smallness. The puppy's relaxed and informal pose, looking happily right out at the viewer, gives this powerful painting a humorous touch that increases its charm. In the hands of a master such as Rosetsu, plebeian subject matter could become simultaneously delightful and monumental, equally pleasing to viewers with or without much education or artistic background.

Ukiyo-E: Pictures of the Floating World

Not only did newly wealthy merchants patronize painters in the middle and later Edo period, but even artisans and tradespeople could purchase works of art. Especially in the new capital of Edo, bustling with commerce and cultural activities, people savored the delights of their peaceful society. Buddhism had long preached that pleasures were fleeting; the cherry tree, which blossoms so briefly, became the symbol for the transience of earthly beauty and joy. Commoners in the Edo period did not dispute this transience, but they took a new attitude: Let's enjoy it to the full as long as it lasts. Thus the Buddhist phrase *ukiyo* ("floating world") became positive rather than negative.

There was no world more transient than that of the pleasure quarters, set up in specified areas of every major city. Here were found restaurants, bathhouses, and brothels. The heroes of the day were no longer famous samurai or aristocratic poets. Instead, swashbuckling actors and beautiful courtesans were admired. These paragons of pleasure soon became immortalized in paintings and—because paintings were too expensive for common people—in **woodblock prints** known as *ukiyo-e*, "pictures of the floating world" (see "Japanese Woodblock Prints," page 867).

HARUNOBU. At first prints were made in black ink, then colored by hand when the public so desired. The first artist to design prints to be printed in many colors was Suzuki Harunobu (1724–70). His exquisite portrayals of feminine beauty quickly became so popular that soon every artist was designing multicolored *nishiki-e* ("brocade pictures").

One print that displays Harunobu's charm and wit is **GEISHA AS DARUMA CROSSING THE SEA** (FIG. 25–15). Harunobu has portrayed a young woman in a red cloak crossing the water on a reed, a reference to one of the legends about Daruma. To see a young woman peering ahead to the other shore, rather than a grizzled Zen master staring off into space, must have greatly amused the Japanese populace. There was also another layer of meaning in this image because geishas were sometimes compared to Buddhist teachers or deities in their ability to bring ecstasy, akin to enlightenment, to humans. Harunobu's print suggests these meanings, but it also succeeds simply as a portrait of a beautiful woman, with the gently curving lines of drapery suggesting the delicate feminine form beneath.

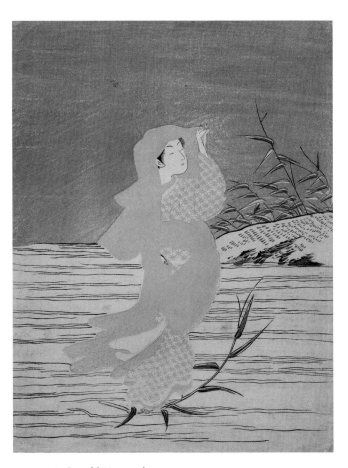

25–15 | Suzuki Harunobu   **GEISHA AS DARUMA CROSSING THE SEA**   Edo period, mid-18th century. Polychrome woodblock print on paper, 10 ⅞ × 8 ¼" (27.6 × 21 cm). Philadelphia Museum of Art.
Gift of Mrs. Emile Geyelin, in memory of Anne Hampton Barnes

The second great subject of *ukiyo-e* were the actors of the new form of popular theater known as *kabuki*. Because women had been banned from the stage after a series of scandalous incidents, male actors took both male and female roles. Much as people today buy posters of their favorite sports, music, or movie stars, so, too, in the Edo period people clamored for images of their pop idols.

HIROSHIGE AND HOKUSAI. During the nineteenth century, landscape joined courtesans and actors as a major theme—not the idealized landscape of China, but the actual sights of Japan. The two great masters of landscape prints were Utagawa Hiroshige (1797–1858) and Katsushika Hokusai (1760–1849). Hiroshige's *Fifty-Three Stations of the Tokaido* and Hokusai's *Thirty-Six Views of Mt. Fuji* became the most successful sets of graphic art the world has known. The woodblocks were printed and printed again until they wore out. They were then recarved, and still more copies were printed. This process continued for decades, and thousands of prints from the two series are still extant.

The Great Wave (SEE FIG. 25–1) is the most famous of the scenes from *Thirty-Six Views of Mt. Fuji.* Hokusai was already

Technique
JAPANESE WOODBLOCK PRINTS

Woodblock prints are called *ukiyo-e* in Japanese, which can be translated as "pictures of the floating world." They represent the combined expertise of three people: the artist, the carver, and the printer. Coordinating and funding the endeavor was a publisher, who commissioned the project and distributed the prints to stores or itinerant peddlers, who would sell them.

The artist supplied the master drawing for the print, executing its outlines with brush and ink on tissue-thin paper. Colors might be indicated, but more often they were understood or decided on later. The drawing was passed on to the carver, who pasted it facedown on a hardwood block, preferably cherrywood, so that the outlines showed through the paper in reverse. A light coating of oil might be brushed on to make the paper more transparent, allowing the drawing to stand out with maximum clarity. The carver then cut around the lines of the drawing with a sharp knife, always working in the same direction as the original brushstrokes. The rest of the block was chiseled away, leaving the outlines standing in relief. This block, which reproduced the master drawing, was called the **key block**. If the print was to be **polychrome**, having multiple colors, prints made from the key block were in turn pasted facedown on blocks that would be used as guides for the carver of the color blocks. Each color generally required a separate block, although both sides of a block might be used for economy.

Once the blocks were completed, the printer took over. Paper for printing was covered lightly with animal glue (gelatin). A few hours before printing, the paper was lightly moistened so that it would take ink and color well. Water-based ink or color was brushed over the block, and the paper placed on top and rubbed with a smooth, padded device called a *baren*, until the design was completely transferred. The key block was printed first, then the colors one by one. Each block was carved with two small marks called **registration marks**, in exactly the same place in the margins, outside of the image area—an L in one corner, and a straight line in another. By aligning the paper with these marks before letting it fall over the block, the printer ensured that the colors would be placed correctly within the outlines. One of the most characteristic effects of later Japanese prints is a grading of color from dark to pale. This was achieved by wiping some of the color from the block before printing, or by moistening the block and then applying the color gradually with an unevenly loaded brush—a brush loaded on one side with full-strength color and on the other with diluted color.

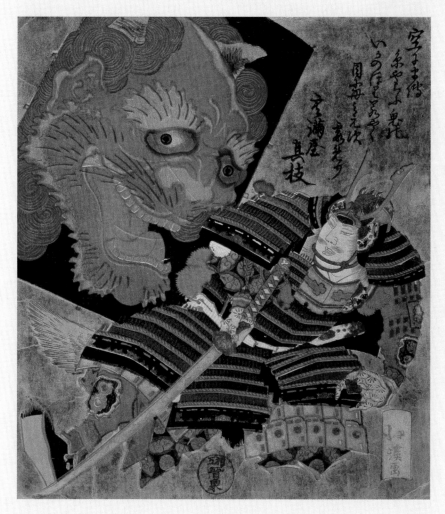

Totoya Hokkei (1780–1850)
RAIKO ATTACKS A DEMON KITE
Edo period, c. 1825. Polychrome woodblock print on paper, 8 ⅜ × 7 ⅓″ (21.4 × 18.6 cm). Collection of the Frank Lloyd Wright Archives, Scottsdale, Arizona. This print, of a luxurious limited-edition type called *surimono*, celebrates the hero Raiko, legendary slayer of demons, and suggests a message for the new year: vanquishing bad luck and ushering in good. The poem in the print reads:

A demon kite
trails its string
so high in the sky
that even young eyes
lose sight of it in the mist

(Translated by John T. Carpenter)

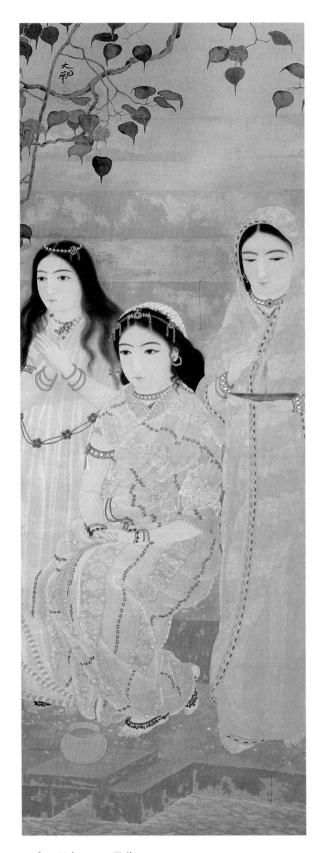

in his seventies, with a fifty-year career behind him, when he designed this image. Such was his modesty that he felt that his Fuji series was only the beginning of his creativity, and he wrote that if he could live until he was 100, he would finally learn how to become an artist.

THE MEIJI AND MODERN PERIODS

Pressure from the West for entry into Japan mounted dramatically in the mid-nineteenth century, and in 1853 the policy of national seclusion was ended. Resulting tensions precipitated the downfall of the Tokugawa shogunate, however, and in 1868 the emperor was formally restored to power, an event known as the Meiji Restoration. The court moved from Kyoto to Edo, which was renamed Tokyo, meaning "Eastern Capital."

Meiji

The Meiji period marked a major change for Japan. After its long isolation, Japan was deluged by the influx of the West. Western education, governmental systems, clothing, medicine, industrialization, and technology were all adopted rapidly into Japanese culture. Teachers of sculpture and oil painting were imported from Italy, while adventurous Japanese artists traveled to Europe and America to study.

A MEIJI PAINTER. Ernest Fenollosa (1853–1908), an American who had recently graduated from Harvard, traveled to Japan in 1878 to teach philosophy and political economy at Tokyo University. Within a few years, he and a former student Okakura Kakuzo (1862–1913) began urging artists to study traditional Japanese arts rather than to focus exclusively on Western art styles and media. Yokoyama Taikan (1868–1958) subsequently developed his personal style within the *Nihonga* (Japanese painting) genre promoted by Okakura. Drawing from Japanese tradition, notably the Rimpa style, Yokoyama avoided outlines and instead defined forms in fields of color. His pictorial space, however, owes something to the Western tradition. Like Okakura, Yokoyama traveled widely. His **FLOATING LIGHTS** (FIG. 25–16) was inspired by a visit to India in 1903, where he observed women engaged in divination on the banks of the Ganges.

Modern Japan

In the push to become a modern industrialized country, Japan did not lose its sense of tradition, even in the days of the strongest Western influence. In modern Japan, artists still choose whether to work in an East Asian style, a Western style, or some combination of the two. Just as Japanese art in earlier periods had both Chinese style and native traditions, so Japanese art today has both Western and native aspects.

25–16 | Yokoyama Taikan **FLOATING LIGHTS**
Meiji period, 1909. One from a pair of hanging scrolls, ink, colors, and gold on silk, 56 ½ × 20 ½ " (143 × 52 cm). The Museum of Modern Art, Ibaraki.

A MODERN CERAMICIST. Perhaps the liveliest contemporary art is ceramics. Japan has retained a widespread appreciation for pottery. Many people still practice the traditional arts of the tea ceremony and flower arranging, both of which require ceramic vessels, and most people own at least one fine ceramic piece. In this atmosphere, many potters earn a comfortable living by making art ceramics, an opportunity not available in other countries. Some ceramicists continue to create raku teabowls and other traditional wares, while others experiment with new styles and new techniques.

Miyashita Zenji (b. 1939), who lives in Kyoto, creates an initial form by constructing an undulating shape out of pieces of cardboard; he then builds up the surface with clay of many different colors, using torn paper to create irregular shapes. When fired, the varied colors of the clay seem to form a landscape, with layers of mountains leading up to the sky. Miyashita's work is modern in shape, yet traditional in its evocation of nature.

Miyashita is representative of the high level of contemporary ceramics in Japan, which is supported by a broad spectrum of educated and enthusiastic collectors and admirers. Objects useful for the tea ceremony or for flower arranging, such as Miyashita's flower vase entitled **WIND** (FIG. 25–17), reflect a continued refinement of traditional taste. There is also strong public interest in contemporary painting, prints, calligraphy, textiles, lacquer, architecture, and sculpture.

A CONTEMPORARY SCULPTOR. One of the most adventurous and original sculptors currently working is Chuichi Fujii (b. 1941). Born into a family of sculptors in wood, Fujii found himself as a young artist more interested in the new materials of plastic, steel, and glass. However, in his mid-

thirties he took stock of his progress and decided to begin again, this time with wood. At first he carved and cut into the wood, but he soon realized that he wanted to allow the material to express its own natural spirit, so he devised an ingenious new technique that preserved the individuality of each log while making of it something new. Fujii first studies the log to come to terms with its basic shape. Next, he inserts hooks into the log and runs wires between them. Every day he tightens the wires, over a period of months gradually pulling the log into a new shape. When he has bent the log to the shape he envisioned, Fujii makes a cut and sees whether his sculpture will stand. If he has miscalculated, he discards the work and begins again.

Here, Fujii has created a circle, one of the most basic forms in nature but never before seen in such a thick tree trunk (FIG. 25–18). The work strongly suggests the *enso*, the circle that Zen monks painted to express the universe, the all, the void, the moon—and even a tea cake. Yet Fujii does not try to proclaim his links with Japanese culture. He says that while his works may seem to have some connections with traditional Japanese arts, he is not conscious of them.

The artist has achieved something entirely new, yet his work also embodies the love of asymmetry, respect for natural materials, and dramatic simplicity encountered throughout the history of Japanese art.

A CONTEMPORARY PAINTER. In the 1990s, art in Japan merged with that in the West, with tradition and creativity playing out in new ways. Takashi Murakami (b. 1962), who lives and works in New York as well as in Japan, is prominent among artists who have taken Japan's *manga* and *anime* art forms, derived from the *ukiyo-e* tradition, as an inspiration for

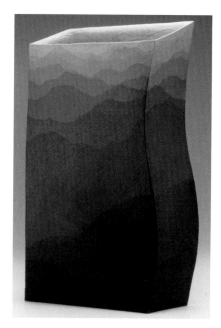

25–17 | Miyashita Zenji **WIND**
c. 1989. Stoneware, 21⅞ × 12¾ × 5⅛" (55.4 × 32.4 × 13 cm).
Spencer Museum of Art, The University of Kansas, Lawrence.
Gift of the Friends of the Art Museum/Helen Foresman Spencer Art Acquisition Fund

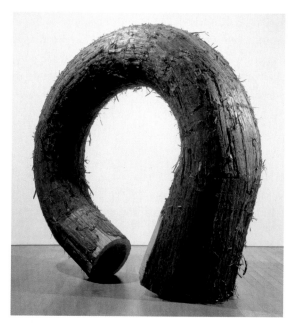

25–18 | Chuichi Fujii **UNTITLED '90**
1990. Cedar wood, height 7′5 ½" (2.3 m).
Hara Museum of Contemporary Art, Tokyo.

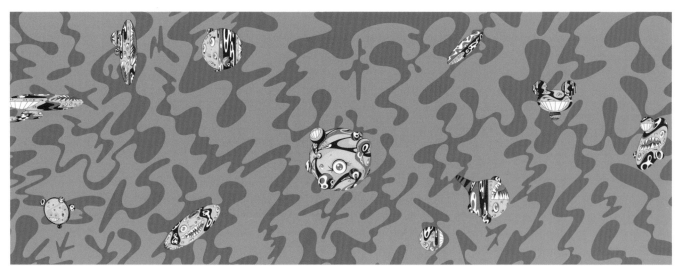

25–19 | Takashi Murakami **MAGIC BALL (POSITIVE)**
1999. Seven panels, acrylic on canvas mounted on board, 94 ½ × 248 ¼ × 2 ¾″ (240 × 630 × 7 cm).
Collection: Galerie 20.21, Essen.

painting and sculpture. These forms' close involvement with popular culture has a strong precedent in the *ukiyo-e* tradition. The emphasis on undulating lines and flat forms—to the point of a denial of pictorial space—also has its root in that Edo period style. Murakami's floating motifs (FIG. 25–19) reference *anime* and at the same time satirize its international consumer culture.

IN PERSPECTIVE

Muromachi, Momoyama, and Edo—six hundred years of Japanese culture—saw profound social and political changes. The arts felt these shifts through changing patterns of patronage of arts, yet all the while distinctive aesthetic orientations matured.

Evocative ink landscapes and Zen dry gardens, based on traditions imported from China, developed as the deeply artistic expressions in Japan. In these art forms the bold brushstrokes or subtle washes, and the general aesthetic of monochrome ink complements a strong appreciation of nature, its materials, and its forms. Wood, clay, and straw, or naturally shaped rocks provide patterns and textures with no need of obvious embellishment.

During the same periods, Japanese art inspired exquisite and exacting craftsmanship. Decoration in gold played a distinctive role in the painted screens that defined interior spaces as well as in the ornamentation of lacquer ware and other useful objects. Forms from nature became abstract and stylized patterns. Representation was often distilled to the simplicity of fluctuating line and flat shapes of color.

Japanese art of these periods was also invested with whimsy or even paradox. A sense of humor shows: sometimes easily accessible and at other times in works of art so sophisticated that they could only be understood by those with a deep knowledge of both Japanese and Chinese literature. In Japan, the patronage of art has long reflected a pluralistic cultural atmosphere. With that has come an ability to refine forms to greater and greater subtlety or, in contrast, to startle the viewer with audacious surprises.

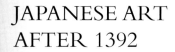

JAPANESE ART
AFTER 1392

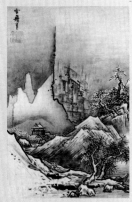

SESSHU
WINTER LANDSCAPE
C. 1470S

1300

◄ **Muromachi (Ashikaga)** 1392–1573

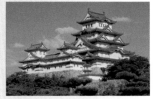

HIMEJI CASTLE
HYOGO 1601–09

1500

◄ **Momoyama** 1568–1615

◄ **Edo (Tokugawa)** 1615–1868

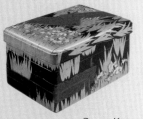

OGATA KORIN
LACQUER BOX
LATE 17TH–EARLY 18TH CENTURY

1700

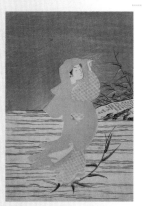

SUZUKI HARUNOBU
GEISHA AS DARUMA
CROSSING THE SEA
MID-18TH CENTURY

◄ **Meiji** 1868–1911

1900

◄ **Taisho** 1911–1926
◄ **Showa** 1926–1989

◄ **Occupation** 1945–1952

◄ **Heisei** 1989–Present

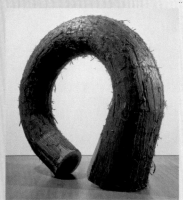

CHUICHI FUJII
UNTITLED '90
1990

2000

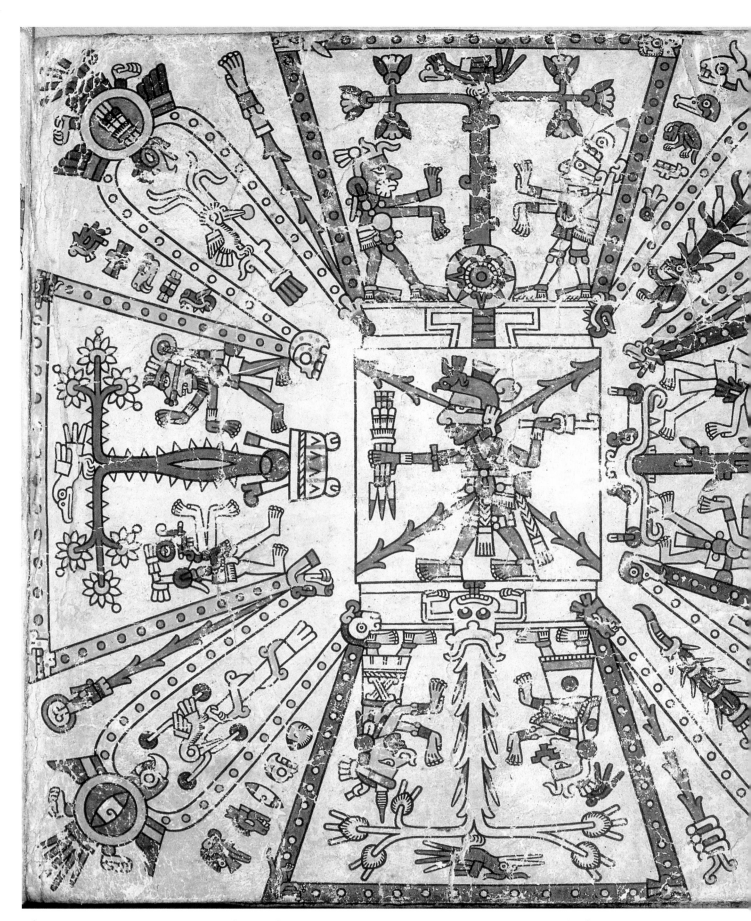

26–1 | A VIEW OF THE WORLD Page from Codex Fejervary-Mayer. Aztec, c. 1400–1519/21. Paint on animal hide, each page 6⅞ × 6⅞″ (17.5 × 17.5 cm), total length 13′3″ (4.04 m). The National Museums and Galleries on Merseyside, Liverpool, England.

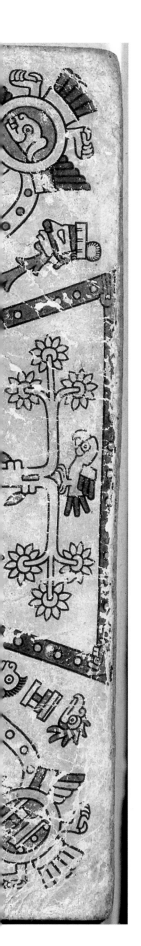

CHAPTER TWENTY-SIX

ART OF THE AMERICAS AFTER 1300

26

Early in November 1519, the army of the Spanish conquistador Hernán Cortés beheld for the first time the great Aztec capital of Tenochtitlan. The shimmering city, which seemed to be floating on the water, was built on islands in the middle of Lake Texcoco in the Valley of Mexico, and linked by broad causeways to the mainland. One of Cortés's companions later recalled the wonder the Spanish felt at that moment: "When we saw so many cities and villages built on the water and other great towns and that straight and level causeway going towards [Tenochtitlan], we were amazed . . . on account of the great towers and [temples] and buildings rising from the water, and all built of masonry. And some of our soldiers even asked whether the things that we saw were not a dream" (cited in Berdan, page 1).

The startling vision that riveted Cortés's soldiers was indeed real, a city of stone built on islands—a city that held many treasures and many mysteries. Much of the period before the conquistadors' arrival remains enigmatic, but a rare manuscript that survived the Spanish conquest of Mexico depicts the preconquest worldview of the native peoples. At the center of the image is the ancient fire god Xiuhtecutli (FIG. 26–1). Radiating from him are the four directions—each associated with a specific color, a deity, and a tree with a bird in its branches. In each corner, to the right of a U-shaped band, is an attribute of Tezcatlipoca, the Smoking Mirror, an omnipotent, primal deity who could see humankind's thoughts and deeds—in the upper right a head, in the upper left an arm, in the lower left a foot, and in the lower right bones. Streams of blood flow from these attributes back to the fire god in the center. Such images are filled with important, symbolically coded information—even the dots refer to the number of days in one aspect of the Mesoamerican calendar—and they were integral parts of the culture of the Americas.

When the first European explorers and adventurers arrived in 1519, the Western Hemisphere was already inhabited from the Arctic Circle to Tierra del Fuego by peoples with long and complex histories and rich and varied cultural traditions. This chapter focuses on the arts of the indigenous peoples of the Americas (MAP 26–1) just prior to, and in the wake of, their encounter with an expansionist Europe.

Two great empires—the Aztec in Mexico and the Inca in South America—had risen to prominence in the fifteenth century at about the same time that European adventurers began to explore the oceans in search of new trade routes to Asia. In the encounter that followed, the Aztec and Inca empires were destroyed.

THE AZTEC EMPIRE

The Mexica people who lived in the remarkable city that Cortés found in the early sixteenth century were then rulers of much of the land that took their name, Mexico. Their rise to power had been recent and swift. Only 400 years earlier, according to their own legends, they had been a nomadic people living northwest of the Valley of Mexico on the shores of the mythical Aztlan. The term *Aztec* derives from the word *Aztlan*.

After a period of migration, the Aztecs arrived in the Valley of Mexico in the thirteenth century. They eventually settled on an island in Lake Texcoco where they had seen an eagle perching on a prickly pear cactus (tenochtli), a sign that their legends told them would mark the end of their wandering. They called the place Tenochtitlan. The city was situated on a collection of islands linked by human-made canals in a grid pattern.

In the fifteenth century, the Aztecs—joined by allies in a triple alliance—began an aggressive campaign of expansion. The tribute they exacted from all over central Mexico transformed Tenochtitlan into a glittering capital. As the Spanish conquistador Hernán Cortés approached Tenochtitlan in November 1519, he and his soldiers marveled at the stone buildings, towers, and temples that seemed from a distance to rise from the water like a mirage.

Religion

Aztec religion was based on a complex pantheon that combined the Aztec deities with more ancient ones that had long been worshiped in central Mexico. According to Aztec belief, the gods had created the current universe at the ancient city of Teotihuacan in the Valley of Mexico (see Chapter 12). The continued existence of the world depended on human actions, including rituals of bloodletting and human sacrifice. The end of each round of fifty-two years in the Mesoamerican calendar was a particularly dangerous time that required a special fire-lighting ritual. Sacrificial victims sustained the sun god, Huitzilopochtli, in his daily course through the sky. Huitzilopochtli was the son of the Earth mother Coatlicue. When Coatlicue conceived Huitzilopochtli by holding within her chest a ball of hummingbird feathers (the soul of a fallen warrior) that had dropped from the sky, her other children—the stars and the moon—jealously conspired to kill her. When they attacked, Huitzilopochtli emerged from his mother's body fully grown and armed, drove off his half brothers, and destroyed his half sister, the moon goddess Coyolxauhqui. Every day at dawn, the Sun God fights off the darkness, killing the stars (his 400 brothers) and the moon (his sister).

Tenochtitlan

An idealized representation of the city of Tenochtitlan and its sacred ceremonial precinct (**FIG. 26–2**) was drawn by Aztec scribes for Spanish administrators. It forms the first page of the *Codex Mendoza*, prepared for the Spanish viceroy in the sixteenth century. An eagle perched on a prickly pear cactus—the symbol of the city—fills the center of the page.

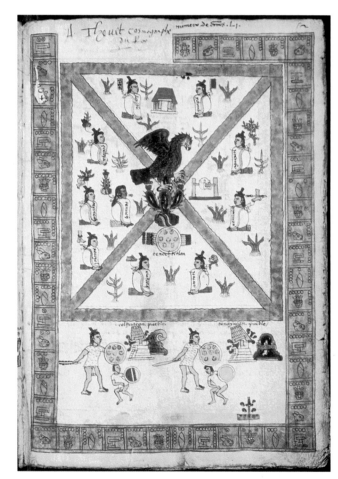

26–2 | **THE FOUNDING OF TENOCHTITLAN**
Page from *Codex Mendoza*. Aztec, 16th century. Ink and color on paper, 12⅜ × 8⅞" (21.5 × 31.5 cm). The Bodleian Library, University of Oxford, England.
MS. Arch Selden. A.1.fol. 2r

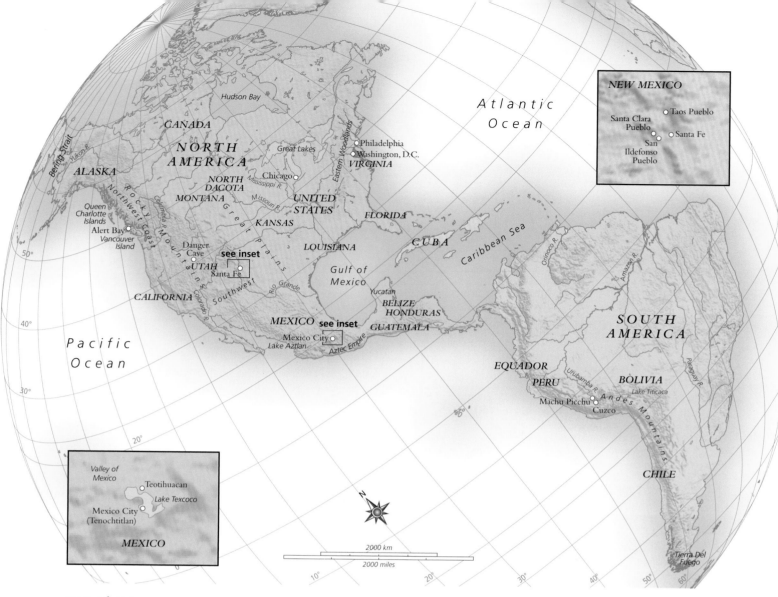

MAP 26–1 | **THE AMERICAS AFTER 1300**

Diverse peoples spread throughout the Americas, each shaping a distinct culture in the area it settled.

Waterways divide the city into four quarters, which are further subdivided into wards, as represented by the seated figures. The victorious warriors at the bottom of the page represent Aztec conquests.

The focal point of the sacred precinct—symbolized in FIGURE 26–2 by the temple or house at the top of the page—was the Great Pyramid, a 115- to 130-foot-high, four-tiered pyramid with two temples on top: a red and black temple dedicated to Huitzilopochtli and a blue temple for Tlaloc, the god of rain and fertility. Two steep staircases led up the west face of the pyramid from the plaza in front. Sacrificial victims climbed these stairs to the Temple of Huitzilopochtli, where priests threw them over a stone, quickly cut open their chests, and pulled out their still-throbbing hearts, hearts whose beating insured the survival of the sun, the gods, and the Aztecs. Their bodies were then rolled down the stairs and dismembered. Thousands of severed heads were said to have been kept on a skull rack in the plaza, represented in FIGURE 26–2 by the rack with a single skull to the right of the eagle.

During the winter rainy season the sun rose behind the Temple of Tlaloc, and during the dry season it rose behind the Temple of Huitzilopochtli. The double temple thus united two natural forces, sun and rain, or fire and water. During the spring and autumn equinoxes, the sun rose between the two temples, illuminating the Temple of Quetzalcoatl, the feathered serpent, an ancient creator god associated with time (the calendar), civilization, and the arts.

TWO GODDESSES. Sculptures of serpents and serpent heads on the Great Pyramid in Tenochtitlan associated it with the place where the Sun God slew the moon goddess, Coyolxauhqui. A huge circular relief of the dismembered goddess lay at the foot of the temple stairs, as if the enraged and triumphant Huitzilopochtli had cast her there like a sacrificial victim (FIG. 26–3). Her torso is in the center, surrounded by her head and limbs. A rope around her waist is attached to a skull. She has bells on her cheeks and balls of down in her hair. She wears a magnificent headdress and has distinctive ear ornaments composed of disks, rectangles, and triangles. The sculpture is two-dimensional in concept—a flat surface with a deeply cut background.

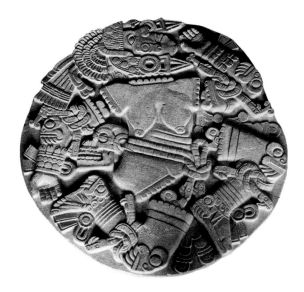

26–3 THE MOON GODDESS COYOLXAUHQUI ("SHE OF THE GOLDEN BELLS")
The Sacred Precinct, now the Museo Templo Mayor, Tenochtitlan. Aztec, 1469 (?). Stone, diameter 10'10" (3.33 m). Museo Templo Mayor, Mexico City.

This disk was discovered in 1978 by workers from a utility company who were excavating in central Mexico City.

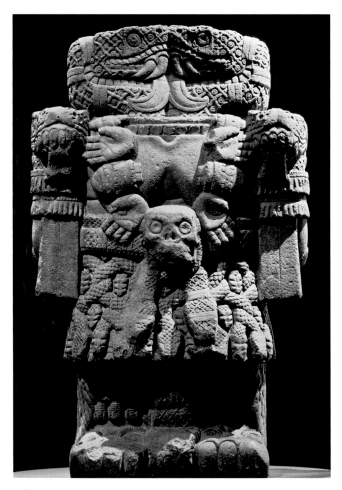

26–4 THE GODDESS COATLICUE
Aztec, 1487–1520. Basalt, height 8'6" (2.65 m).
Museo Nacional de Antropología, Mexico City.

Standing high above the disk of the vanquished moon goddess was an imposing statue of Coatlicue, mother of Huitzilopochtli (FIG. 26–4). A sixteenth-century Spaniard described seeing such a statue covered with blood inside the Temple of the Sun. Coatlicue means "she of the serpent skirt," and this broad-shouldered figure with clawed hands and feet has a skirt of twisted snakes. A pair of serpents, symbols of gushing blood, rise from her neck to form her head. Their eyes are her eyes; their fangs, her tusks. The writhing serpents of her skirt also form her body. Around her stump of a neck hangs a necklace of sacrificial offerings—hands, hearts, and a dangling skull. Despite the surface intricacy, the sculpture's simple, bold, and blocky forms create an impression of solidity. The colors with which it was originally painted would have heightened its dramatic impact.

Indeed Aztec art was colorful. An idea of its iridescent splendor is captured in the feather headdress said to have been given by Moctezuma to Cortés, and thought to be the one listed in the inventory of treasures Cortés shipped to Charles V, the Habsburg emperor in Spain in 1519. Featherwork was one of the glories of Mesoamerican art but very few of these extremely fragile artworks survive. "Moctezuma's Crown," as it was called, was originally a conqueror's trophy, and only recognized as "art" in recent times (FIG. 26–5). It is made of brilliant green, red, white, and blue feathers of the quetzal bird, macaw parrot, and other lesser birds, fastened to a reed frame. The feathers were gathered in small bunches, their quills reinforced with reed tubes, and then sewn to the frame in overlapping layers. Featherworkers were esteemed craftspersons. A song in praise of the feather artist says, "He is whole; he has a face and a heart. The good feather artist is skillful, is master of himself; it is his duty to humanize the desires of the people. He works with feathers, chooses them, arranges them, paints them with different colors, joins them together." (Sorge Gruziriski, *The Aztecs, Discoveries*, New York: Abrams. English translation, 1992, p. 153.)

The Aztec empire was short lived. Within two years of their arrival in Mexico, the Spanish conquistadors overran Tenochtitlan. They built their own capital, Mexico City, over its ruins and established their own cathedral on the site of Tenochtitlan's sacred precinct.

THE INCA EMPIRE IN SOUTH AMERICA

At the beginning of the sixteenth century the Inca Empire was one of the largest states in the world. It extended more than 2,600 miles along western South America, encompassing most of modern Peru, Ecuador, Bolivia, and northern Chile and reaching into present-day Argentina. Like the Aztec Empire, its rise was rapid and its destruction sudden.

The Incas called their empire the "Land of the Four Quarters." At its center was their capital, Cuzco, "the navel of

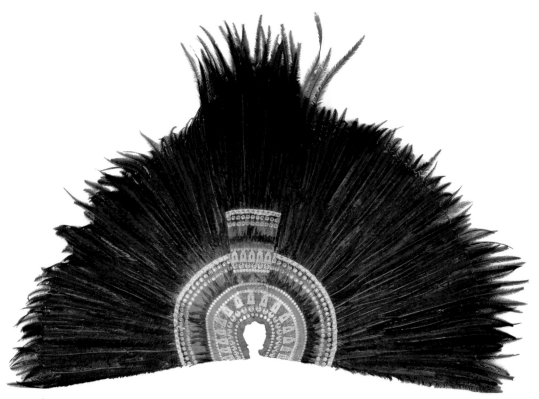

26–5 | **FEATHER HEADDRESS OF MOCTEZUMA**
Before 1519. Quetzal, macaw, and other feathers on a reed frame.
Museum für Völkerkunde, Vienna.

the world," located high in the Andes Mountains. The Inca state was one of many small competing kingdoms that emerged in the highlands. In the fifteenth century the Incas began to expand, suddenly and rapidly, and had subdued most of their vast domain—through conquest, alliance, and intimidation—by 1500.

To hold this linguistically and ethnically diverse empire together, the Inca ("Inca" refers to both the ruler and to the people) relied on religion, an efficient bureaucracy, and various forms of labor taxation, in which the payment was a set amount of time spent performing tasks for the state. As part of their labor tax, people were required to work the lands of the gods and the state for part of each year. In return the state provided gifts through their local leaders and sponsored lavish ritual entertainments. Men might serve periodically on public-works projects—building roads and terracing hillsides, for example—or in the army. Women wove cloth, a commodity that Inca people considered more precious than gold. The Inca might relocate whole communities to best exploit the resources of the empire. Ranks of storehouses at Inca administrative centers assured the state's ability to feed its armies and supply its workers. No Andean civilization ever developed writing, but the Inca kept detailed accounts on knotted and colored cords, called *quipu*.

THE INCA ROAD SYSTEM. To move their armies and speed transport and communication within the empire, the Incas built more than 23,000 miles of roads. These varied from 50-foot-wide thoroughfares to 3-foot-wide paths. Two main north–south roads, one along the coast and the other through the highlands, were linked by east–west roads. Travelers journeyed on foot, using llamas as pack animals. Stairways helped them negotiate steep mountain slopes, and rope suspension bridges allowed river gorge crossings. The main road through the Pacific coastal desert had walls to protect it from blowing sand. All along the roads, storehouses and lodgings—more than a thousand have been found—were spaced a day's journey apart. A relay system of runners could carry messages between Cuzco and the farthest reaches of the empire in about a week.

Masonry

Cuzco, a capital of great splendor, was home to the Inca, ruler of the empire. The city was a showcase of the finest Inca masonry, some of which can still be seen in the present-day city. This masonry has survived earthquakes that have destroyed later structures. Fine **INCA MASONRY** consisted of either rectangular blocks or irregular polygonal blocks (**FIG. 26–6**). In both types, adjoining blocks were painstakingly shaped to fit tightly together without mortar (see "Inca Masonry," page 878). Their stone faces might be slightly beveled along their edges so that each block presented a "pillowed" shape expressing its identity, or walls might be smoothed into a continuous flowing surface in which the individual blocks form a seamless whole. In contrast to the massive walls, Inca buildings had gabled, thatched roofs.

Elements of Architecture
INCA MASONRY

Working with the simplest of tools—mainly heavy stone hammers—and using no mortar, Inca builders created stonework of great refinement and durability: roads and bridges that linked the entire empire, built-up terraces for growing crops, and structures both simple and elaborate. At Machu Picchu (SEE FIGS. 26–6, 26–7), all buildings and terraces within its 3-square-mile extent were made of granite, the hard stone occurring at the site. Commoners' houses and some walls were constructed of irregular stones that were carefully fitted together. Some walls and certain domestic and religious structures were erected using squared-off, smooth-surfaced stones laid in even rows. At a few Inca sites, the stones used in construction were boulder-size: up to 27 feet tall.

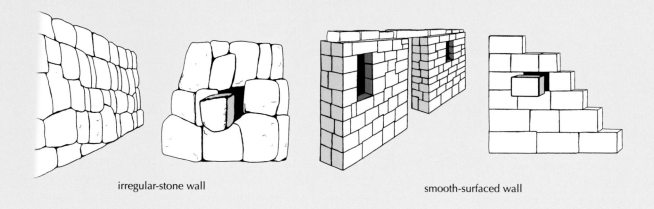

irregular-stone wall

smooth-surfaced wall

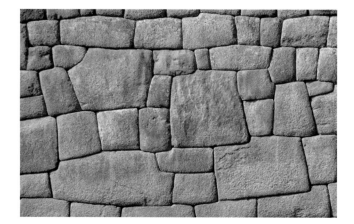

26–6 | **INCA MASONRY, DETAIL OF A WALL IN MACHU PICCHU**
Peru. Inca, 1450–1530.

Doors, windows, and niches were trapezoid shaped, narrower at the top than the bottom. The effort expended on stone construction by the Inca was prodigious.

MACHU PICCHU. **MACHU PICCHU**, one of the most spectacular archaeological sites in the world, provides an excellent example of Inca architectural planning (FIG. 26–7). At 9,000 feet above sea level, it straddles a ridge between two high peaks in the eastern slopes of the Andes and looks down on the Urubamba River. Stone buildings, today lacking only their thatched roofs, occupy terraces around central plazas, and narrow agricultural terraces descend into the valley. The site, near the eastern limits of the empire, was the estate of the Inca Pachacuti (ruled 1438–71). Its temples and sacred stones —some, left natural, were erected in courtyard shrines—suggest that the site also had an important religious function.

Textiles

The production of fine textiles had been an important art in the Andes from the time of the Paracas culture (see Chapter 12), beginning about 1000 BCE. Among the Incas, textiles of cotton and camelid fibers (from llama, vicuna, and alpaca) were a primary form of wealth. One form of labor taxation required the manufacture of fibers and cloth, and textiles as well as agricultural products filled Inca storehouses. Cloth was deemed a fitting offering for the gods, so fine garments were draped around golden statues, and even three-dimensional images were constructed of cloth.

TUNICS. The patterns and designs on garments were not simply decorative but also carried symbolic messages, including indications of a person's ethnic identity and social rank. In the elaborate **TUNIC** in FIGURE 26–8, each square represents a miniature tunic, but the meanings of the individual patterns

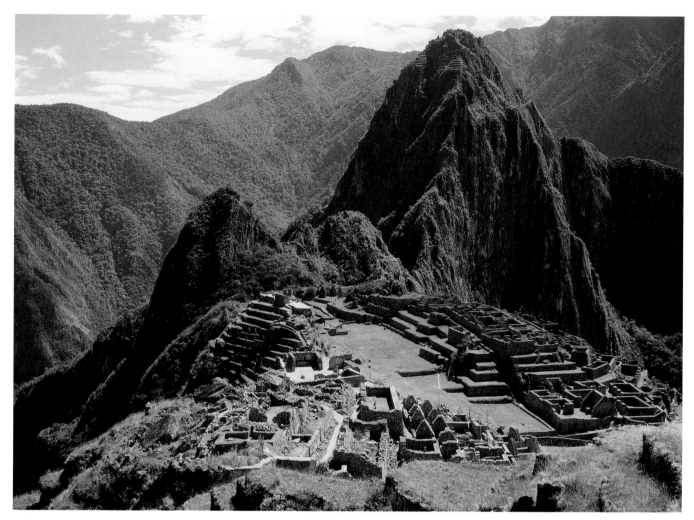

26–7 | **MACHU PICCHU**
Peru. Inca, 1450–1530.

are not yet completely understood. The four-part motifs may refer to the Land of the Four Quarters. The diagonal key motif is often found on tunics with horizontal border stripes but its meaning is not known. The checkerboard patterns are thought to designate military officers and royal escorts. While we may not be sure what was meant in every case, patterns and colors appear to have been standardized like uniforms in order to convey information at a glance.

Metalwork

Following Cortés's example, Francisco Pizarro led an expedition to South America in 1532. He and his men seized the Inca ruler, Atahualpa, held him for ransom, and then treacherously strangled him. They marched on to Cuzco and seized it in 1533.

The Spanish were far less interested in Inca cloth than in their vast quantities of gold and silver. The Inca valued objects made of gold and silver not for their precious metal, but because they saw in them symbols of the sun and the moon. They are said to have called gold the "sweat of the sun" and silver the "tears of the moon." On the other hand, the

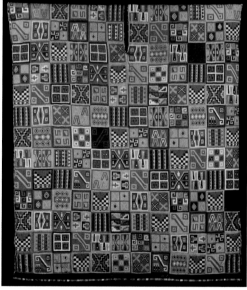

26–8 | **TUNIC**
Peru. Inca, c. 1500. Wool and cotton, 35⅞ × 30″ (91 × 76.5 cm). Dumbarton Oaks Research Library and Collections, Pre-Columbian Collection, Washington, D.C.

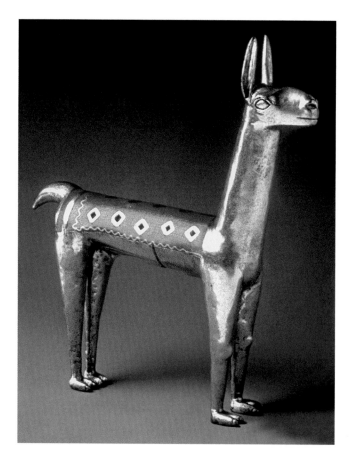

26–9 | LLAMA

From Bolivia or Peru, found near Lake Titicaca, Bolivia. Inca, 15th century. Cast silver with gold and cinnabar, 9 × 8½ × 1¾″ (22.9 × 21.6 × 4.4 cm). American Museum of Natural History, New York.

Spanish exploration of the New World was propelled by feverish tales of native treasure. Whatever gold and silver objects the Spanish could lay their hands on, they melted down to enrich their royal coffers. Only a few small figures buried as offerings, like the little llama (FIG. 26–9), escaped the conquerors. The llama was thought to have a special connection with the sun, with rain, and with fertility, and a llama was sacrificed to the sun every morning and evening in Cuzco. A white llama was kept as the symbol of the Inca. Dressed in a red tunic and wearing gold jewelry, this llama passed through the streets of Cuzco during April celebrations. According to Spanish commentators, these processions included life-size gold and silver images of llamas, people, and gods.

The Aftermath of the Spanish Conquest

Native American populations in Mexico and Peru declined sharply after the conquest because of the exploitative policies of the conquerors and the ravages of smallpox and other diseases that spread from Europe and against which the indigenous people had no immunity. European missionaries suppressed local beliefs and practices and worked to spread Roman Catholicism throughout the Americas. While increas-

ing numbers of Europeans began to settle and dominate the land, native arts did not end with the Spanish conquest. Traditional arts, including fine weaving, continue to this day.

NORTH AMERICA

In America north of Mexico, from the upper reaches of Canada and Alaska to the southern tip of Florida, existed many different peoples with widely varying cultures. Much of their artwork was small, portable, fragile, and impermanent. In previous times these artworks were not appreciated for their aesthetic qualities, but were collected as anthropological artifacts or curiosities. As a consequence, one often must visit anthropology and natural history museums to view works of indigenous art. Today this attitude has changed, and Native American artworks have entered collections as art and are displayed in such prestigious places as the National Museum of the American Indian in Washington, D.C. Today work of an increasing number of young Native American artists can be seen alongside Euro-American artists in mainstream art galleries. We will look at art from only four North American cultural areas: the Eastern Woodlands, the Great Plains, the Northwest Coast, and the Southwest (SEE MAP 26–2).

The Eastern Woodlands

In the eastern woodlands, most tribes lived in stable villages, and they combined hunting, gathering, and agriculture for their livelihood. In the sixteenth century, skilled politicians appeared among them. The Iroquois formed a powerful confederation of five northeastern Native American nations, and they played a prominent military and political role until after the American Revolution. The Huron and Illinois also formed sizable confederacies.

The arrival in the seventeenth century on the Atlantic coast of a few boatloads of Europeans seeking religious freedom, land to farm, and a new life for themselves brought major changes. Trade with these settlers gave the Woodlands peoples access to things they valued, while on their part, the colonists learned native forms of agriculture, hunting, and fishing—skills they needed in order to survive. The arrival of the Europeans also had a negative impact, since they brought diseases, especially smallpox, with them. Disease wiped out entire Native populations. The lands seemed an untended wilderness to the Europeans, although in the first years of colonization some people remarked on the presence of abandoned fields and villages.

Native Americans traded furs for such useful items as metal tools, cookware, needles, and cloth, and they especially prized European glass beads and silver. They associated glass beads, and other shiny, reflective objects and materials, with ancient cultural values of self-knowledge, introspection, and understanding. These trade items largely replaced older materials, such as crystal, copper, and shell. The traditional meanings and values of

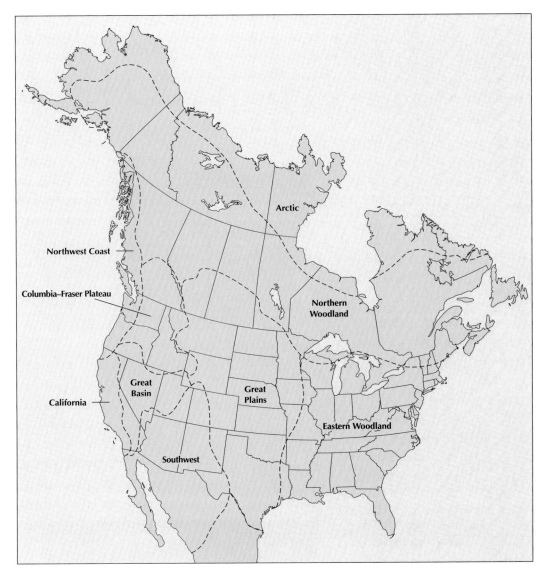

MAP 26–2 | NORTH AMERICAN CULTURAL AREAS

beads and similar items survive today from the ancestral mound-building civilizations of Eastern North America in contemporary celebratory and ceremonial powwow dress.

WAMPUM. Woodlands peoples made belts and strings of cylindrical purple and white shell beads called *wampum.* The Iroquois and Delaware peoples used wampum to keep records (the purple and white patterns served as memory devices) and exchanged belts of wampum to conclude treaties (FIG. 26–10). Few actual wampum treaty belts have survived, so this one associated with an unwritten treaty when the land now comprising the State of Pennsylvania was

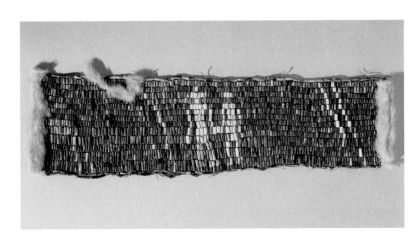

26–10 | WAMPUM BELT, TRADITIONALLY CALLED WILLIAM PENN'S TREATY WITH THE DELAWARE
1680's. Shell beads. Royal Ontario Museum, Canada.
HD6364

Technique
BASKETRY

Basketry is the weaving of reeds, grasses, and other plant materials to form containers. In North America the earliest evidence of basketwork, found in Danger Cave, Utah, dates to as early as 8400 BCE. Over the subsequent centuries, Native American women, notably in California and the American Southwest, developed basketry into an art form that combined utility with great beauty.

There are three principal basket-making techniques: coiling, twining, and plaiting. *Coiling* involves sewing together a spiraling foundation of rods with some other material. *Twining* is the sewing together of a vertical warp of rods. *Plaiting* employs weaving strips over and under each other.

The coiled basket shown here was made by the Pomo of California. According to Pomo legend, the Earth was dark until their ancestral hero stole the sun and brought it to Earth in a basket. He hung the basket first just over the horizon, but, dissatisfied with the light it gave, he kept suspending it in different places across the dome of the sky. He repeats this process every day, which is why the sun moves across the sky from east to west. In the Pomo basket, the structure of coiled willow and bracken fern root produces a spiral surface into which the artist worked sparkling pieces of clamshell, trade beads, and the soft

tufts of woodpecker and quail feathers. The underlying basket, the glittering shells, and the soft, moving feathers make this an exquisite container. Such baskets were treasured possessions, cremated with their owners at death.

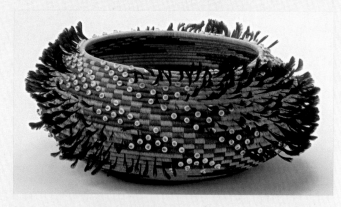

FEATHERED WEDDING BASKET
Pomo. c. 1877. Willow, bulrush, fern, feather, shells, glass beads. Height 5½" (14 cm), diameter 12" (36.5 cm). Philbrook Museum, Tulsa, Oklahoma.
Clark Field Collection (1948.39.37)

---

ceded by the Delawares in 1682 is especially prized. The belt with two figures of equal size holding hands suggests the mutual respect enjoyed by the Delaware and Penn's Society of Friends (Quakers), a respect that later collapsed into land fraud and violence. In general, wampum strings and belts had the power of legal agreement and also symbolized a moral and political order.

QUILLWORK. Woodlands art focused on personal adornment—tattoos, body paint, elaborate dress—and fragile arts such as quillwork. Quillwork involved dyeing porcupine and bird quills with a variety of natural dyes, soaking the quills to soften them, and then working them into rectilinear, ornamental surface patterns on deerskin clothing and on birchbark items like baskets and boxes. A Sioux legend recounts how a mythical ancestor, Doublewoman ("double" because she was both beautiful and ugly, benign and dangerous), appeared to a woman in a dream and taught her the art of quillwork. As the legend suggests, quillwork was a woman's art form, as was basketry (see "Basketry," above). The Sioux **BABY CARRIER** (FIG. 26–11) is richly decorated with symbols of protection and well-being, including bands of antelopes in profile and thunderbirds—flying with their heads turned and tails outspread. The thunderbird was an especially beneficent symbol, thought to be capable of protecting against both human and supernatural adversaries.

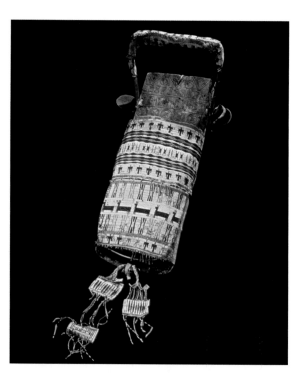

26–11 | BABY CARRIER
The Upper Missouri River area. Eastern Sioux, 19th century. Board, buckskin, porcupine quill, length 31" (78.8 cm). Department of Anthropology, Smithsonian Institution Libraries, Washington, D.C.
(Catalogue No. 7311)

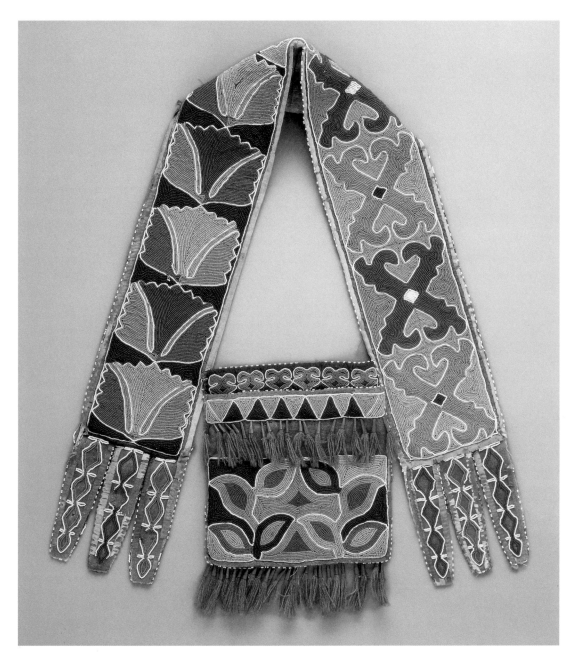

26–12 | SHOULDER BAG
Delaware people. Kansas. c. 1860. Wool fabric, cotton fabric and thread, silk ribbon, and glass beads, 23 × 7¾" (58.5 × 19.8 cm). The Detroit Institute of Arts.
Founders Society Purchase (81.216)

BEADWORK. In spite of the use of shell beads in wampum, decorative beadwork did not become commonplace until after European contact. In the late eighteenth century, Native American artists began to acquire European colored-glass beads, and in the nineteenth century they favored the tiny seed beads from Venice and Bohemia. Early beadwork mimicked the patterns and colors of quillwork. In the nineteenth century it largely replaced quillwork and incorporated European designs. About 1830 Canadian nuns introduced the young women in their schools to embroidered European floral motifs, and the native embroiderers began to adapt these designs as well as European needlework techniques and patterns from European garments into their own work. Functional aspects of garments might be transformed into purely decorative motifs; for example, a pocket would be replaced by an area of beadwork shaped like a pocket. A **SHOULDER BAG** from Kansas, made by a Delaware woman (**FIG. 26–12**), is covered with curvilinear plant motifs in contrast to the

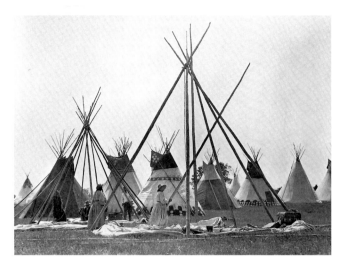

26–13 | **BLACKFOOT WOMEN RAISING A TEPEE**
Photographed c. 1900. Montana Historical Society, Helena, Montana.

rectilinear patterns of traditional quillwork. White lines outline brilliant pink and blue leaf-shaped forms, heightening the intensity of the colors, which alternate within repeated patterns. The Delaware bag exemplifies the evolution of beadwork design.

The Great Plains

Between the Eastern Woodlands region and the Rocky Mountains to the west lay an area of prairie grasslands called the Great Plains. On the Great Plains, two differing ways of life developed, one a relatively recent and short lived (1700–1870) nomadic lifestyle—dependent on the region's great migrating herds of buffalo for food, clothing, and shelter—and the other, a much older sedentary and agricultural lifestyle. Horses, from wild herds descended from feral horses brought to America by Spanish explorers in the sixteenth and seventeenth centuries, made travel and a nomadic life easier for the dispossessed eastern groups that moved to the plains.

European settlers on the eastern seaboard put increasing pressure on the Eastern Woodlands peoples, seizing their farmlands and forcing them westward. Both Native Americans and backcountry settlers were living in loosely village-based, farming societies and thus were competing for the same resources. The resulting interaction of Eastern Woodlands artists with one another and with Plains artists led in some cases to the emergence of a new hybrid style, while other artists consciously fought to maintain their own cultures.

PORTABLE ARCHITECTURE. The nomadic Plains peoples hunted buffalo for food and hides from which they created clothing and a light, portable dwelling known as a **TEPEE** (FIG. 26–13). The tepee was well adapted to withstand the strong and constant wind, and the dust and violent storms of the prairies. The framework of a tepee consisted of a stable pyramidal frame of three or four long poles, filled out with about twenty additional poles, in a roughly egg-shaped plan. The framework was covered with hides (or, later, with canvas) to form a conical structure. The hides were specially prepared to make them flexible and waterproof. A typical tepee required about eighteen hides; the largest, about thirty-eight hides. An opening at the top served as the smoke hole for a central hearth. The tepee leaned slightly into the prevailing west wind while the flap-covered door and smoke hole faced east, away from the wind. An inner lining covered the lower part of the walls and the perimeter of the floor to protect the occupants from drafts.

Tepees were the property and responsibility of women, who set them up at new encampments and lowered them when the group moved on. Blackfoot women could set up their huge tepees in less than an hour. Women painted, embroidered, quilled, and beaded tepee linings, backrests, clothing, and equipment. The patterns with which tepees were decorated, as well as their proportions and colors, varied from nation to nation, family to family, and individual to individual. In general, the bottom was covered with the traditional motifs of the people, and the center section held personal images. When disassembled and packed to be dragged by a horse to another location, the tepee served as a platform for transporting other possessions. The Sioux arranged their tepees in two half circles—one for the sky people and one for the earth people—divided along an east–west axis. When the Blackfoot people gathered in the summer for their ceremonial Sun Dance, their encampment contained hundreds of tepees in a circle a mile in circumference.

PLAINS INDIAN PAINTING. Plains men recorded their exploits in paintings on tepee linings and covers and on buffalo-hide robes. The earliest surviving painted buffalo-hide robe illustrates a battle fought in 1797 by the Mandan (of what is now North Dakota) and their allies against the Sioux (FIG. 26–14). The painter, trying to capture the full extent of a conflict in which five nations took part, shows a party of warriors in twenty-two separate episodes. The party is led by a man with a pipe and an elaborate eagle-feather headdress, and the warriors are armed with bows and arrows, lances, clubs, and flintlock rifles. Details of equipment and emblems of rank—headdresses, sashes, shields, feathered lances, powder horns for the rifles—are depicted carefully. Horses are shown in profile with stick legs, C-shaped hooves, and either clipped or flowing manes.

The figures stand out clearly against the light-colored background of the buffalo hide. The painter pressed lines into the hide, then filled in with black, red, green, yellow, and brown pigments. He drew the warriors as stick figures with rectangular torsos and tiny round heads. A strip of colored porcupine quills runs down the spine of the buffalo hide. The robe would have been worn draped over the shoulders of the powerful warrior whose deeds it commemorates. As the wearer moved, the painted horses and warriors would seem to come alive, transforming the warrior into a living representation of his exploits.

Life on the Great Plains changed abruptly in 1869, when the Euro-Americans finished the transcontinental railway linking the east and west coasts of the United States and providing easy access to Native American lands. Between

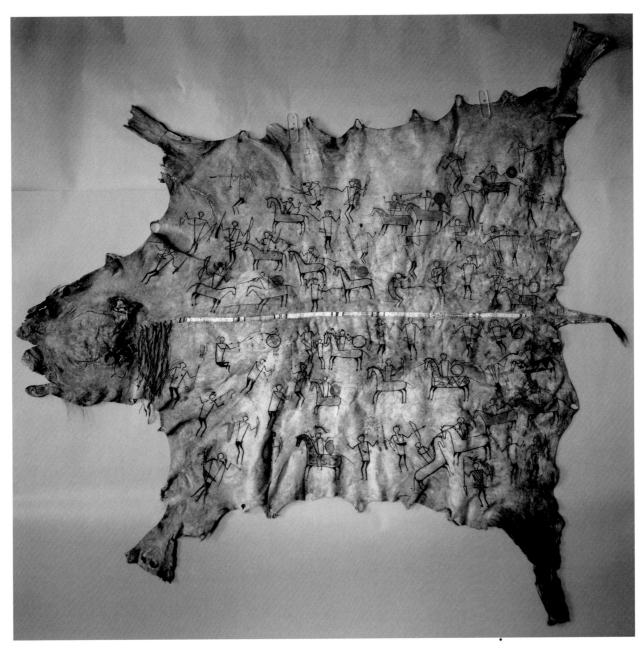

26–14 | **BATTLE-SCENE, HIDE PAINTING**
Mandan. North Dakota. 1797–1800. Tanned buffalo hide, dyed porcupine quills, and black, red, green, yellow, and brown pigment, 7'10" × 8'6" (2.44 × 2.65 m). Peabody Museum of Archaeology, Harvard University, Cambridge, Massachusetts.
(99-12-10/53121)

This robe, collected in 1804 by Meriwether Lewis and William Clark on their 1804–06 expedition into western lands acquired by the United States in the Louisiana Purchase, is the earliest documented example of Plains painting. It was one of a number of Native American artworks that Lewis and Clark sent to President Thomas Jefferson. Jefferson displayed the robe in the entrance hall of his home at Monticello, Virginia.

1871 and 1890, Euro-American hunters had killed off most of the buffalo, and soon ranchers and then farmers moved into the Great Plains. The U.S. government forcibly moved the outnumbered and outgunned Native Americans to reservations, land considered worthless until the later discovery of oil and, in the case of the Black Hills, gold.

The Northwest Coast

From southern Alaska to northern California, the Pacific coast of North America is a region of unusually abundant resources. Its many rivers fill each year with salmon returning to spawn. Harvested and dried, the fish could sustain large populations throughout the year. The peoples of the Northwest Coast—among them the Tlingit, the Haida, and the Kwakwaka'wakw (formerly spelled Kwakiutl)—exploited this abundance to develop a complex and distinctive way of life in which the arts played a central role.

ANIMAL IMAGERY. Northwest Coast people lived in extended family groups (clans) that claimed descent from a mythic animal or animal-human ancestor. A family derived its name and the right to use certain animals and spirits as totemic emblems, or crests, from its mythic ancestor. These emblems appeared prominently in Northwest Coast art, notably in carved cedar house poles and the tall, freestanding poles (mortuary poles) erected to memorialize dead chiefs. Chiefs, who were males in the most direct line of descent from the mythic ancestor, administered a family's spiritual and material resources. They validated their status and garnered prestige for themselves and their families by holding ritual feasts known as potlatches, during which they gave valuable gifts to the invited guests. Shamans, who were sometimes also chiefs, mediated between the human and spirit worlds. Some shamans were female, giving them unique access to specific aspects of the spiritual world.

The people lived in large, elaborately decorated communal houses made of massive timbers and thick planks. Carved and painted partition screens separated the chief's quarters from the rest of the house. The Tlingit screen illustrated here (FIG. 26–15) came from the house of Chief Shakes of Wrangell (d. 1916), whose family crest was the grizzly bear. The image of a rearing grizzly painted on the screen is itself made up of smaller bears and bear heads that appear in its ears, eyes, nostrils, joints, paws, and body. The images within the image enrich the monumental symmetrical design. The oval door opening is a symbolic vagina; passing through it reenacts the birth of the family from its ancestral spirit.

TEXTILES. Blankets and other textiles produced by the Chilkat Tlingit had great prestige among the Northwest Coast people (FIG. 26–16). Both men and women worked on the blankets. Men drew the patterns on boards, and women wove the patterns into the blankets, using shredded cedar

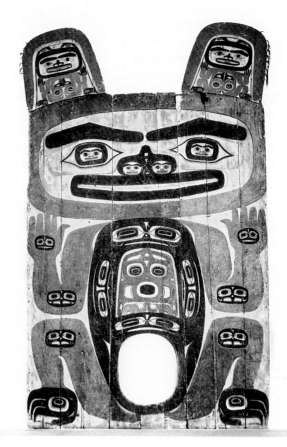

26–15 | **GRIZZLY BEAR HOUSE-PARTITION SCREEN**
The house of Chief Shakes of Wrangell, Canada. Tlingit people. c. 1840. Cedar, native paint, and human hair, 15 × 8′ (4.57 × 2.74 m). Denver Art Museum, Denver, Colorado.

bark and mountain-goat wool. The weavers did not use looms; instead, they hung cedar warp threads from a rod and twisted colored goat wool back and forth through them to make the pattern. The ends of the warp formed the fringe at the bottom of the blanket.

The small face in the center of the blanket shown here represents the body of a large stylized creature, perhaps a sea bear (a fur seal) or a standing eagle. Above the body are the creature's large eyes; below it and to the sides are its legs and claws. Characteristic of Northwest painting and weaving, the images are composed of two basic elements: the **ovoid**, a slightly bent rectangle with rounded corners, and the **formline**, a continuous, shape-defining line. Here, subtly swelling black formlines define shapes with gentle curves, ovoids, and rectangular C shapes. When the blanket was worn, its two-dimensional shapes would have become three-dimensional, with the dramatic central figure curving over the wearer's back and the intricate side panels crossing over his shoulders and chest.

MASKS. Many Native American cultures stage ritual dance ceremonies to call upon guardian spirits. The participants in Northwest Coast dance ceremonies wore elaborate costumes and striking carved and painted wooden masks. Among the most elaborate masks were those used by the Kwakwaka'wakw in their Winter Ceremony, in which they initiated members into the shamanistic Hamatsa society (see "Hamatsa Masks," page 888). The dance reenacted the taming of Hamatsa, a cannibal spirit, and his three attendant bird spirits. Magnificent carved and painted masks transformed the dancers into Hamatsa and the bird attendants who searched for victims to eat. Strings allowed the dancers to manipulate the masks so that the beaks opened and snapped shut with spectacular effect. Isolated in museums as "art," the masks doubtless lose some of the shocking vivacity they have in performance; nevertheless their bold forms and color schemes retain power and meaning that can be activated by the viewer's imagination.

The Southwest

The Native American peoples of the southwestern United States include, among others, the Pueblo (sedentary village-dwelling groups) and the Navajo. The Pueblo groups are heirs of the Ancestral Puebloans (Anasazi) and Hohokam cultures, which developed a fully settled, agricultural way of life

around 700. Earlier societies had developed agriculture in the Southwest as early as 3500 BCE. The Ancestral Puebloans built apartmentlike villages and cliff dwellings whose ruins are found throughout the Four Corners region (New Mexico, Colorado, northern Arizona, and Utah) of the American Southwest. The Navajo, who arrived in the region sometime during the eleventh century or even later, developed a semi-sedentary way of life based on agriculture and (after the introduction of sheep by the Spanish) sheepherding. Being

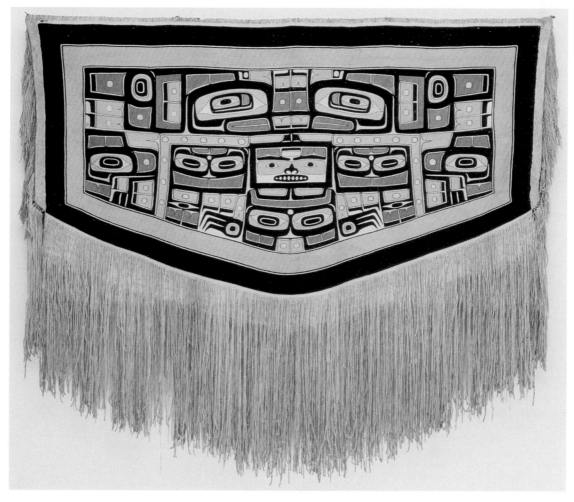

26–16 | **CHILKAT BLANKET**
Tlingit people. Before 1928. Mountain-goat wool and shredded cedar bark, 55⅛ × 63¾" (140 × 162 cm). American Museum of Natural History, New York.

THE ⦿BJECT SPEAKS

HAMATSA MASKS

During the harsh winter season, when spirits are thought to be most powerful, many northern people seek spiritual renewal through their ancient rituals—including the potlatch, or ceremonial gift giving, and the initiation of new members into the prestigious Hamatsa Society. With snapping beaks and cries of "Hap! Hap! Hap!" ("Eat! Eat! Eat!"), Hamatsa, the people-eating spirit of the north, and his three assistants—horrible masked monster birds—begin their wild, ritual dance. The dancing birds threaten and even attack the Kwakwaka'wakw people who gather for the Winter Ceremony.

In the Winter Ceremony, youths are captured, taught the Hamatsa lore and rituals, and then in a spectacular theater-dance performance are "tamed" and brought back into civilized life. All the members of the community, including singers, gather in the main room of the great house, which is divided by a painted screen (SEE FIG. 26–15). The audience members fully participate in the performance; in early times, they brought containers of blood so that when the bird-dancers attacked them, they could appear to bleed and have flesh torn away.

Whistles from behind the screen announce the arrival of the Hamatsa (danced by an initiate), who enters through the central hole in the screen in a flesh-craving frenzy. Wearing hemlock, a symbol of the spirit world, he crouches and dances wildly with outstretched arms as attendants try to control him. He disappears but returns again, now wearing red cedar and dancing upright. Finally tamed, a full member of society, he even dances with the women.

Then the masked bird-dancers appear—first Raven-of-the-North-End-of-the-World, then Crooked-Beak-of-the-End-of-the-World, and finally the untranslatable Huxshukw, who cracks open skulls with his beak and eats the brains of his victims. Snapping their beaks, these masters of illusion enter the room backward, their masks pointed up as though the birds are looking skyward. They move slowly counterclockwise around the floor. At each change in the music they crouch, snap their beaks, and let out their wild cries of "Hap! Hap! Hap!" Essential to the ritual dances are the huge carved and painted wooden masks, articulated and operated by strings worked by the dancers. Among the finest masks are those by Willie Seaweed (1873–1967), a Kwakwaka'wakw chief, whose brilliant colors and exuberantly decorative carving style determined the direction of twentieth-century Kwakwaka'wakw sculpture.

The Canadian government, abetted by missionaries, outlawed the Winter Ceremony and potlatches in 1885, claiming the event was injurious to health, encouraged prostitution, endangered children's education, damaged the economy, and was cannibalistic. But the Kwakwaka'wakw refused to give up their "oldest and best" festival—one that spoke powerfully to them in many ways, establishing social rank and playing an important role in arranging marriages. By 1936, the government and the missionaries, who called the Kwakwaka'wakw "incorrigible," gave up. But not until 1951 could the Kwakwaka'wakw people gather openly for winter ceremonies, including the initiation rites of the Hamatsa Society.

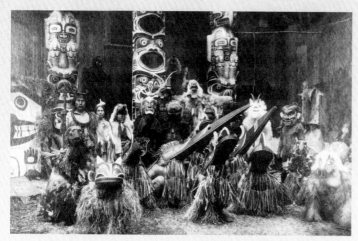

Edward S. Curtis   **HAMATSA DANCERS, KWAKWAKA'WAKW**
Canada. Photographed 1914. Smithsonian Institution Libraries, Washington, D.C.

The photographer Edward S. Curtis (1868–1952) devoted thirty years to documenting the lives of Native Americans. This photograph shows participants in a film he made about the Kwakwaka'wakw. For the film, his Native American assistant, Richard Hunt, borrowed family heirlooms and commissioned many new pieces from the finest Kwakwaka'wakw artists. Most of the pieces are now in museum collections. The photograph shows carved and painted posts, masked dancers (including those representing people-eating birds), a chief at the left (holding a speaker's staff and wearing a cedar neck ring), and spectators at the right.

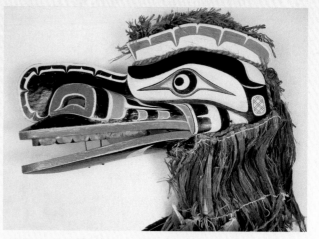

Attributed to Willie Seaweed
KWAKWAKA'WAKW BIRD MASK
Alert Bay, Vancouver Island, Canada. Prior to 1951.
Cedar wood, cedar bark, feathers, and fiber,
10 × 72 × 15″ (25.4 × 183 × 38.1 cm). Collection of the Museum of Anthropology, Vancouver, Canada.
(A6120)

The name "Seaweed" is an anglicization of the Kwakwaka'wakw name *Siwid,* meaning "Paddling Canoe," "Recipient of Paddling," or "Paddled To"—referring to a great chief to whose potlatches guests paddled from afar. Willie Seaweed was not only the chief of his clan, but a great orator, singer, and tribal historian who kept the tradition of the potlatch alive during years of government repression.

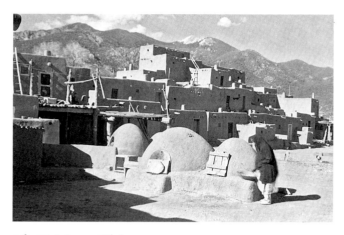

26–17 | Laura Gilpin **TAOS PUEBLO**
Tewa. Taos, New Mexico. Photographed 1947. Amon Carter Museum, Fort Worth, Texas.
© 1979 Laura Gilpin Collection (neg. # 2528.1)

Laura Gilpin, photographer of the landscape, architecture, and people of the American Southwest, began her series on the Pueblos and Navajos in the 1930s. She published her work in four volumes of photographs between 1941 and 1968.

among the very few Native American tribal groups whose reservations are located on their actual ancestral homelands, both groups have managed to maintain the continuity of their traditions despite Euro-American pressure. Today, their arts reflect the adaptation of traditional forms to new technologies, new mediums, and the influences of the dominant American culture that surrounds them.

THE PUEBLOS. Some Pueblo villages, like those of their ancient ancestors, consist of multistoried dwellings of considerable architectural interest to today's environmentalists. One of these, **TAOS PUEBLO**, shown here in a photograph taken in 1947 by the American photographer of the Southwest, Laura Gilpin (1891–1979), is located in north-central New Mexico **(FIG. 26–17)**. The northernmost of the surviving Pueblo communities, Taos once served as a trading center between Plains and Pueblo peoples. Taos burned in 1690 but was rebuilt about 1700 and has often been modified since. "Great Houses" (multifamily dwellings) stand on either side of Taos Creek. Bordering on a plaza that opens toward the neighboring mountains, they rise in a stepped fashion to provide a series of roof terraces that can serve as viewing platforms. The plaza and roof terraces are centers of communal life and ceremony, as can be seen in Pablita Velarde's painting of the winter solstice celebrations (SEE FIG. 26–19).

CERAMICS. Pottery traditionally was a woman's art among Pueblo peoples. Wares were made by coiling and other hand-building techniques, and then fired at low temperature in wood bonfires. The best-known twentieth-century Pueblo potter was Maria Montoya Martinez (1887–1980) of San Ildefonso Pueblo in New Mexico. Inspired by prehistoric blackware pottery that was unearthed at nearby archaeological excavations, she and her husband, Julian Martinez (1885–1943), developed a distinctive ceramics style decorated with matte (dull, nongloss) black forms on a lustrous black background **(FIG. 26–18)**. Maria made pots covered with a slip that was then burnished. Using additional slip, Julian

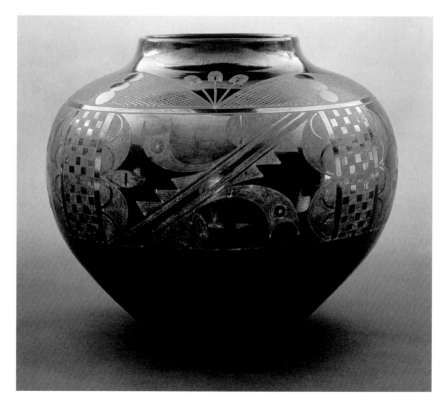

26–18 | Maria Montoya Martinez and Julian Martinez **BLACKWARE STORAGE JAR**
San Ildefonso Pueblo, New Mexico. c. 1942. Ceramic, height 18¾" (47.6 cm), diameter 22½" (57.1 cm). Museum of Indian Arts and Culture/Laboratory of Anthropology, Museum of New Mexico, Santa Fe.

Art and Its Context
NAVAJO NIGHT CHANT

This chant accompanies the creation of a sand painting during a Navajo curing ceremony. It is sung toward the end of the ceremony and indicates the restoration of inner harmony and balance.

In beauty (happily) I walk.
With beauty before me I walk.
With beauty behind me I walk.

With beauty below me I walk.
With beauty above me I walk.
With beauty all around me I walk.
It is finished (again) in beauty.
It is finished in beauty.

(Cited in Washington Mathews, *American Museum of Natural History Memoir, no. 6.* New York, 1902, page 145.)

---

painted the pots with designs that interpreted traditional Pueblo imagery in the then fashionable Art Deco style. After firing, the burnished ground became a lustrous black and the slip painting retained a matte surface. By the 1930s, production of blackware in San Ildefonso had become a communal enterprise. Family members and friends all worked making pots, and Maria signed all the pieces so that, in typical pueblo communal solidarity, everyone profited from the art market.

THE SANTA FE INDIAN SCHOOL. In the 1930s Anglo-American art teachers and dealers worked with Native Americans of the Southwest to create a distinctive, stereotypical "Indian" style in several mediums—including jewelry, pottery, weaving, and painting—to appeal to tourists and collectors. A leader in this effort was Dorothy Dunn (1903–91), who taught painting in the Santa Fe Indian School, an off-reservation government boarding school in New Mexico, from 1932 to 1937. Dunn inspired her students to create a painting style that combined the outline drawing and flat colors of folk art, the decorative qualities of Art Deco, and "Indian" subject matter. She and her students formed the Studio School. Restrictive as the school was, Dunn's success made painting a viable occupation for young Native American artists.

Pablita Velarde (1918–2006), from Santa Clara Pueblo in New Mexico and a 1936 graduate of Dorothy Dunn's school, was only a teenager when one of her paintings was selected for exhibition at the Chicago World's Fair in 1933. Thereafter, Velarde began to document Pueblo ways of life in a large series of murals for Bandelier National Monument. **KOSHARES OF TAOS** (FIG. 26–19) illustrates a moment during a ceremony celebrating the winter solstice when koshares, or clowns, take over the plaza from the Katsinas. Katsinas—the supernatural counterparts of animals, natural phenomena like clouds, and geological features like mountains—are central to traditional Pueblo religion. Katsinas manifest themselves in the human dancers who impersonate them during the winter

solstice ceremony, as well as in the small figures known as Katsina dolls that are given to children as educational aids in learning to identify the masks. Velarde's painting combines bold, flat colors and a simplified decorative line with European perspective. Her paintings, with their Art Deco abstraction, influenced the popular idea of the Indian style in art.

THE NAVAJOS. Navajo women are renowned for their skill as weavers. According to Navajo mythology, the universe itself is a weaving, its fibers spun by Spider Woman out of sacred cosmic materials. Spider Woman taught the art of weaving to Changing Woman (a Mother Earth figure who changes through the seasons), and she in turn taught it to Navajo women. The earliest Navajo blankets have simple horizontal stripes, like those of their Pueblo neighbors, and are limited to the white, black, and brown colors of natural sheep's wool. Over time, the weavers developed finer techniques and introduced more intricate patterns. In the mid-nineteenth century, they began unraveling the colored fibers from commercially manufactured and dyed blankets and reusing the yarn in their own work. By 1870–90 they were weaving spectacular blankets that were valued as prestige items among the Plains peoples as well as Euro-American collectors.

SAND PAINTING. Another traditional Navajo art, sand painting, is the exclusive province of men. Sand paintings are made to the accompaniment of chants by shaman-singers in the course of healing and blessing ceremonies, and they have great sacred significance (see "Navajo Night Chant," above). The paintings depict mythic heroes and events; and as ritual art, they follow prescribed rules and patterns that ensure their power. To make them, the singer dribbles pulverized colored stones, pollen, flowers, and other natural colors over a hide or sand ground. The rituals are intended to cure by restoring harmony to the world. The paintings are not meant to be seen by the public and certainly not to be displayed in

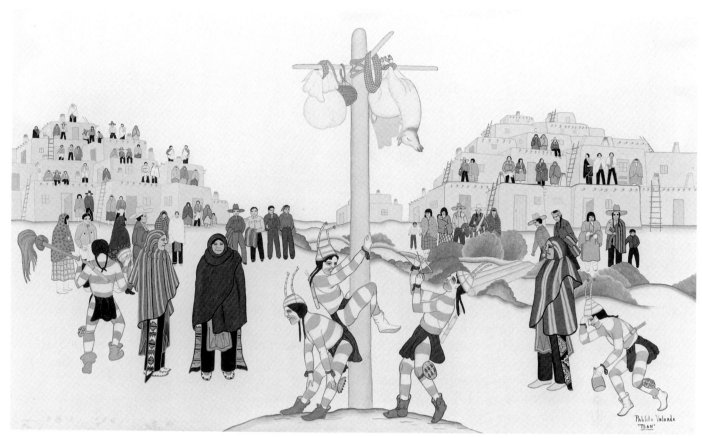

26–19 | Pablita Velarde **KOSHARES OF TAOS**
Santa Clara Pueblo, New Mexico. 1946–47. Watercolor on paper, 13⅞ × 22⅞″ (35.3 × 56.9 cm). Philbrook
Museum of Art, Tulsa, Oklahoma.
Museum Purchase (1947.37)

museums. They are meant to be destroyed by nightfall of the day on which they are made.

In 1919 a respected shaman-singer named Hosteen Klah (1867–1937) began to incorporate sand-painting images into weaving, breaking with the traditional prohibitions. Many Navajos took offense at Klah both for recording the sacred images and for doing so in what was traditionally a woman's art form. Klah had learned to weave from his mother and sister. The Navajo traditionally recognize at least three genders and perhaps as many as five or more; Hosteen Klah was a *nadle*, or Navajo third-gender. Hence, he could learn both female and male arts; that is, he was trained both to weave and to heal. Hosteen Klah was not breaking artistic barriers in a conventional sense, but rather exemplifying the complexities of the traditional Navajo gender system. Klah's work was ultimately accepted because of his great skill and prestige.

The **WHIRLING LOG CEREMONY** sand painting, woven into tapestry (**FIG. 26–20**), depicts part of the Navajo creation myth. The Holy People create the Earth's Surface and divide it into four parts. They create humans, and bring forth corn, beans, squash, and tobacco—the four sacred plants. A male-female pair of humans and one of the sacred plants stands in each of the four quarters, defined by the central cross. The four Holy People (the tall sticklike figures) surround the

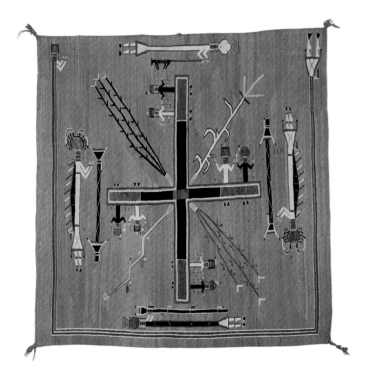

26–20 | Hosteen Klah **WHIRLING LOG CEREMONY**
Sand painting; tapestry by Mrs. Sam Manuelito. Navajo,
c. 1925. Wool, 5′5″ × 5′10″ (1.69 × 1.82 m). Heard
Museum, Phoenix, Arizona.

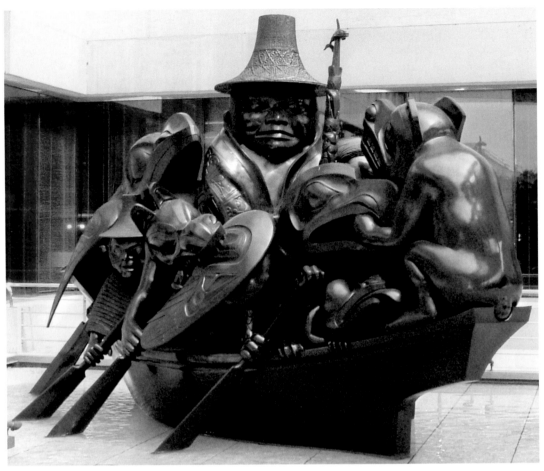

26–21 | Bill Reid **THE SPIRIT OF HAIDA GWAII**
Haida, 1991. Bronze, approx. 13 × 20′ (4 × 6 m). Canadian Embassy, Washington, D.C.

image, and the guardian figure of Rainbow Maiden frames the scene on three sides. Since the open side represents the east, her head is in the northeast corner and her feet are in the southeast. Like all Navajo artists, Hosteen Klah hoped that the excellence of the work would make it pleasing to the spirits. Recently shaman-singers have made permanent sand paintings on boards for sale, but they usually introduce slight errors in them to render the paintings ceremonially harmless.

A NEW BEGINNING

The Institute of American Indian Arts (IAIA), founded in 1962 in Santa Fe and attended by Native American students from all over North America, supports Native American aspirations in the arts today just as Dorothy Dunn's Studio School had in the 1930s. Staffed by major Native American artists, the school encourages the incorporation of indigenous ideals in the arts without creating an official "style." As alumni achieved distinction and the IAIA museum in Santa Fe established a reputation for excellence, the institute has led Native American art into the mainstream of contemporary art (see Chapter 31).

Other artists, such as the Canadian Haida artist Bill Reid (1920–98), have sought to sustain and revitalize traditional art in their work. For example, trained as a woodcarver, painter, and jeweler, Reid revived the art of carving totem poles and dugout canoes in the Haida homeland of Haida Gwaii— "Islands of the People"—known on maps today as the Queen Charlotte Islands. Late in life he began to create large-scale sculpture in bronze. With their black patina, these works recall traditional Haida carvings in shiny black argillite.

An imposing piece, Reid's **THE SPIRIT OF HAIDA GWAII** now stands outside the Canadian Embassy in Washington, D.C. (**FIG. 26–21**). This sculpture, which Reid viewed as a metaphor for modern Canada's multicultural society, depicts a boatload of figures from the natural and mythic worlds struggling to paddle forward.

The dominant figure is a shaman in a spruce-root basket hat and Chilkat blanket holding a speaker's pole. On the prow, the place reserved for the chief in a war canoe, sits the Bear. He faces backward rather than forward, and is bitten by an Eagle, with formline-patterned wings. The Eagle, in turn, is bitten by the Seawolf. The Eagle and the Seawolf, together with the man behind them, nevertheless continue paddling.

At the stern, steering the canoe, is the Raven, the trickster in Haida mythology. The Raven is assisted by Mousewoman, the traditional guide and escort of humans in the spirit realms. According to Reid, the work represents a "mythological and environmental lifeboat," where "the entire family of living things . . . whatever their differences, . . . are paddling together in one boat, headed in one direction."

THE NATIONAL MUSEUM OF THE AMERICAN INDIAN. In 1989 Congress established the National Museum of the American Indian within the Smithsonian Institution. After many years of discussion and negotiation, the art of indigenous peoples is finally achieving full recognition by the museum establishment. Championed by curator/collectors such as Ralph T. Coe, exhibitions of contemporary as well as traditional Native American arts are held in major American and European museums. In September of 2004, the **NATIONAL MUSEUM OF THE AMERICAN INDIAN** finally opened on the Mall in Washington, D.C., directly below Capitol Hill and across from the National Gallery of Art (FIG. 26–22).

Inspired by the colors, textures, and forms of the American Southwest, the museum building establishes a new presence of Native Americans on the Mall. Symbolizing the Native ethic of environmental concern, the National Museum of the American Indian is surrounded by boulders ("Grandfather Rocks"), water, and plantings that recall the varied landscapes of North America, including wetlands, meadows, forest, and traditional cropland with corn, squash, and tomatoes. These are not gardens; rather they are intended to evoke indigenous environments. The entrance to the museum on the east side faces the morning sun and recalls the orientation of prairie tepees. Inside the building a Sun Marker of stained glass in the south wall throws its dagger of light across the vast atrium as the day progresses. Once again the great spirits of Earth and sky take form in a creation of the art of the Americas.

IN PERSPECTIVE

After 1492, the arrival of Europeans completely altered the destiny of the Americas. In Mesoamerica and South America the break with the past was sudden and violent; in North America the change took place more gradually, but the outcome was much the same. In both North and South America, natives succumbed to European disease to which they had no immunity, especially smallpox, leading to massive population loss and social disruption. Many present-day Native American ethnic groups, however, were formed by combinations of various survivor groups.

In the south, the Spanish came as conquerors to exploit the wealth of the New World. Aztecs, Incas, and others, who were heirs to long-established building traditions, had built huge ceremonial complexes and housing for substantial

Defining Art
CRAFT OR ART?

In many world cultures, the distinction between "fine art" and "craft" does not exist. The traditional Western academic hierarchy of materials—in which marble, bronze, oil, and fresco are valued more than terra cotta and watercolor—and the equally artificial hierarchy of subjects—in which history painting, including religious history, stands supreme—are irrelevant to non-Western art.

The indigenous peoples of the Americas did not produce objects as works of art. In their eyes all pieces were utilitarian objects, adorned in ways necessary for their intended purposes. A work was valued for its effectiveness and for the role it played in society. Some, like a Sioux baby carrier (SEE FIG. 26-11), enrich mundane life with their aesthetic qualities. Others, such as Pomo baskets (see "Basketry," page 882), commemorate important events. The function of an Inca tunic may have been to identify or confer status on its owner or user through its material value or symbolic associations. And as with art in all cultures, many pieces have had great spiritual or magical power. Such works of art cannot be fully comprehended or appreciated when they are seen only on pedestals or encased in glass boxes in museums or galleries. They must be imagined, or better yet seen, as acting in their societies. How powerfully might our minds and emotions be engaged if we saw Kwakwaka'wakw (Kwakiutl) masks functioning in religious drama, changing not only the outward appearance, but also the very essence of the individual.

At the beginning of the twentieth century, European and American artists broke away from the academic bias that extolled the classical heritage of Greece and Rome. They found new inspiration in the art—or craft, if you will—of many different non-European cultures. Artists explored a new freedom to use absolutely any material or technique that effectively challenged outmoded assumptions and opened the way for a free and unfettered delight in, and understanding of, Native American art as well as the art of other non-Western cultures. The intellectual community as well as collectors, dealers, and critics have come to appreciate the non-Western aesthetics and to treasure forgotten and ignored arts on their own terms. And the more recent twentieth- and twenty-first-centuries conception of art as a multimedia adventure has helped validate works of art once seen only in ethnographic collections and in the homes of private collectors. Today objects once called "primitive" are recognized as great works of art and acknowledged to be an essential dimension of a twenty-first-century worldview. The line between "art" and "craft" seems more artificial and less relevant than ever before.

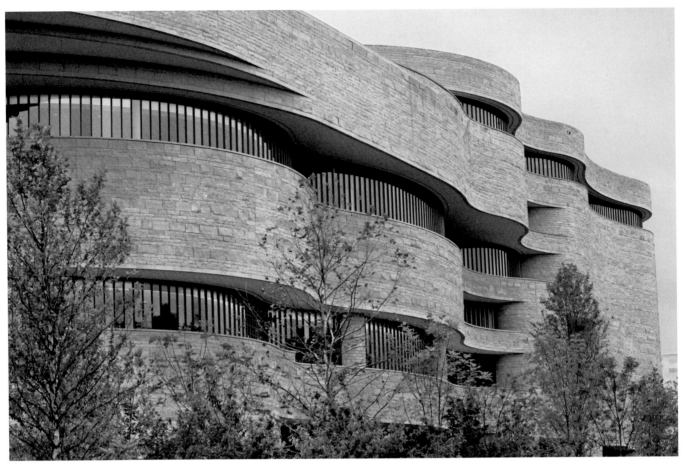

26–22 | **NATIONAL MUSEUM OF THE AMERICAN INDIAN**
The Smithsonian Institution, Washington, D.C. Opened September, 2004. Architectural design: GBQC in association with Douglas Cardinal (Blackfoot). Architectural consultants: Johnpaul Jones (Cherokee-Choctaw) and Ramona Sakiestewa (Hopi). Landscape consultant: Donna House (Navajo-Oneida), ethno-botanist.

populations in cities. They had also performed feats of engineering in road networks and in drainage and irrigation works. Their monumental sculpture in stone and ceramic survived the Spanish onslaught, as did some examples of their magnificent textiles, but their plentiful objects in silver and gold were almost all melted down and carted off. Some traditional arts, especially in weaving and pottery, continue to the present day.

In North America, the Europeans came not as military men seeking riches to plunder, but as families seeking land to farm. Unlike the Spaniards, they found no large cities with urban populations to resist them. However, although they imagined that the lands they settled were an untended wilderness, in fact nearly all of North America was populated and possessed by indigenous peoples. Over the next 400

years, by means of violence, bribery, and treaties, the English colonies and, in turn, the United States displaced nearly all Native Americans from their ancestral homelands. What indigenous art Euro-Americans encountered they viewed as a curiosity, not art.

During the past century, the indigenous arts of the Americas have undergone a reevaluation that has renewed the conception of what constitutes "American art," especially as diverse artists continue to revive indigenous traditions, revisit native outlooks, and restate ancient truths in new ways. After being pushed to the brink of extinction, Native American cultures are now experiencing a revival in both North and South America, as Native Americans assert themselves politically, and as Euro-Americans come to appreciate the connections between native history and the land.

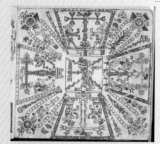

AZTEC, A VIEW OF THE WORLD
PAGE FROM *CODEX FEJERVARY-MAYER*
c.1400–1519/21

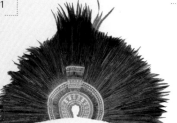

AZTEC, FEATHER HEADDRESS
OF MONTEZUMA
BEFORE 1519

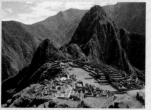

INCA, MACCHU-PICCHU
PERU
450–1530

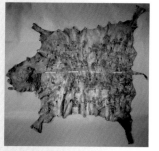

BATTLE-SCENE, HIDE PAINTING
MANDAN, NORTH DAKOTA
1797–1800

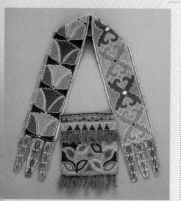

SHOULDER BAG
DELAWARE, KANSAS
c.1860

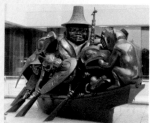

HAIDA, BILL REID
THE SPIRIT OF HAIDA GWAII
1991

ART OF THE AMERICAS AFTER 1300

1300

◄ **Eastern Woodlands Culture**
c. 1300

1400

◄ **Aztec Empire at Its Height**
c. 1400–1519/21
◄ **Inca Empire at Its Height**
c. 1438–1532

1500

◄ **Cortés Conquers Aztec Empire**
c. 1519–24
◄ **Pizarro Conquers Inca Empire**
c. 1532

1600

1700

◄ **Plains Nomadic Culture** 1700–1870

1800

◄ **Louisiana Purchase** 1803

◄ **Transcontinental Railway Complete**
1869
◄ **Winter Ceremony Outlawed**
1885–1951

1900

2000

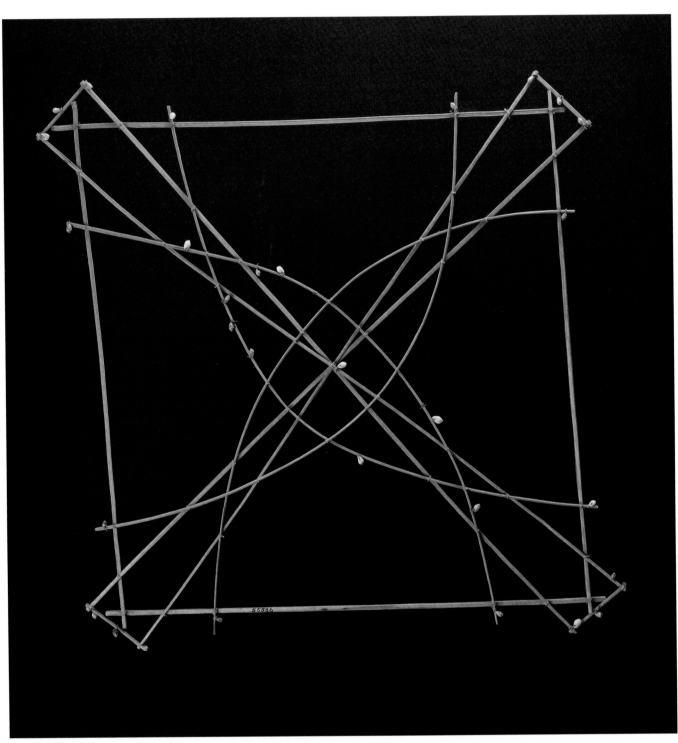

27-1 | *WAPEPE* **NAVIGATION CHART**   Marshall Islands, Micronesia. 19th century. Sticks, coconut fiber, shells. 29½ × 29½" (75 × 75 cm).

CHAPTER TWENTY-SEVEN

ART OF PACIFIC CULTURES

27

The low-lying coral atolls that make up the Marshall Islands of Micronesia are spaced like two strands of green pearls across the shimmering blue cloth of the Pacific (SEE MAP 27–1). Distances from island to island are not great; the longest is not much more than 75 miles. But the low elevation of the shores means that a canoe traveling from one to the next is out of sight of land for most of the voyage. Renowned for their navigational skill, Marshallese sailors relied on celestial navigation (navigating by the sun and moon and stars) as well as a detailed understanding of the ocean currents and trade winds that prevail around their islands. To teach navigation to younger generations, Marshall Islands elders traditionally used "stick charts"—maps that included land, but also the path from one island to the next, the water a sailor would cross in his voyage.

In common use until the 1950s, the stick chart (FIG. 27–1), called a *mattang* or *wapepe*, was a schematic diagram of the prevailing ocean currents and the characteristic wave patterns encountered on a journey from one island to another. The currents are represented by sticks held together by coconut fibers; the shells mark islands on the route. The arrangement of sticks around a shell indicates a zone of distinctive waves shaped by the effect of an island deflecting the prevailing wind. Recognizing such refracted waves enables a navigator to sense the proximity of land without being able to see it, and to discern the least difficult course for making landfall. Since any given navigational course would encounter these ocean patterns in a particular way depending on its starting point and destination, each chart was applicable to one particular itinerary only. The charts were not taken out to sea, but were used as teaching devices to help memorize the ocean patterns between islands. Although such an object is primarily functional, its combination of clarity, simplicity, and abstraction have aesthetic impact. This *wapepe* was collected by the expedition of the USS *Albatross* in 1899–1900.

Every society has its own way of picturing the world. Born of an intimate familiarity with the sea, and constructed from simple materials readily at hand, the stick charts of the Marshall Islands envision a voyage in a conceptual diagram denoting the varying texture of wind and water between islands.

THE PEOPLING OF THE PACIFIC

On a map with the Pacific Ocean as its center, only the peripheries of the great landmasses of Asia and the Americas appear. More than one-third of the earth's surface is taken up by this vast expanse. The area of Oceania includes four distinct but connected cultural-geographic areas: Australia, Melanesia, Micronesia, and Polynesia (MAP 27–1). Australia includes the continent as well as the island of Tasmania to the southeast. Melanesia (meaning "black islands," a reference to the dark skin color of its inhabitants) includes New Guinea and the string of islands that extend eastward from it as far as Fiji and New Caledonia. Micronesia ("small islands"), to the north of Melanesia, is a region of small islands, including the Marianas. Polynesia ("many islands") is scattered over a huge, triangular region defined by New Zealand in the south, Easter Island in the east, and the Hawaiian Islands to the north. The last region on earth to be inhabited by humans, Polynesia covers some 7.7 million square miles, of which fewer than 130,000 square miles are dry land—and most of that is New Zealand. With the exception of temperate New Zealand, with its marked seasons and snow-capped mountains, Oceania is in the tropics, that is, between the Tropic of Cancer in the north and the Tropic of Capricorn to the south.

Australia, Tasmania, and New Guinea formed a single continent during the last Ice Age, which began some 2.5 million years ago. About 50,000 years ago, when the sea level was about 330 feet lower than it is today, people moved to this continent from Southeast Asia, making at least part of the journey over open water. Some 27,000 years ago humans were settled on the large islands north and east of New Guinea as far as San Cristobal, but they ventured no farther for another 25,000 years. By about 4000 BCE—possibly as early as 7000 BCE—the people of Melanesia were raising pigs and cultivating taro, a plant with edible rootstocks. As the glaciers melted, the sea level rose, flooding low-lying coastal land. By around 4000 BCE a 70-mile-wide waterway, now called the Torres Strait, separated New Guinea from Australia, whose aboriginal (native) people continued their hunting and gathering way of life into the twentieth century.

The settling of the rest of the islands of Melanesia and the westernmost islands of Polynesia—Samoa and Tonga—coincided with the spread of the Lapita culture, named for a site in New Caledonia. The Lapita people spread throughout the islands of Melanesia beginning around 1500 BCE. They were farmers and fisherfolk who cultivated taro and yams and brought with them dogs, pigs, and chickens, animals that these colonizers needed for food. They also carried with them the distinctive ceramics whose remnants today enable us to trace the extent of their travels. Lapita potters produced dishes, platters, bowls, and jars. Sometimes they covered their wares with a red **slip**, and they often decorated them with bands of incised and stamped patterns—dots, lines, and hatching—heightened with white lime. Most of the decoration was entirely geometric, but some was figurative. The human face that appears in the example shown (FIG. 27–2) is among the earliest representations of a human being in Oceanic art. The Lapita people were skilled shipbuilders and

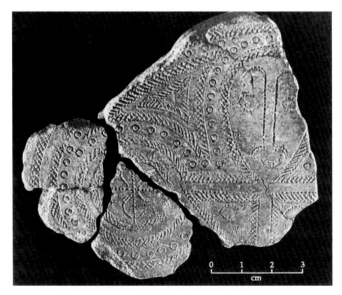

27–2 | **FRAGMENTS OF A LARGE LAPITA JAR**
Venumbo Reef, Santa Cruz Island, Solomon Islands, Melanesia. c. 1200–1100 BCE. Clay, height of human face approx. 1½" (4 cm).

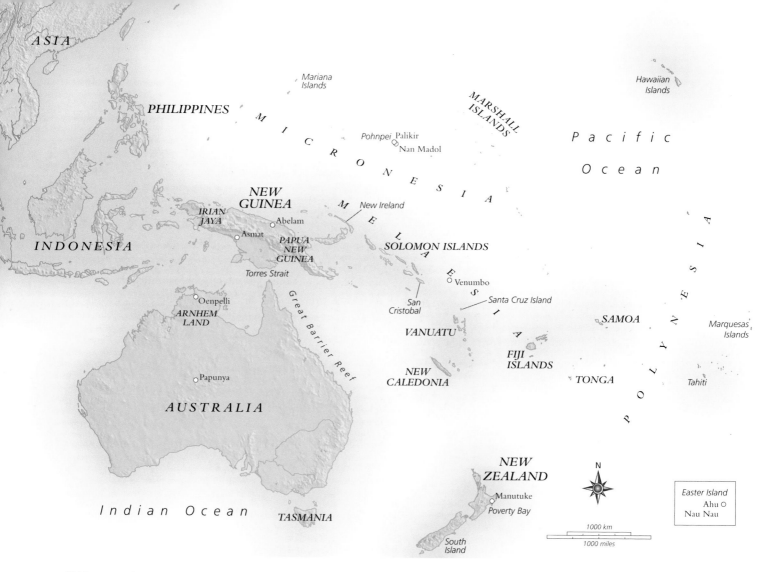

MAP 27–1 | **PACIFIC CULTURAL-GEOGRAPHIC REGIONS**

The Pacific cultures are found in four vast areas: Australia, Melanesia, Micronesia, and Polynesia.

navigators and engaged in interisland trade. Over time the Lapita culture lost its widespread cohesion and evolved into various local forms. Its end is generally dated to the early centuries of the Common Era.

Polynesian culture emerged in the eastern Lapita region on the islands of Tonga and Samoa. Around the beginning of the first millennium CE, daring Polynesian seafarers, probably in double-hulled sailing canoes, began settling the scattered islands of Far Oceania and eastern Micronesia. Voyaging over open water, sometimes for thousands of miles, they reached Hawaii and Easter Island after about 500 CE and settled New Zealand around 800/900–1200 CE.

While the continued contact between eastern Melanesia (Vanuatu and the surrounding islands) and Polynesian peoples allowed for cross-cultural borrowings, there are distinctions between these areas and within the regions as well. The islands that make up Micronesia, Melanesia, and Polynesia include both low-lying coral atolls and the tall tops of vol-

canic mountains that rise from the ocean floor. Raw materials available to residents of these islands vary greatly, and islander art and architecture utilize these materials in different ways. The soil of volcanic islands can be very rich and thus can support densely populated settlements with a local diversity of plants and animals. On the other hand, coral atolls do not generally have very good soil and thus cannot support large populations. In a like manner, volcanic islands can provide good stone for tools and building (as at Nan Madol; SEE FIG. 27–8), while coral is sharp but not particularly hard, and the strongest tools on a coral atoll are often those made from giant clam shells. Generally, the diversity of both plants and animals decreases from west to east among the Pacific Islands.

The arts of this vast and diverse region display an enormous variety that is closely linked to a community's ritual and religious life. In this context, the visual arts were often just one strand in a rich weave that also included music, dance, and oral literature.

AUSTRALIA

The aboriginal inhabitants of Australia, or Aborigines, were nomadic hunter-gatherers closely attuned to the varied environments in which they lived until European settlers disrupted their way of life. They did not cultivate any crops, and their only modification of the landscape was regular controlled burning of the underbrush, which encouraged new plant life and attracted animals.

The Aborigines' traditional life is intimately connected with the concept of the Dreamtime, the period before humans existed. The world had begun as flat, but spirit beings shaped it into mountains, sand hills, creeks, and water holes. These spirits grew old and eventually went back to the sleep from which they had awoken at the Dreamtime, but their continuing influence is felt in climatic phenomena such as the monsoon season. Each animal and human is thought to have two souls, one mortal and one immortal, the latter associated with a particular ancestral spirit. These totemic ancestors are identified with specific places, which are honored as sacred sites. Social organization and mythology of the Aborigines are vividly represented in their arts. The goal of many aboriginal paintings is restoring contact with the Dreamtime.

Arnhem Land

While the Aborigines lived throughout the continent, some of their earliest remains are found in the north, in tropical Arnhem Land. In Arnhem Land the native people continued what was essentially a paleolithic lifestyle until well into the twentieth century. Their rich ceremonial life included ritual body painting as well as the ornamentation of implements and the interiors of bark houses. The rock paintings of Western Arnhem Land are particularly famous, and they illustrate images that are often associated with the Dreamtime.

X-RAY STYLE ROCK PAINTING. One of the most distinctive characteristics of traditional aboriginal imagery is the **x-ray style** depiction of animals. When depicting an x-ray style ani-

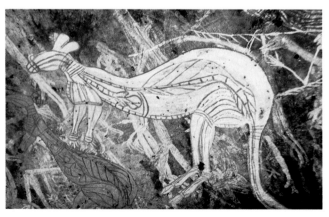

27–3 | **MIMIS AND KANGAROO**
Prehistoric rock art, Oenpelli, Arnhem Land, Australia. Older painting 18,000-7000 BCE. Red and yellow ocher and white pipe clay.

mal, the artist would draw bones and internal organs—including the spinal column, the heart, and the stomach—over the silhouetted form. In the picture shown here (FIG. 27–3), all four of the kangaroo's legs have been drawn, and the ears have been placed symmetrically on top of its head. In some images both eyes appear in the head, which is shown in profile. The x-ray style was still prevalent in western Arnhem Land when European settlers arrived in the nineteenth century. This rock painting, however, dates much earlier, to perhaps as early as 18,000 years ago, roughly the same time as cave paintings were being produced in Western Europe. As here, frequently these rock paintings show a later image superimposed on an earlier one. The earlier painting is of skinny, sticklike humans that the Aborigines call *mimis* ("ancestral spirits").

BARK PAINTING. Eventually, as a means of communicating with outsiders and as an aid to education and memory, tribal elders recorded origin myths, rituals, and significant places and objects by painting on the bark stripped from eucalyptus trees. Bark painters from western Arnhem Land continued to use the x-ray style, but in eastern Arnhem Land, the bark painters, especially the Yolngu-speakers, developed a style based on ritual body painting.

The Yolngu rarely reveal the full meaning of a painting to outsiders, but in general they depict origin myths and ritual activities. A modern bark painting by Mithinarri Gurruwiwi (FIG. 27–4) represents a part of the origin myth of eastern Arnhem Land as interpreted by the Gälpu clan of the Yolngu people. The first humans—the Wäwilak Sisters—walked about with their digging sticks, singing, dancing, naming things, and populating the land with their children. But they offended the Wititj (Olive Serpent), who swallowed them but was then called before a council of serpents representing all the clans. Wititj had to admit wrongdoing and regurgitate the humans. This conference of snakes signifies both the origin of ritual activities and the spreading of the Wäwilak story to other clans. At the center of the bark painting, a dark rectangle represents Wititj's water hole, the Gälpu clan's ceremonial center and the home of the Yolngu people before and after their time on earth—both unborn souls and the dead. Wititj coils protectively around the water, slithering in and out of his hole. Wititj is represented twice again at the top of the painting among the water lilies, and at the bottom he attends the conference, with goannas (large lizards) and other serpents. The ancestral snakes are associated with water—rain, water holes, thunder and lightning—and fertility, so Wititj is covered with dots representing eggs. The dotted water lilies also remind us of the fertility of well-watered land. The Wäwilak sisters' story is sacred, and some Yolngus believe that only the initiated clan members should see such paintings. Ritual life and the meaning of ceremonial designs still remain private, and only designated artists have rights to reproduce clan narratives and designs.

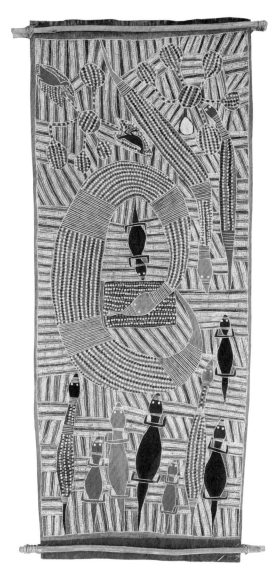

27–4 | Mithinarri Gurruwiwi **THE CONFERENCE OF SERPENTS FROM THE WÄWILAK MYTH**
Eastern Arnhem Land, Australia. 1963. Natural pigments (ochers and clay) on eucalyptus bark, 53⅞ × 22⅖" (137 × 58.5 cm). Kluge-Ruhe Aboriginal Art Collection, University of Virginia, Charlottesville.

The surface of the painting shimmers with brilliant dotting and cross-hatching. This characteristic cross-hatching, known as *rarrk*, originated in the designs painted on male chests and thighs as part of initiation ceremonies; consequently, what may appear to be simple decoration—the angle of the lines, their color, and the alternation of continuous and broken lines—has a more profound meaning for the Yolngu. In this painting, geometric forms represent abstract ideas as well as underlying structures and meanings, while recognizable figures are used to tell stories and to represent occurrences.

Aboriginal artists today may paint with acrylic paint on canvas instead of with ocher, clay, and charcoal on rock and eucalyptus bark, but their imagery has remained relatively constant, and their explanations of their work provide insight into the meaning of prehistoric images.

MELANESIA

In Melanesia the people usually rely at least partially on agriculture, and as a result they live in permanent settlements, many of which feature spaces set aside for ritual use. As in Australia, the arts were intimately involved with belief and provided a means for communicating with supernatural forces. Rituals and ritual arts were primarily the province of men, who devoted a great deal of time to both. In some societies most of the adult males were able to make ritual objects. Women, although barred from ritual arts, gained prestige for themselves and their families through their skill in the production of other kinds of goods, such as bark cloth. To be effective, ritual objects had to be well made, but they were often allowed to deteriorate after they had served their ceremonial function.

New Guinea

New Guinea, the largest island in the Pacific (and at 1,500 miles long and 1,000 miles wide, the second-largest island in the world), is today divided between two countries. The eastern half of the island is part of the modern nation of Papua New Guinea; the western half is Irian Jaya, a province of present-day Indonesia. Located near the equator and with mountains that rise to 16,000 feet, the island inhabitants utilize a variety of environments, from coastal mangrove marshes to grasslands, from dense rain forests to swampy river valleys. The population is equally diverse, with coastal fishermen, riverine hunters, slash-and-burn agriculturalists, and more stable farming communities in the highlands. Between New Guinea itself and the smaller neighboring islands more than 700 languages have been identified.

THE TAMBERAN HOUSE OF THE ABELAM OF PAPUA NEW GUINEA. The Abelam, who live in the foothills of the mountains on the north side of Papua New Guinea, raise pigs and cultivate yams, taro, bananas, and sago palms. In traditional Abelam society, people live in extended families or clans in hamlets. Wealth among the Abelam is measured in pigs, but men gain status from participation in a yam cult that has a central place in Abelam society and in the iconography of its art and architecture. The yams that are the focus of this cult—some of which reach an extraordinary 12 feet in length—are associated with clan ancestors and the potency of their growers. Village leaders renew their relationship with the forces of nature that yams represent during the Long Yam Festival, which is held at harvest time and involves processions, masked figures, singing, and the ritual exchange of the finest yams.

An Abelam hamlet includes sleeping houses, cooking houses, storehouses for yams, a central space for rituals, and a *tamberan* house. The term refers to something that the uninitiated are not allowed to view. In this ceremonial structure the images and objects associated with the yam cult and with

Art and Its Context
BOATS IN OCEANIA

Among island dwellers, boats are essential. In the Pacific their forms varied, depending on their purpose and the materials available. For example, a canoe for fishing in a calm lagoon would have different requirements from a battle canoe used for attacking across the open sea. Canoes ranged in size from simple dugouts and single outriggers (used throughout Polynesia) to double-hull canoes, which in Tahiti could carry up to 300 men. In the Gambier Islands of Polynesia, the Mangarevans did not traditionally build canoes at all; rather their ocean journeys were made on large rafts that could be fitted together to compose ocean-going platforms. Elsewhere in Polynesia, on coral atolls where plant life was limited, there were few large trees to use in canoe building. In the Tuamotu Islands, residents overcame this deficiency by making canoes out of small wooden planks sewn together with coconut fiber rope. Many canoes were paddled, but others had sails, or were powered by a combination of sail and paddle.

Some Melanesian and Polynesian canoes were relatively unornamented either because they were purely functional canoes and did not require ornamental elaboration to perform their task, or because of the circumstances of their use. For example, Hawaiian canoes tend to be uncarved because the oceans around the islands can be very violent and any carving would interfere with the streamlined form needed for safe control in high seas.

The most elaborate canoes were ocean-going sailing and war canoes. As the public political and martial face of the community, islanders wanted such boats to make a dramatic impression. Their prows and sterns were larger than needed to cut through the water, and they were often decorated with elaborate images of animals and humans as well as spirals and geometric shapes. In addition, many decorations were embellished with inlaid shell and painted designs. The most dramatic war canoes came from New Zealand and from the islands just north and east of New Guinea.

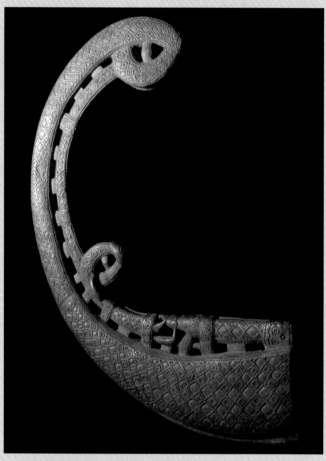

CANOE PROW
Kaniet Manus Province, Papua New Guinea.
Wood, length 18⅛″ (46 cm). Otago Museum, Dunedin.
D24.702

clan identity are kept hidden from women and uninitiated boys. Men of the clan gather in the *tamberan* house to organize rituals and conduct community business, and—in the past—to plan raiding parties. The prestige of a hamlet is linked to the quality of its *tamberan* house and the size of its yams. Constructed on a frame of poles and rafters and roofed with split cane and thatch, *tamberan* houses are built with a triangular floor plan, the side walls meeting at the back of the building. The façade is elaborately painted and carved (FIG. 27–5). In this example, built about 1961, red, ocher, white, and black faces of male spirits make up the bottom and middle rows on the façade, and at the top the figure is said to represent a female flying witch. This last figure is associated with the feminine power of the house itself. The projecting pole at the top of the house is the only male element of the architecture, and is said to be the penis of the house. The small door at the lower right is a female element, a womb; entering and exiting the house is the symbolic equivalent to death and rebirth. The Abelam believe the paint itself has magical qualities. Regular, ritual repainting revitalizes the images and ensures their continued potency.

Every stage in the construction of a *tamberan* house is accompanied by ceremonies, which are held in the early morning while women and boys are still asleep. The completion of a house is celebrated with elaborate fertility rituals and an all-night dance. Women participate in these inaugural ceremonies and are allowed to enter the new house, which afterward is ritually cleansed and closed to them.

ANCESTRAL SPIRIT POLES OF THE ASMAT OF IRIAN JAYA. The Asmat, who live in the grasslands on the southwest coast, were known in the past as warriors and headhunters. They identified trees with human beings, their fruit with human heads. Fruit-eating birds were thus the equivalent of headhunters, and were often represented in war and mortuary arts, as was the praying mantis, because the female of the species bites off the head of the male while mating. To honor the dead the Asmat erected memorial poles covered with elaborate sculpture (FIG. 27–6). The poles are known as *mbis*, and the rituals surrounding them are intended to reestablish the balance between life and death. The Asmat believe that *mbis* house the souls of the recent dead, and they place them in front of the men's house of the village so the souls can observe the rituals there. After the *mbis* ceremonies, the poles are abandoned and allowed to deteriorate.

In the past, once the poles had been carved, villagers would organize a headhunting expedition so that they could place an enemy head in a cavity at the base of each pole. The base, with its abstract voids for enemy heads, represents the twisting roots of the banyan tree. Above the base, figures representing tribal ancestors support figures of the recent dead.

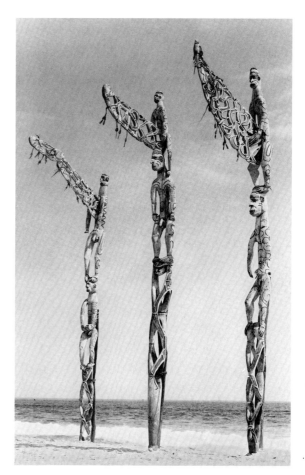

27–6 ASMAT ANCESTRAL SPIRIT POLES (MBIS)
Faretsj River, Irian Jaya, Indonesia, New Guinea. c. 1960. Wood, paint, palm leaves, and fiber, height approx. 18' (5.48 m). Photograph in the Metropolitan Museum of Art, New York.
The Michael C. Rockefeller Memorial Collection, Gift of Nelson A. Rockefeller and Mrs. Mary C. Rockefeller, 1965 (1978.412.1248-50)

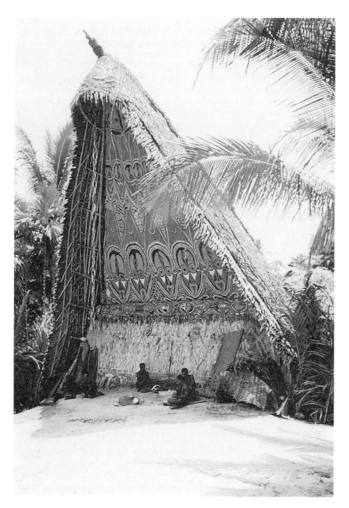

27–5 EXTERIOR OF *TAMBERAN* HOUSE
Kinbangwa village, Sepik River, Papua New Guinea, New Guinea. Abelam, 20th century. Carved and painted wood, with ocher pigments on clay ground.

The bent pose of the figures associates them with the praying mantis; birds are shown breaking open nuts. The large, lacy phalluses emerging from the figures at the top of the poles symbolize male fertility, and the surface decoration suggests tattoos and scarification (patterned scars), common body ornamentation in Melanesia.

New Ireland

New Ireland is one of the large eastern islands of the nation of Papua New Guinea. The northern people on the island practice a complex set of integrated cultural traditions known as *malanggan*, which are ceremonies that honor one's family and the family into which one marries. *Malanggan* are integral to honoring the dead, and one of the most important aspects of the traditions are elaborate funerary rituals for which striking painted carvings and masks are made. *Malanggan* involve an entire community as well as its neighbors and serve to validate social relations and property claims.

Although preparations are hidden from women and children, everyone participates in the actual ceremonies.

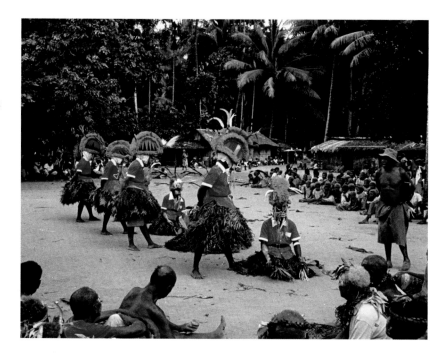

27–7 | DANCERS WEARING *TATANUA* MASKS
Pinikindu Village, central New Ireland, Papua
New Guinea, New Guinea. 1979. Masks:
wood, vegetable fibers, trade cloth, and pigments, approx. 17 × 13″ (43 × 33 cm).

Arrangements begin with the selection of trees to be used for
the *malanggan* carvings. In a ceremony marked by a feast of
taro and pork, the logs are cut, transported, and ritually
pierced. Once the carvings are finished, they are dried in the
communal men's house, polished, and then displayed in a
malanggan house in the village *malanggan* enclosure. Here the
figures are painted and eyes made of sea-snail shell are
inserted. The works displayed in a *malanggan* house include
figures on poles and freestanding sculpture representing
ancestors and the honored dead, as well as masks and ritual
dance equipment.

TATANUA DANCE MASKS. One of the many ceremonies that
make up the *malanggan* in New Ireland is a dance called
tatanua that commemorates the dead. The term *tatanua* can be
used to refer to the dance itself as well as the distinctive hel-
met masks worn by the male dancers. *Tatanua* masks represent
one of the three souls of the dead (FIG. 27–7). They are
carved and painted with simple, repetitive motifs such as ladders, zigzags, and stylized feathers. Traditional paint colors are
applied in a ritually specified order: first lime white for magic
spells; then red ocher to recall the spirits of those who died
violently; then black from charcoal or burned nuts, a symbol
of warfare; and finally yellow and blue from vegetable materials. The left and right sides of the magnificent crest of plant
fiber are different colors, perhaps a reflection of a long-ago
hairstyle in which the hair was cut short and left naturally
black on one side and dyed yellow and allowed to grow long
on the other. The contrasting sides of the masks allow dancers
to present a different appearance by turning from side to side.
A good performance of the *tatanua* dance is considered a
demonstration of strength, while a mistake can bring laughter
and humiliation.

MICRONESIA

The majority of Micronesia's inhabited islands are small, low-
lying coral atolls. But in the western region several are volcanic in origin. The basalt cliffs of the island of Pohnpei provided the building material for one of the largest and most
remarkable stone architectural complexes in Oceania.

NAN MADOL. Nan Madol, on its southeast coast, consists of
92 artificial islands set within a network of canals covering
about 170 acres (MAP 27–2). Seawalls and breakwaters 15 feet
high and 35 feet thick protect the area from the ocean. When
it was populated, openings in the breakwaters gave canoes
access to the ocean and allowed seawater to flow in and out
with the tides, flushing clean the canals. While other similar
complexes have been identified in Micronesia, Nan Madol is
the largest and most impressive, reflecting the importance of
the kings who ruled from the site. The artificial islands and
the buildings atop them were built between the early thirteenth and seventeenth centuries, until the dynasty's political
decline. The site had been abandoned by the time Europeans
discovered it in the nineteenth century.

Nan Madol was an administrative and ceremonial center
as well as a home for as many as 1,000 people at one time.
The powerful kings drew upon the labor force to construct a
monumental city. Both the buildings and the underlying
islands themselves are built of massive pieces of stone set in
alternating layers of log-shaped stones and boulders of pris-
matic basalt. The largest of the artificial islets is more than 100
yards long, and one basalt cornerstone alone is estimated to
have weighed about 50 tons. The stone logs were split from
the cliffs by alternately heating the stone and dousing it with
water. Most of the islands are oriented northeast-southwest,
receiving the benefit of the cooling prevailing winds.

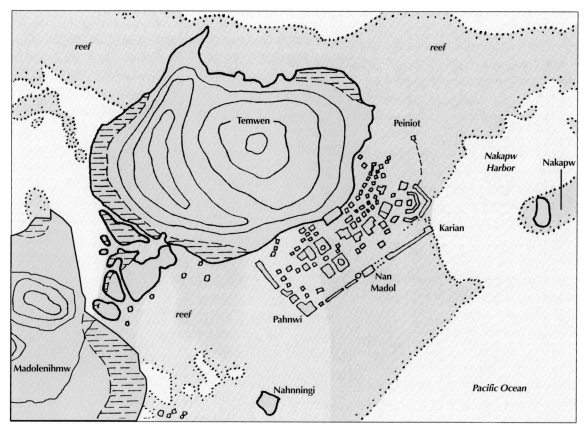

MAP 27–2 | **THE COMPLEX OF NAN MADOL**
Pohnpei, Federated States of Micronesia. c. 1200/1300–c. 1500/1600.

The royal mortuary compound, which once dominated the southeast side of Nan Madol (**FIG. 27–8**), has walls rising in subtle upward and outward curves to a height of 25 feet. To achieve the sweeping, rising lines, the builders increased the number of stones in the header courses (those with the ends of the stones laid facing out along the wall) relative to the stretcher courses (those with the lengths of the stones laid parallel to the wall) as they came to the corners and entryways. The plan of the structure consists simply of progressively higher rectangles within rectangles—the outer walls leading by steps up to interior walls that lead up to a central courtyard with a small, cubical tomb.

POLYNESIA

The settlers of the far-flung islands of Polynesia developed distinctive cultural traditions but also retained linguistic and cultural affinities that reflect their common origin. Traditional Polynesian society was generally far more stratified than Melanesian society, and Polynesian art objects served as indicators of rank and status. Valued both as material objects and for the status they conferred, Polynesian artworks often were handed down as heirlooms from generation to generation.

In addition to being the last area of the Pacific to have been settled by humans, Polynesia was the last area mapped and colonized by Europeans. The most informative early explorations were led by the English captain James Cook, who made three voyages to the Pacific in the 1760s and 1770s. His expeditions mapped the Great Barrier Reef of

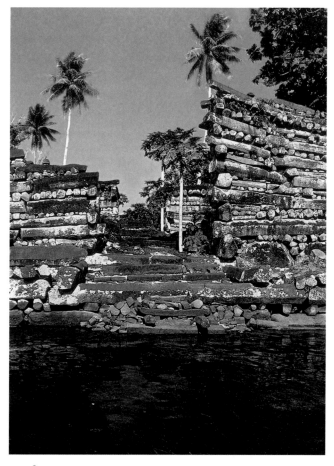

27–8 | **ROYAL MORTUARY COMPOUND, NAN MADOL**
Pohnpei, Federated States of Micronesia. Basalt blocks, wall height up to 25′ (7.62 m).

Australia and both islands of New Zealand in addition to "finding" the Hawaiian Islands. These were voyages of discovery, and scientific study was a major activity and goal. In addition to astronomers, botanists, and other scientists, Cook brought artists to the Pacific to record visual images of the new plants, animals, places, and peoples that were encountered. Our earliest images of some of the peoples of the Pacific come from these artists.

European contact had a profoundly disruptive effect on society and art in Polynesia, as elsewhere in Oceania. Explorers, and later whalers, traded for or otherwise took objects of cultural importance, often misunderstanding the significance of the items they transported back to Europe and North America. The income derived from sales to European collectors quickly affected the production of such artworks, gradually debasing their original significance in their own cultural context and turning these artworks into mere commercial objects for the tourist trade.

Missionaries followed the explorers and their impact on the art of the Pacific Islands was just as dramatic. They encouraged the abandonment and even destruction of objects used in ritual context. They also promoted changes in the subject matter of religious art. Even attire changed significantly under the influence of Christian settlers, who insisted on much more coverage of the body than had been common previously, particularly in the case of women who had often gone bare-breasted before European contact.

Easter Island

Easter Island is the most isolated inhabited locale in Oceania, some 2,300 miles west of the coast of South America and 1,200 miles from Pitcairn Island, the nearest Polynesian outpost. Three volcanoes, one at each corner, make up the small triangular island. Originally known to its native inhabitants as Te Pito o te Henúa (Navel of the World) and now known as Rapanui, the name "Easter Island" was given by Captain Jacob Roggeveen, the Dutch explorer who first landed on the island on Easter Sunday in 1722.

MONUMENTAL MOAI. Easter Island is the site of Polynesia's most impressive sculpture. Stone temples, or *marae*, with stone altar platforms, or *ahu*, are common throughout Polynesia. Most of the *ahu* are built near the coast, parallel to the shore. About 900 CE, Easter Islanders began to erect huge stone figures on *ahu*, perhaps as memorials to dead chiefs. Nearly 1,000 of the figures, called *moai*, have been found, including some unfinished in the quarries where they were being made. Carved from tufa, a yellowish brown volcanic stone, most are about 36 feet tall, but one unfinished figure measures almost 70 feet. In 1978 several figures were restored to their original condition, with red tufa topknots on their heads and white coral eyes with stone pupils (FIG. 27–9). The heads have deep-set eyes under a prominent brow ridge; a

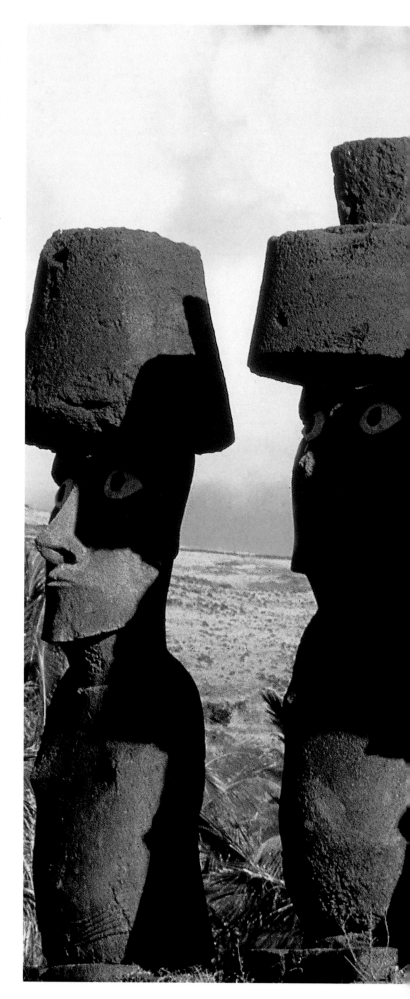

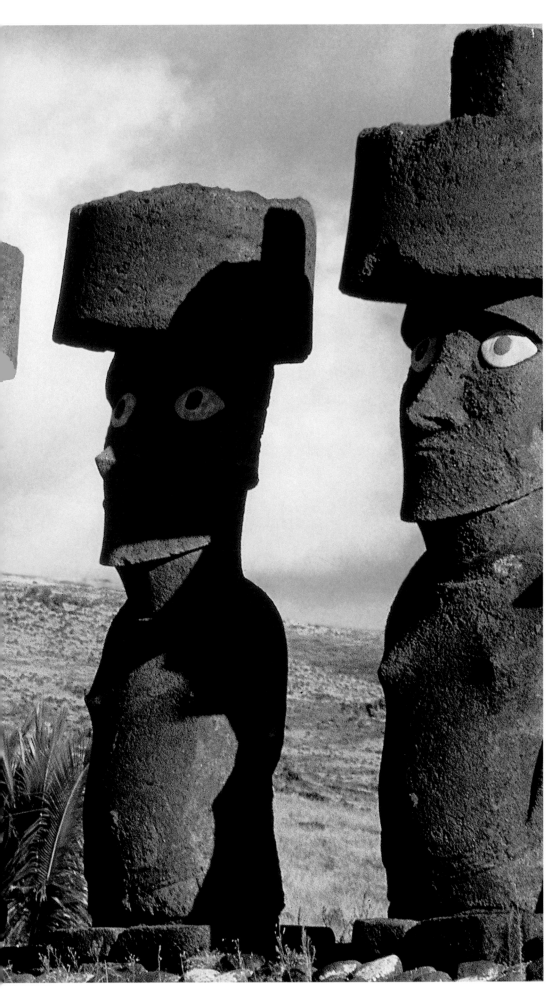

27–9 | *MOAI* **ANCESTOR**
FIGURES (?) Ahu Nau Nau,
Easter Island, Polynesia.
c. 1000–1500, restored 1978.
Volcanic stone (tufa), average
height approx. 36′ (11 m).

THE OBJECT SPEAKS

FEATHER CLOAK

When the Hawaiian King Kamehameha presented a feathered cape to the English explorer George Vancouver for King George III, it was a gift appropriate for a king. Like England, the stratified society of Polynesia had an elite social class to which people were born and from which they could not fall, no matter what events entangled them. The feathered cloak was an emblem of that status, and the right to wear it was restricted to members of the highest social level. The clothing is called *'Ahu 'ula* ("red cloak"), which refers to the red color associated with royalty in Hawaii, much in the same way as purple was the color of royalty in the Byzantine Empire. Draped over the wearers' shoulders, such cloaks create a sensuously textured and colored abstract design. When the garment shown here is worn, the symmetrical arrangement of paired crescents join to create matching decorations on front and back.

Feathers were used for decorating not just cloaks, but also helmets, capes, blankets, and garlands (*leis*), all of which conferred status and prestige. Tall feather pompons (*kahili*) mounted on long slender sticks were symbols of royalty. Even the effigies of gods that Hawaiian warriors carried into battle were made of light, basketlike structures covered with feathers. The feathered capes and cloaks worn by Hawaiian chiefs in war and ceremony indicated the relative status of the chief within the highly stratified Polynesian society. The most valuable capes and cloaks were full length and made with red, black, and yellow feathers. Shorter ones and capes using green feathers and feathers from less-desirable birds marked upper-class members of a lower rank.

The annual tribute paid to the king by his subjects included feathers. These went to the king who then redistributed them to his chiefs. Members of the upper class, while not guaranteed a feather cloak, had the right to accumulate feathers for making one. The greater a chief's prestige, the closer he was to the king, and thus the more access he had to the tribute feathers that were the king's to bestow. The yellow feathers used in cloaks were especially prized because they were particularly rare. While several birds in Hawaii had yellow feathers, only the tail feathers of the mamo bird (now extinct) were considered desirable. These birds were snared, their tail feathers plucked, and then released. Each bird gave only a few feathers, usually no more than eight, in any given year. Thus the labor necessary to obtain them was intensive, and the limitation to a particular type of bird created an artificial scarcity of yellow feathers, making a full-length cloak with wide areas of yellow even more valuable. At the same time, the use of red indicated featherwork as being the property of the highest social classes, so the feathered cloaks of red and yellow symbolically express both social and economic power.

The cloak's foundation consisted of coconut fiber netting onto which bundles of feathers were tied. Unlike tapa cloth, these cloaks were so closely associated with the spiritual power (*mana*) of the chief that they could be made only by men, who were surrounded by sacred protective objects as they worked. While they knotted the cloaks, the makers recited the chief's genealogy, imbuing the object with the power of the ancestors.

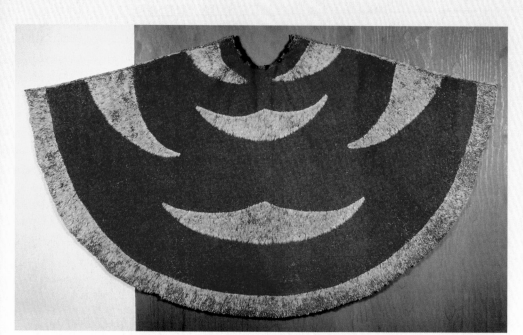

FEATHER CLOAK, KNOWN AS THE KEARNY CLOAK
Hawaii. c. 1843. Red, yellow, and black feathers, *olona* cordage, and netting, length 55¾" (143 cm).
Bishop Museum, Honolulu.

King Kamehameha III (ruled 1825–54) presented this cloak to Commodore Lawrence Kearny, commander of the frigate USS *Constellation*.

long, concave, pointed nose; a small mouth with pursed lips; and an angular chin. The extremely elongated earlobes have parallel engraved lines that suggest ear ornaments. The figures have schematically indicated breastbones and pectorals, and small arms with hands pressed close to the sides, but no legs.

Easter Islanders stopped erecting *moai* around 1500 and entered a period of warfare among themselves, apparently because overpopulation was straining the island's available resources. Most of the *moai* were knocked down and destroyed during this period. The island's indigenous population, which may at one time have consisted of as many as 10,000 people, was nearly eradicated by Peruvian slave traders in the nineteenth century. The smallpox and tuberculosis they brought with them precipitated an epidemic that left only about 600 Easter Island inhabitants alive.

Marquesas Islands

The first inhabitants of Easter Island probably were voyagers from the Marquesas Islands, almost 2,000 miles to the west. The Marquesas are made up of several volcanic islands in two groups, one north of the other. Only six of the islands are inhabited. The natives were noted for their warfare, the culmination of which was often cannibalism. Contact with outsiders beginning in 1595 decimated the Marquesans. The worst century for declining population began in 1800, when there were an estimated 90,000 people living on the islands. By 1900 census figures show the population had dropped to about 3,500, and the native population reached its low of less than 2,000 by 1930. Even with their local traditions of violence and warfare, the greatest threat to the native way of life had come from outside, with diseases such as smallpox brought by visitors to the islands.

WAR CLUB. Traditional fighting in the Marquesas was hand-to-hand and warriors used elaborate regalia to convey their rank and status. A 5-foot-long ironwood war club (FIG. 27–10) is lavishly decorated, with a Janus-like double face at the end. The high, arching eyebrows frame sunburst eyes whose pupils are tiny faces. Other patterns seem inspired by human eyes and noses. The overlay of low relief and engraved patterns suggests tattooing, a highly developed art in Polynesia (FIG. 27–11).

New Zealand

New Zealand was the last part of Polynesia to be settled. The first inhabitants had arrived by about the tenth century, and their descendants, the Maori, numbered in the hundreds of thousands by the time of European contact in the seventeenth and eighteenth centuries.

PORTRAIT OF A MAORI. Captain Cook's first expedition explored the coast of New Zealand in 1769. Sydney Parkinson (1745?–71), one of the artists on the voyage, documented aspects of Maori life and art at the time. An unsigned drawing

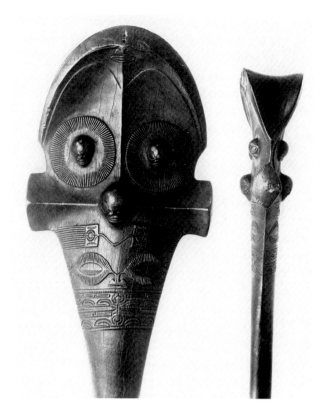

27–10 | **WAR CLUB**
Marquesas Islands, Polynesia. Early 19th century.
Ironwood, length approx. 5′ (1.52 m).
Peabody Essex Museum, Salem, Massachusetts.

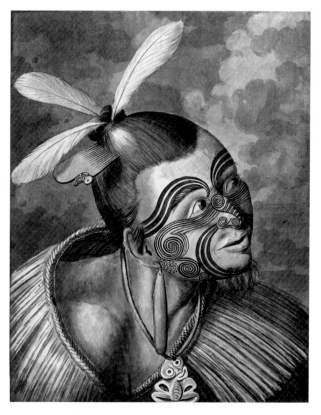

27–11 | Sydney Parkinson **PORTRAIT OF A MAORI 1769**
Wash drawing, 15 ½ × 11 ⅝″ (39.37 × 29.46 cm), later engraved and published as plate XVI in Parkinson's *Journal*, 1773. The British Library, London.

by Parkinson (FIG. 27–11) shows a Maori with facial tattoos (*moko*) wearing a headdress with feathers, a comb, and a *hei-tiki* (a carved pendant of a human figure).

Combs similar to the one in the drawing can still be found in New Zealand. The long ear pendant is probably made of greenstone, a form of jade found on New Zealand's South Island that varies in color from off-white to very dark green. The Maori considered greenstone to have supernatural powers. The *hei-tiki* hanging on a cord around the man's neck would have been among his most precious possessions. Such tiki figures, which represented legendary heroes or ancestor figures, gained power from their association with powerful people. The tiki in this illustration has an almost embryonic appearance, with its large tilted head, huge eyes, and seated posture. Some tiki had large eyes of inlaid shell.

The art of tattoo was widespread and ancient in Oceania; bone tattoo chisels have even been found in Lapita sites. Both men and women were tattooed, and in modern traditional societies, both men and women do the tattooing on members of their own gender. Maori men generally had tattoos on the face and on the lower body between the waist and the knees. Women were tattooed around the mouth and on the chin. The typical design of men's facial tattoos, like the striking one shown here, consisted of broad, curving parallel lines from nose to chin and over the eyebrows to the ears. Small spiral patterns adorned the cheeks and nose. Additional spirals or other patterns were placed on the forehead and chin and in front of the ears. A formal, bilateral symmetry controlled the design. Maori men considered their *moko* designs to be so personal that they sometimes signed documents with them. Ancestor carvings in Maori meetinghouses also have distinctive *moko*. According to Maori mythology, tattooing, as well as weaving and carving, was brought to them from the underworld, the realm of the Goddess of Childbirth. *Moko* might thus have a birth-death symbolism that links the living with their ancestors.

CARVED LINTEL. The Maori are especially known for their wood carving, which is characterized by a combination of massive underlying form with delicate surface ornament. This combination is found in small works like the *hei-tiki* in Parkinson's drawing as well as in the larger-scale sculpture that adorned storehouses and meetinghouses in Maori hilltop villages.

A carved lintel, probably collected on Captain Cook's second voyage in 1773, is one of the earliest surviving Maori sculptures in North America (FIG. 27–12). From its place over a doorway, the sculpture confirmed the power and prestige of its owners. The composition revolves around a central figure, a standing tiki. The fearsome square head glares at the world with glittering blue and green haliotis shell pupils set in triangular eyes under heavy eyebrows. Flaring nostrils and an open figure-eight shaped mouth with protruding tongue add to the terrifying aspect of the figure. The tongue gesture is defiant and aggressive. Massive arms and legs swell under a dense pattern of surface ornament and end in clawlike hands and feet. The tiki clutches a whale or fish. Glittering shell eyes help to sort out other fantastic, interlocking creatures, whose forms are nearly lost under the continuous spirals of surface ornament. The wood itself glows with a rich reddish-brown color, produced by rubbing the surface with a mixture of red clay and shark-liver oil, which colors and waterproofs the lintel.

MAORI MEETINGHOUSE. Only this lintel remains of what must have been an important building, but in the Museum of New Zealand in Wellington a meetinghouse carved by the master carver Raharuhi Rukupo in 1842–43 has been restored and re-erected.

This meetinghouse was built by Rukupo as a memorial to his brother (FIG. 27–13). Rukupo, who was an artist, diplomat, warrior, priest, and early convert to Christianity, built the house with a team of eighteen wood carvers. Although they used European metal tools, they worked in the technique and style of traditional carving done with stone tools. They finished the carved wood as usual, by rubbing it with a combination of red clay and shark-liver oil.

The whole structure symbolizes the sky father. The ridgepole is his backbone, the rafters are his ribs, and the slanting **bargeboards**—the boards attached to the projecting end of the gable—are his outstretched enfolding arms. His head and face are carved at the peak of the roof. The curvilinear patterns on the rafters were made with a silhouetting technique. Artists first painted the rafters white, then outlined the patterns, and finally painted the background red or black,

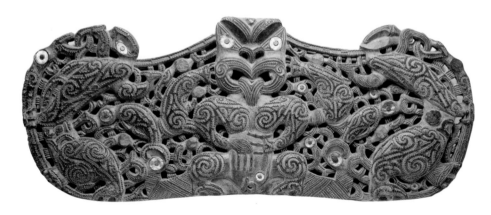

27–12 | CARVED LINTEL
New Zealand, Polynesia. Maori, 18th century. Totara wood and haliotis shell, 40¼ × 15¾ × 2″ (102.2 × 40 × 5.1 cm). Nelson-Atkins Museum of Art, Kansas City, Missouri.
Gift of Mr. and Mrs. Morton Sosland [76-57]

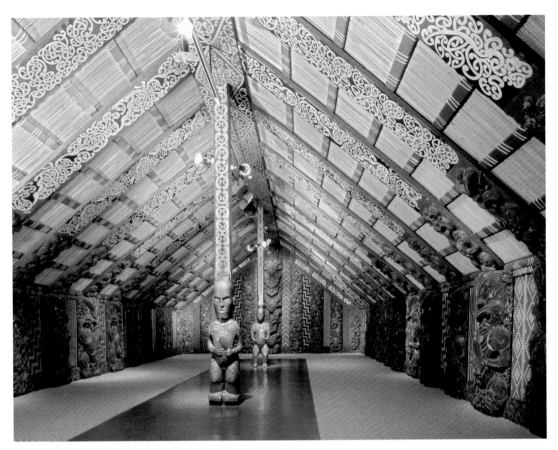

27–13 Raharuhi Rukupo, master carver **TE-HAU-KI-TURANGA (MAORI MEETINGHOUSE)**
Manutuke Poverty Bay, New Zealand. 1842–43, restored in 1935. Wood, shell, grass, flax, and
pigments. The Museum of New Zealand Te Papa Tongarewa, Wellington.
Neg. B18358

leaving the patterns in white. Characteristically Maori is the koru pattern, a curling stalk with a bulb at the end that is said to resemble the young tree fern.

Relief figures of ancestors—Raharuhi Rukupo included a portrait of himself among them—cover the support poles, wall planks, and the lower ends of the rafters. The ancestors, in effect, support the house. They were thought to take an active interest in community affairs and to participate in the discussions held in the meetinghouse. Like the *hei-tiki* in FIGURE 27–11, the figures have large heads. Flattened to fit within the building planks and covered all over with spirals, parallel and hatched lines, and tattoo patterns, they face the viewer head on with glittering eyes of blue-green inlaid shell. Their tongues stick out in defiance from their grimacing mouths, and they squat in the posture of the war dance.

Lattice panels made by women fill the spaces between the wall planks. Because ritual prohibitions, or taboos, prevented women from entering the meetinghouse, they worked from the outside and wove the panels from the back. They created the black, white, and orange patterns from grass, flax, and flat slats. Each pattern has a symbolic meaning: chevrons represent the teeth of the monster Taniwha; steps represent the stairs of heaven climbed by the hero-god Tawhaki; and diamonds represent the flounder.

Considered a national treasure by the Maori, this meetinghouse was restored in 1935 by Maori artists from remote areas who knew the old, traditional methods and is now preserved at the Museum of New Zealand.

Hawaiian Islands

Until about 1200 CE the Hawaiian Islands remained in contact with other parts of Polynesia; thereafter they were isolated, and the rigidly stratified Hawaiian society divided into several independent chiefdoms. Their isolation came to an end in 1778 with the arrival of the explorer Captain James Cook, who named them the Sandwich Islands after one of his patrons, the Earl of Sandwich. His first arrival coincided with a season of celebration in honor of the Hawaiian god Lono, and Captain Cook was regarded as a representative or emissary from that god. However his ship was damaged by a storm at sea shortly after leaving Hawaii and he went back for repairs. During the return visit relations with the Hawaiians were less cordial, and Cook was killed in a confrontation with them.

At the time of Cook's visit the islands were governed by several independent chiefdoms. In 1810 one ruler, Kamehameha I (c. 1758–1819), consolidated the islands into a unified kingdom. His family ruled until 1872, and the monarchy itself lasted until the dethronement of Queen

Lili'uokalani in 1893. Throughout the nineteenth century the influence of United States missionaries and economic interests increased, and Hawaii's traditional religion and culture declined. The United States annexed Hawaii in 1898, and the territory became a state in 1959.

When the Polynesians settled in Hawaii, they brought with them the production of bark cloth. This cloth, known as *tapa* or *kapa*, was usually made by women, sometimes with the assistance of men in obtaining the bark or in the decoration of the completed cloth. The bark used in the cloth was stripped from certain trees, particularly the "paper-mulberry" (not a true mulberry tree, but widely cultivated in the Pacific islands). It was washed in seawater, dried, and then softened by being soaked again in salt water and rinsed in fresh water. Layers of bark were folded over and beaten together, building up the cloth in a process of felting. In Hawaii the faces of the wooden mallets used for beating the cloth were incised with complex patterns, which left impressions in the cloth like watermarks, viewable when the cloth is held up to the light.

The traditional Hawaiian women's dress consisted of a sheet of bark cloth wrapped around the body either below or above the breasts. The example shown here (FIG. 27–14) belonged to Queen Kamamalu. Such garments were highly prized and considered to be an appropriate diplomatic gift. The queen took bark-cloth garments with her when she and King Kamehameha II made a state visit to London in 1823.

Bark cloth, with its easily available material and simple method of manufacture, is a common medium throughout Polynesia and Melanesia. Plain and decorated cloth was used for clothing, sails, mats, and ceremonial objects. Although there was great diversity in the islands of the Pacific, the restricted natural resources on any one archipelago and limited contact with outsiders meant that residents developed distinctive art styles for such products as tapa cloth even when the material used was essentially the same from one island to the next.

Various thicknesses and qualities of bark cloth were used for different purposes. Melanesians in one region of Vanuatu even made lightweight bark cloth for use as mosquito netting. Often the roughest, heaviest cloth would be used for mats, but clothing too was often quite rough. In Tikopia in the Solomon Islands, for example, a man's waist cloth was known to be uncomfortably scratchy for the first day or so.

The decoration of bark cloth varied. It could be dyed with turmeric or mud. It was sometimes exposed to smoke to turn it black or dark brown. Fine bark cloth was sometimes decorated in red or black with repeated geometric patterns made with tiny bamboo stamps or painted with freehand designs. The cloth could also be worked into a kind of appliqué, in which a layer of cutout patterns, usually in red, was beaten onto a light-colored backing sheet.

While bark cloth's most common use is functional, as clothing and for such items as mats and sails, tapa was also used for symbolic purposes, for example, to wrap wooden or wicker frames to make human effigies for display during festivals in the Marquesas and Easter Island. In addition to presenting clothing as a royal gift, pieces of bark cloth were exchanged for political advantage. In western Polynesia very large pieces, 7 to 10 feet across and hundreds of feet long, traditionally were given in ceremonial exchanges of valuables.

RECENT ART IN OCEANIA

Many contemporary artists in Oceania, in a process anthropologists call *reintegration*, have responded to the impact of European culture by adapting traditional themes and subjects to new mediums and techniques. The work of a Hawaiian quilt maker and an Australian aboriginal painter provide two examples of this process.

A QUILT FROM HAWAII. Missionaries encouraged women in the production of fiber arts, even though traditionally both men and women participated to varying extents in the making of such objects. Fabric patchwork and quilting were introduced to the Hawaiian Islands in 1820, and Hawaiian women were soon making distinctive, multilayered stitched quilts. Over time, as European-type cloth became increasingly available, the new arts replaced bark cloth in prestige, and today they are held in high esteem. Quilts are brought out for display and given as gifts to mark holidays and rites of passage, such as weddings, anniversaries, and funerals. They are also important gifts for establishing bonds between individuals and communities.

Royal Symbols, by contemporary quilter Deborah (Kepola) U. Kakalia, is a luxurious quilt with a two-color pattern remi-

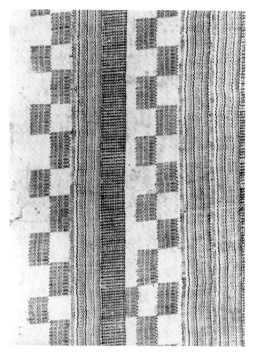

27–14 | **SKIRT ORIGINALLY BELONGING TO QUEEN KAMA-MALU** Hawaii. 1823-24. Paper mulberry (wauke) bark, stamped patterns, 12'3″ × 5'6″ (3.77 × 1.7 m). Bishop Museum, Honolulu.
Gift of Evangeline Priscilla Starbuck, 1927 (C.209)

niscent of bark-cloth design (FIG. 27–15). It combines heraldic imagery from both Polynesian and European sources to communicate the artist's proud sense of cultural identity. The crowns, the rectangular feather standards (kahili) in the corners, and the boldly contrasting red and yellow colors—derived from traditional featherwork—are symbols of the Hawaiian monarchy, even though the crowns have been adapted from those worn by European royalty. The kahili are ancient Hawaiian symbols of authority and rule, and the eight arches arranged in a cross in the center symbolize the uniting of Hawaii's eight inhabited islands into a single kingdom. The quilt's design, construction, and strong color contrasts are typically Hawaiian. The artist created the design the way children create paper snowflakes, by folding a piece of red fabric into eight triangular layers, cutting out the pattern, and then unfolding it. The red fabric was then sewn onto a yellow background and quilted with a technique known as contour stitching, in which the quilter follows the outlines of the design layer with parallel rows of tiny stitches. This technique, while effectively securing the layers of fabric and batting together, also creates a pattern that quilters liken to breaking waves.

AUSTRALIAN ABORIGINE ACRYLIC ON CANVAS. In Australia, Aborigine artists have adopted canvas and acrylic paint for rendering imagery traditionally associated with more ephemeral mediums like bark, body, and sand painting. Sand painting is an ancient ritual art form that involves creating large colored designs on bare ground. These paintings are done with red and yellow ochers, seeds, and feathers arranged on the ground in dots and other symbolic patterns. They are used to convey tribal lore to young initiates. Led by an art teacher named Geoffrey Bardon, a group of Aborigines

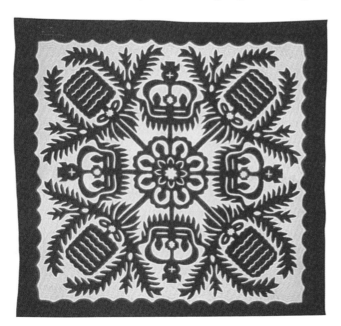

27–15 | Deborah (Kepola) U. Kakalia **ROYAL SYMBOLS**
1978. Quilt of cotton fabric and synthetic batting, appliqué, and contour stitching, 6'6¼" × 6'4½" (1.98 × 1.96 m).
Courtesy of Joyce D. Hammond, Joyce D. Hammond Collection

Sequencing Works of Art

c. 1000–1500	*Moai* ancestor figures (?) originally built, Easter Island
1842–43	Raharuhi Rukupo,.Te-Hau-ki-Turanga, New Zealand
c. 1960	Asmat ancestral spirit poles (*mbis*), New Guinea
1978	Deborah (Kepola) U. Kakalia, *Royal Symbols*
1978	Clifford Possum Tjapaltjarri, *Man's Love Story*

expert in sand painting formed an art cooperative in 1971 in Papunya, in central Australia. Their success in transforming their ephemeral art into a painted mural on the school wall encouraged community elders to allow others, including women, to try their hand at painting, which soon became an economic mainstay for many aboriginal groups in the central and western Australia desert.

Clifford Possum Tjapaltjarri (c. 1932–2002), a founder of the Papunya cooperative who gained an international reputation after an exhibition of his paintings in 1988, worked with his canvases on the floor, as in traditional sand painting, using ancient patterns and colors, principally red and yellow ochers as well as touches of blue. The superimposed layers of concentric circles and undulating lines and dots in a painting like *Man's Love Story* (FIG. 27–16) create an effect of shifting colors and lights.

The painting seems entirely abstract, but it actually conveys a narrative involving two mythical ancestors: One of these ancestors came to Papunya in search of honey ants; the white U shape on the left represents him seated in front of a water hole with an ants' nest, represented by the concentric circles. His digging stick lies to his right, and white sugary leaves lie to his left. The straight white "journey line" represents his trek from the west. The second ancestor, represented by the brown-and-white U-shaped form, came from the east, leaving footprints, and sat down by another water hole nearby. He began to spin a hair string (a string made from human hair) on a spindle (the form leaning toward the upper right of the painting) but was distracted by thoughts of the woman he loved, who belonged to a kinship group into which he could not marry. When she approached, he let his hair string blow away (represented by the brown flecks below him) and lost all his work. Four women (the dotted U shapes) from the group into which he could marry came with their digging sticks and sat around the two men. Rich symbolism also fills other areas of the painting: The white footprints are those of another ancestral figure following a woman, and the wavy line at the top is the path of yet another ancestor. The black, dotted oval area indicates the site where young men were taught this story. The long horizontal bars are mirages. The wiggly shapes represent caterpillars, and the dots represent seeds, both forms of food.

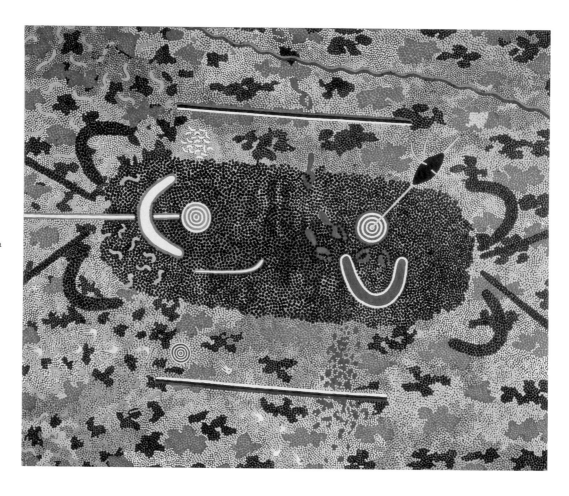

27–16 | Clifford Possum Tjapaltjarri
MAN'S LOVE STORY
1978. Synthetic polymer paint on canvas, 6'11¾" × 8'4¼" (2.15 × 2.57 m). Art Gallery of South Australia, Adelaide.
Visual Arts Board of the Australia Council Contemporary Art Purchase Grant, 1980

The point of view of this work may be that of someone looking up from beneath the surface of the earth rather than looking down from above. To begin the work Clifford Possum Tjapaltjarri first painted the landscape features and the impressions left on the earth by the figures—their tracks, direction lines, and the U-shaped marks they left when sitting. Then, working carefully, dot by dot, he captured the vast expanse and shimmering light of the arid landscape. The painting's resemblance to modern Western painting styles such as Abstract Expressionism, gestural painting, pointillism, or Color Field painting (Chapter 32) is accidental. Clifford Possum's work is rooted in the mythic, narrative traditions of his people. Although few artifacts remain from prehistoric times on the Pacific islands, throughout recorded history artists such as Possum have worked with remarkable robustness, freshness, and continuity. They have consistently created arts that express the deepest meanings of their culture.

IN PERSPECTIVE

Artists in the Pacific include the natives of Australia as well as the island groups of Melanesia, Micronesia, and Polynesia. The islands were the last region of the earth to be perma-

nently settled, with some areas of Polynesia only inhabited during the last 1,000 years. There is great diversity among the cultures in these areas, reflecting the dramatic variation in the environment and resources available to native societies.

The small and sometimes isolated populations in the Pacific are intimately connected to their environment, utilizing the limited raw materials available to them to produce distinctive artworks closely linked to their religious lives and rituals. Clothing and body decorations such as body painting and tattooing are used to reflect social status and ethnic identity. Some of the scattered island groups of Micronesia and Polynesia produced dramatic stonework carved without metal tools, including monumental architecture and large-scale stone sculpture. In parts of Australia, Aborigines lived as hunter-gatherers into the twentieth century. Their art reflects the continuity in their way of life and a deep spiritual connection to the landscape from antiquity through modern times. The largest island in Melanesia, New Guinea, has the most diverse environment in the Pacific. The combination of the environmental circumstances and the tens of thousands of years during which people lived there have allowed a wide variety of cultures to develop, each group speaking its own language and producing its own style of art.

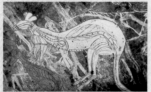

MIMIS AND KANGAROO
18,000–7000 BCE

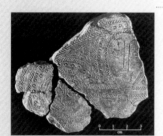

**FRAGMENTS OF A LARGE
LAPITA JAR**
C. 1200–1100 BCE.

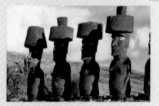

MOAI FIGURES
C. 1000–1500 CE

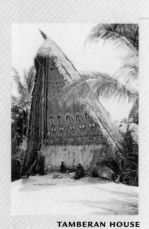

TAMBERAN HOUSE
20TH CENTURY

ART OF PACIFIC CULTURES

915

7000
BCE

◄ **Farming Culture in Melanesia**
c. 7000 BCE

4000

◄ **Australia Separates from Melanesia**
c. 4000 BCE

2000

◄ **Lapita Culture in Melanesia**
c. 1500 BCE

1000

I
CE

◄ **Polynesians Settle Micronesia**
c. 1 CE

◄ **Hawaii, Easter Island Settled**
After 500 CE

◄ **New Zealand Settled**
c. 800/900–1200 CE

1000

2000

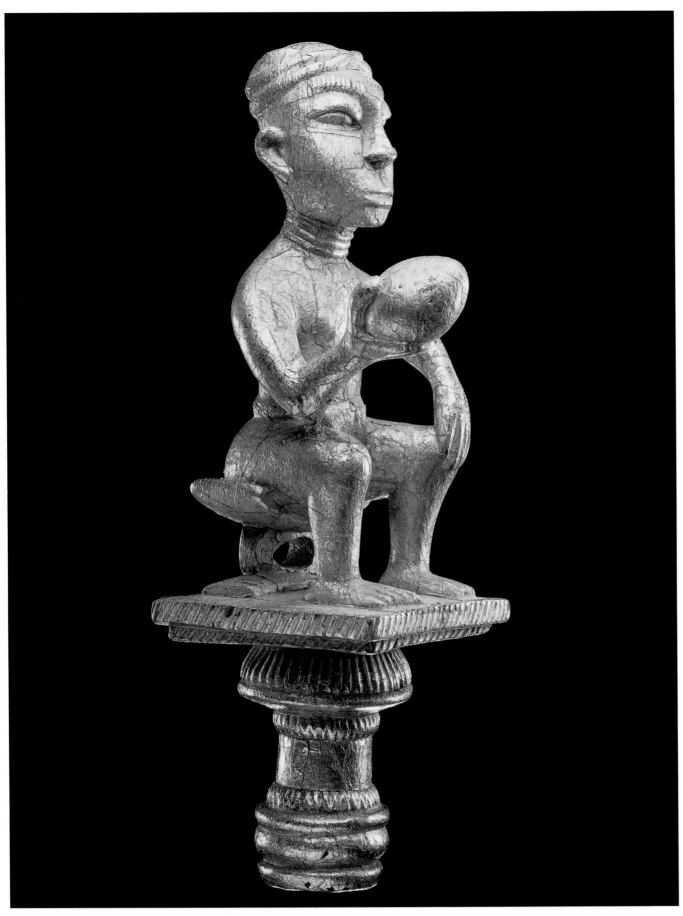

28–1 | Attributed to Kojo Bonsu **FINIAL OF A SPOKESPERSON'S STAFF (OKYEAME POMA)** From Ghana. Ashanti culture. 1960s–70s. Wood and gold, height 11¼" (28.57 cm). Sarah Da Vanzo Collection, Johannesburg, South Africa.

ART OF AFRICA IN THE MODERN ERA

28

Political power is like an egg, says an Ashanti proverb. Grasp it too tightly and it will shatter in your hand; hold it too loosely and it will slip from your fingers. Whenever the *okyeame*, or spokesperson, for one twentieth-century Ashanti ruler was conferring with that ruler or communicating the ruler's words to others, he held a staff with this symbolic caution on the use and abuse of power prominently displayed on the gold-leaf–covered finial (FIG. 28–1).

A staff or scepter is a nearly universal symbol of authority and leadership. Today in many colleges and universities a ceremonial mace is still carried by the leader of an academic procession, and it is often placed in front of the speaker's lectern, as a symbol of the speaker's authority. The Ashanti spokespersons who carry their image-topped staffs are part of this widespread tradition.

Since the fifteenth century, when the first Europeans explored Africa, objects such as this staff have been shipped back to Western museums of natural history or ethnography, where they were catalogued as curious artifacts of "primitive cultures." Toward the end of the nineteenth century, however, changes in Western thinking about African culture gradually led more and more people to appreciate the inherent aesthetic qualities of these unfamiliar objects and at last to embrace them fully as art. In recent years scholars have further enhanced the appreciation of traditional African arts by exploring their meaning from the point of view of the people who made them.

If we are to understand African art such as this staff on its own terms, we must take it out of the glass case of the museum where we usually encounter it and imagine the artwork playing its vital role in a human community. Indeed, this is true of any work of art produced anywhere in the world. When we recognize in an artwork the true expression of values and beliefs, our imaginations cross a bridge to understanding.

TRADITIONAL AND CONTEMPORARY AFRICA

The second-largest continent in the world, Africa is a land of enormous diversity (MAP 28–1). Geographically, it ranges from vast deserts to tropical rain forest, from flat grasslands to spectacular mountains and dramatic rift valleys. Cultural diversity in Africa is equally impressive. More than 1,000 African languages have been identified and grouped by scholars into five major linguistic families. Various languages represent unique cultures, with their own history, customs, and art forms.

Before the nineteenth century, the most important outside influence to pervade Africa had been the religious culture of Islam, which spread gradually and largely peacefully through much of West Africa and along the East African coast (see "Foundations of African Cultures," page 921). The modern era, in contrast, begins with the European exploration during the nineteenth century and subsequent colonization of the African continent, developments that brought traditional African societies into sudden and traumatic contact with the "modern" world that Europe had largely created.

European ships first visited sub-Saharan Africa in the fifteenth century. For the next several hundred years, however, European contact with Africa was almost entirely limited to coastal areas, where trade, including the tragic slave trade, was carried out. Between the sixteenth and nineteenth centuries, over 10 million slaves were taken from Africa to colonies in North and South America and the Caribbean islands. Countries that participated in the Atlantic slave trade included Great Britain, Portugal, France, Spain, Denmark, Holland, and the United States.

During the nineteenth century, as the slave trade was gradually eliminated, European explorers began to investigate the unmapped African interior in earnest. They were soon followed by Christian missionaries, whose reports greatly fueled popular interest in the continent. Drawn by the potential wealth of Africa's natural resources, European governments began to seek territorial concessions from African rulers. Diplomacy soon gave way to force, and toward the end of the century, competition among rival European powers fueled the so-called scramble for Africa, during which England, France, Germany, Belgium, Italy, Spain, and Portugal raced to lay claim to whatever part of the continent they could. By 1914 virtually all of Africa had fallen under colonial rule.

In the years following World War I, nationalistic movements arose across Africa. Their leaders generally did not advocate a return to earlier forms of political organization but rather demanded the transformation of colonial divisions into modern nation-states governed by Africans. From the 1950s through the mid-1970s, one colony after another gained its independence, and the present-day map of Africa took shape. Today, the continent is composed of over fifty independent countries.

Change has been brought about by contact between one people and another since the beginning of time, and art in Africa has both affected and been affected by such contacts. During the early twentieth century, the art of traditional African societies played a role in revitalizing Western art. The formal inventiveness and expressive power of African sculpture were sources of inspiration for European artists trying to rethink strategies of representation. Conversely, contemporary African artists, who have come of age in the postcolonial culture that mingles European and African elements, can draw easily on influences from many cultures, both African and non-African. These artists have established a firm place in the lively international art scene along with their European, American, and Asian counterparts, and their work is shown as readily in Paris, Tokyo, New York, and Los Angeles as it is in the African cities of Abidjan, Johannesburg, Kinshasa, and Dakar.

From the time of the first European explorations and continuing through the colonial era, quantities of art from traditional African societies were shipped back to Western museums—not art museums, at first, but museums of natural history or ethnography, which exhibited the works as curious artifacts of "primitive" cultures. Toward the end of the nineteenth century, however, profound changes in Western thinking about art gradually led people to appreciate the aesthetic qualities of tradition-based African "artifacts" and finally to embrace them fully as art. Art museums, both in Africa and in the West, began to collect African art seriously and methodically. Together with the living arts of African peoples today, these collections afford us a rich sampling of African art in the nineteenth and twentieth centuries.

Numerous tradition-based societies persist in Africa, both within and across contemporary political borders, and art continues to play a vital role in the spiritual and social life of the community. This chapter explores African art in light

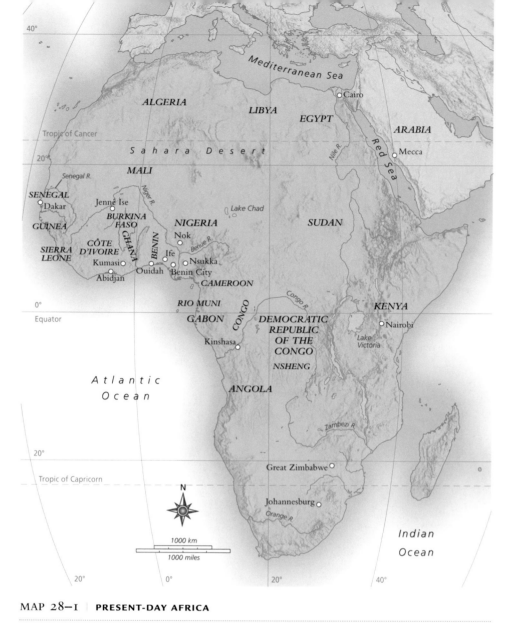

MAP 28–1 | **PRESENT-DAY AFRICA**

The vast continent of Africa is home to over fifty countries and innumerable cultures.

of how it addresses some of the fundamental concerns of human existence. Those concerns—rather than geographical region or time frame—form the backdrop against which we look at artworks in this chapter, as African art can be more fully understood within contexts of production and use.

Living Areas

Shelter is a basic human concern, yet each culture approaches it in a unique way that helps define that culture. The farming communities of the Nankani people in the border area between Burkina Faso and Ghana, in West Africa, have developed a distinctive painted adobe architecture. The mud and adobe buildings of their walled compounds are low and single storied with either flat roofs that form terraces or conical roofs. Each compound is surrounded by a defensive wall with a single entrance on the west side. Each building inside the enclosure is arranged so that it has a direct view of the entrance. Some buildings are used only by men, others only

by women. For example, Nankani men are in charge of the ancestral shrine near the entrance of the compound, the corral for cattle, and the granary; they have rectangular houses. The inner courtyards, outdoor kitchen, and round houses are women's areas (FIG. 28–2). Men build the compound; women paint the buildings inside and out.

The women decorate the walls with horizontal molded ridges called *yidoor*, meaning "rows in a cultivated field" and "long eye" (long life), to express good wishes for the family. They paint the walls with rectangles and squares divided diagonally to create triangular patterns that contrast with the curvature of the walls. The painted patterns are called "braided sling," "broken pottery," "broken gourd," and since the triangular motifs can be seen as pointing up or down, they are sometimes called "filed teeth." The same geometric motifs are used on pottery and baskets, and for scarification of the skin. When people decorate themselves, their homes, and their possessions with the same patterns, art serves to enhance cultural identity.

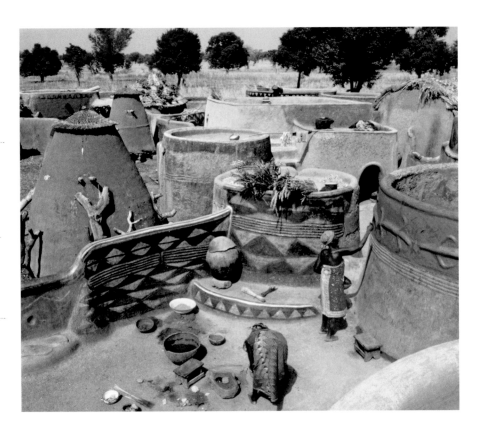

28-2 | NANKANI COMPOUND
Sirigu, Ghana. 1972.

Among the Nankani people, creating living areas is a cooperative but gender-specific project. Men build the structures, women decorate the surfaces. The structures are also gendered. The round dwellings shown here are women's houses located in an interior courtyard; men occupy rectangular flat-roofed houses. The bisected lozenge design on the dwelling to the left is called *zalanga*, the name for the braided sling that holds a woman's gourds and most treasured possessions.

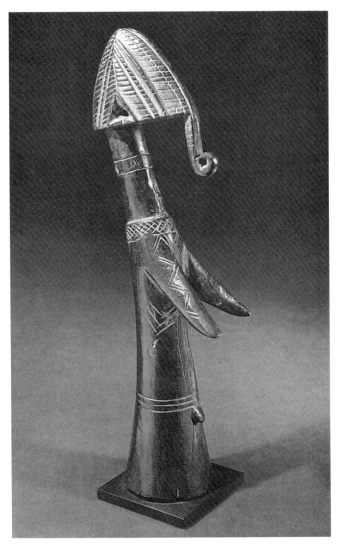

28-3 | DOLL (*BIIGA*)
Burkina Faso. Mossi culture. Mid-20th century. Wood, height 11¼" (28.57 cm). Collection Thomas G. B. Wheelock.

Children and the Continuity of Life

Among the most fundamental of human concerns is the continuation of life from one generation to the next. In tradition-based societies children are especially important: Not only do they represent the future of the family and the community, but they also provide a form of "social security," guaranteeing that parents will have someone to care for them when they are old.

In the often harsh and unpredictable climates of Africa, human life can be fragile. In some areas half of all infants die before the age of 5, and the average life expectancy may be as low as 40 years. In these areas women bear many children in hopes that at least a few will survive into adulthood, and failure to have children is a disaster for a wife, her husband, and her husband's lineage. Women who have had difficulty bearing children appeal for help with special offerings or prayers, often involving the use of art.

Art and Its Context
FOUNDATIONS OF AFRICAN CULTURES

Africa was the site of one of the great civilizations of the ancient world—that of Egypt, which arose along the fertile banks of the Nile River over the course of the fourth millennium BCE and lasted for some 3,000 years. Egypt's rise coincided with the emergence of the Sahara, now the largest desert in the world, from the formerly lush grasslands of northern Africa. Some of the oldest known African art, images inscribed and painted in the mountains of the central Sahara beginning around 8000 BCE, bear witness to this gradual transformation as well as to the lives of the pastoral peoples who once lived in the region.

As the grassland dried, its populations migrated in search of pasture and arable land. Many probably made their way to the Sudan, the broad band of savanna south of the Sahara. During the sixth century BCE, knowledge of iron smelting spread across the Sudan, enabling larger and more complex societies to emerge. One such society was the iron-working Nok culture, which arose in present-day Nigeria around 500 BCE and lasted until about 200 CE. Terra-cotta figures created by Nok artists are the earliest known sculpture from sub-Saharan Africa.

Farther south in present-day Nigeria, a remarkable culture developed in the city of Ife, which rose to prominence around 800 CE. There, from roughly 1000 to 1400, a tradition of naturalistic sculpture in bronze and terra-cotta flourished. Ife was, and remains, the sacred city of the Yoruba people. According to legend, Ife artists brought the techniques of bronze casting to the kingdom of Benin to the southeast. From 1170 to the present century, Benin artists in the service of the court created numerous works in bronze, at first in the naturalistic style of Ife, then in an increasingly stylized and elaborate manner.

With the Arab conquest of North Africa during the seventh and eighth centuries, Islamic travelers and merchants became regular visitors to the Sudan. Largely through their writings, we know of the powerful West African empires of Ghana and Mali, which flourished successively from the fourth through the sixteenth centuries along the great bend in the Niger River. Both grew wealthy by controlling the flow of African gold and forest products into the lucrative trans-Sahara trade. The city of Jenné, in Mali, served not only as a commercial hub but also as a prominent center of Islam.

Peoples along the coast of East Africa, meanwhile, since before the Common Era had participated in a maritime trade network that ringed the Indian Ocean and extended east to the islands of Indonesia. Over time, trading settlements arose along the coastline, peopled by Arab, Persian, and Indian merchants as well as Africans. By the thirteenth century these settlements were important port cities, and a new language, Swahili, had developed from the longtime mingling of Arabic with local African languages. Peoples of the interior organized extensive trade networks to funnel goods to these ports. From 1000 to 1500 many of these interior routes were controlled by the Shona people from the site called Great Zimbabwe. The extensive stone palace compound there stood in the center of a city of some 10,000 at its height. Numerous cities and kingdoms, often of great wealth and opulence, greeted the astonished eyes of the first European visitors to Africa at the end of the fifteenth century.

MOSSI BIIGA. The Mossi people of Burkina Faso carve a small wooden figure called *biiga*, or "child," as a plaything for little girls (FIG. 28–3). The girls feed and bathe the figures and change their clothes, just as they see their mothers caring for younger siblings. At this level the figures are no more than simple dolls. Like many children's dolls around the world, they show ideals of mature beauty, including elaborate hairstyles, lovely clothing, and developed breasts. The *biiga* shown here wears its hair just as little Mossi girls do, with a long lock projecting over the face. But the elongated breasts mark the doll as a mother of many children. Likewise, the scars on the belly mimic those applied to Mossi women following the birth of their first child. Thus, although the doll is called a child, it actually represents the ideal Mossi woman, one who has achieved the goal of motherhood.

Mossi girls do not outgrow their dolls as one would a childhood plaything. When a young woman marries, she brings the doll with her to her husband's home to serve as an

aid to fertility. If she initially has difficulty bearing a child, she carries the doll on her back just as she would a baby. When she gives birth, the doll is placed on a new, clean mat just before the infant is placed there, and when she nurses, she places the doll against her breast for a moment before the newborn receives nourishment.

YORUBA TWIN FIGURES. The Yoruba people of Nigeria have one of the highest rates of twin births in the world. The birth of twins is a joyful occasion, yet it is troubling as well, for twins are more delicate than single babies, and one or both may well die. Many African peoples believe that a dead child continues its life in a spirit world and that the parents' care and affection may reach it there, often through the medium of art. When a Yoruba twin dies, the parents often consult a diviner, a specialist in ritual and spiritual practices, who may tell them that an image of a twin, or *ere ibeji*, must be carved to serve as a dwelling place for the deceased twin's spirit (FIG. 28–4).

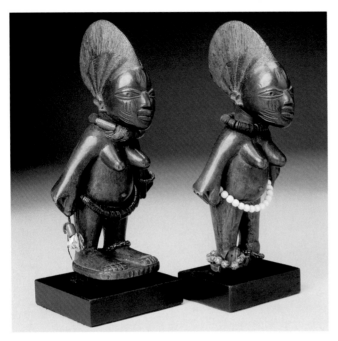

28–4 | TWIN FIGURES (*ERE IBEJI*)
Yoruba culture, from Nigeria. 20th century. Wood, height 7⅞"
(20 cm). The University of Iowa Museum of Art, Iowa City.
The Stanley Collection (×1986.489 and ×1986.488).

As with other African sculpture, patterns of use result in particular
signs of wear. The facial features of *ere ibeji* are often worn down or
even obliterated by repeated feedings and washings. Camwood
powder applied as a cosmetic builds to a thick crust in areas that
are rarely handled, and the blue indigo dye regularly applied to the
hair eventually builds to a thin layer of color.

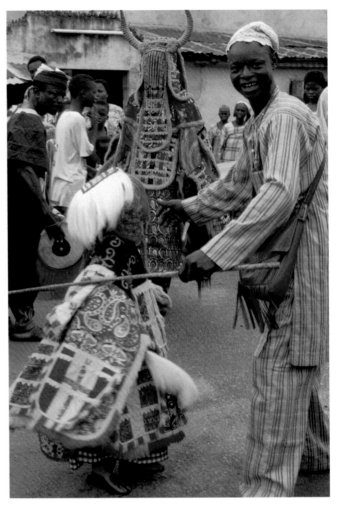

**28–5 | ELDER GUIDING SMALL BOY IN EGUNGUN PERFORM-
ANCE WHILE ADULT EGUNGUN PERFORMER LOOKS ON**
Yoruba culture, Nigeria. Photograph by Margaret Thompson
Drewal. National Museum of African Art, Smithsonian Institu-
tion, Washington, D.C.
Eliot Elisofon Photographic Archive

When the image is finished, the mother brings the artist
gifts. Then, carrying the figure as she would a living child, she
dances home accompanied by the singing of neighborhood
women. She places the figure in a shrine in her bedroom and
lavishes care upon it, feeding it, dressing it with beautiful textiles and jewelry, anointing it with cosmetic oils. The Yoruba
believe that the spirit of a dead twin, thus honored, is appeased
and will look with favor on the surviving family members.

The twins in FIGURE **28–4** are female. They may be the
work of the Yoruba artist Akiode, who died in 1936. Like
most objects that Africans produce to encourage the birth
and growth of children, the figures emphasize health and
well-being. They have beautiful, glossy surfaces to suggest that
they are well fed, as well as marks of adulthood, such as elaborate hair styles and scarification patterns, that will one day
be achieved. They represent hope for the future, for survival,
and for prosperity.

CHILDREN, ART, AND PERFORMANCE. In sub-Saharan Africa, as
elsewhere, children from an early age are intensely interested
in adult roles and activities including art making and the per-
formative arts. In many societies a child's link to a particular
artistic or craft activity is fixed. For example, in Africa, wood
carving is universally a male-dominated activity, while women

are most often involved in pottery production, and individual
children may be apprenticed to a wood carver or potter
according to their gender. But, even beyond such formal
apprenticeships, children are especially interested in the festive
activities of community life, such as masquerade. While mask
making and masquerade performance are usually controlled
by adult associations, children are given space at the edges of
events to experiment with their homemade masks and costumes. Yoruba masquerades such as Gelede or Egungun are
often organized so that children perform first (FIG. 28–5).
Some families even purchase or make elaborate costuming for
their children in a similar style to that worn by adults. Adults
view these early forays into masquerade as a training ground.
As children perform, they are encouraged and gently cor-
rected from the sidelines by family members. The Yoruba of
Nigeria, especially place a significant value on the training of
children into adult performance and aesthetic forms, and children are encouraged to perform from an early age.

Initiation

In contemporary Western societies, initiation into the adult world is extended over several years and punctuated by numerous rites, such as being confirmed in a religion, earning a driver's license, graduating from high school, and reaching the age of majority. All of these steps involve acquiring the knowledge society deems appropriate and accepting the corresponding responsibilities. In other societies, initiation can take other forms, and the acquisition of knowledge is usually supplemented by trials of endurance to prove that the candidate is equal to the responsibilities of adult life.

MASKS OF BWA INITIATION.   The Bwa people of central Burkina Faso initiate young men and women into adulthood following the onset of puberty. The initiates are first separated from younger playmates by being "kidnapped" by older relatives, though their disappearance is explained in the community by saying that they have been devoured by wild beasts. The initiates remove their clothing and sleep on the ground without blankets. Isolated from the community, they are instructed about the world of nature spirits and about the masks that represent them. They learn of the spirit each mask

represents, and they memorize the story of each spirit's encounter with the founding ancestors of the clan. They learn how to construct costumes from hemp to be worn with the masks, and they learn the songs and instruments that accompany the masks in performance. Only boys wear each mask in turn and learn the dance steps that express the character and personality each mask represents. Returning to the community, the initiates display their new knowledge in a public ceremony. Each boy performs with one of the masks, while the girls sing the accompanying songs. At the end of the mask ceremony the young men and young women rejoin their families as adults, ready to marry, to start farms, and to begin families of their own.

Most Bwa masks depict spirits that have taken an animal form, such as crocodile, hyena, hawk, or serpent. Others represent spirits in human form. Among the most spectacular masks, however, are those that represent spirits that have taken neither human nor animal form. Crowned with tall, narrow planks (FIG. 28–6), these masks are covered in **abstract** patterns that are easily recognized by the initiated. The white crescent at the top represents the quarter moon, under which the initiation is held. The white triangles below represent bull

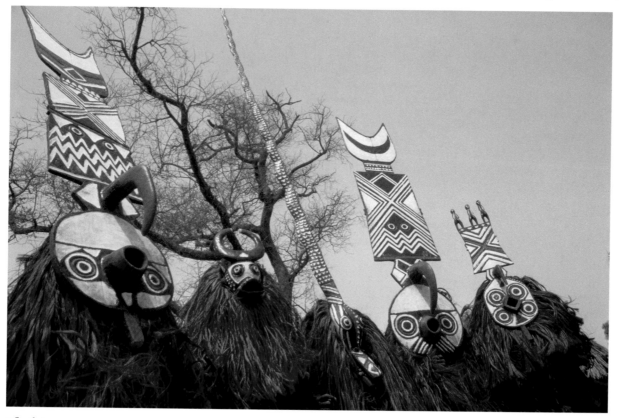

28–6 | **MASKS IN PERFORMANCE**
Dossi, Burkina Faso, Bwa culture, 1984. Wood, mineral pigments, and fiber, height approx. 7' (2.13 m).

The Bwa have been making and using such masks since well before Burkina Faso achieved its independence in 1960. We might assume their use is centuries old, but in this case, the masks are a comparatively recent innovation. The elders of the Bwa family who own these masks state that they, like all Bwa, once followed the cult of the spirit of Do, who is represented by masks made of leaves. In the last quarter of the nineteenth century, the Bwa were the targets of slave raiders from the north and east. Their response to this new danger was to acquire wooden masks from their neighbors, for such masks seemed a more effective and powerful way of communicating with spirits who could help them. Thus, faced with a new form of adversity, the Bwa sought a new tradition to cope with it.

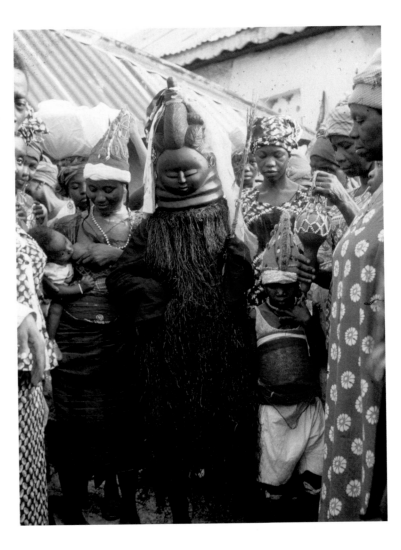

28–7 | **TEMNE NOWO MASQUER-ADE WITH ATTENDANTS**
Photograph by Fred Lamp, 1980.
Sierra Leone.

roarers—sacred sound makers that are swung around the head on a long cord to re-create spirit voices. The large central X represents the scar that every initiated Bwa bears as a mark of devotion. The horizontal zigzags at the bottom represent the path of the ancestors and symbolize adherence to ancestral ways. That the path is difficult to follow is clearly conveyed. The curving red hook that projects in front of the face is said to represent the beak of the hornbill, a bird associated with the supernatural world and believed to be an intermediary between the living and the dead. The mask thus proudly announces the initiate's passage to adulthood while encoding secrets of initiation in abstract symbols of proper moral conduct.

INITIATION TO WOMANHOOD IN WEST AFRICA. Among the Mende, Temne, Vai, and Kpelle peoples of Sierra Leone, the initiation of girls into adulthood is organized by a society of older women called Sande or Bondo. The initiation culminates with a ritual bath in a river, after which the initiated return to the village to meet their future husbands. At the ceremony, the Sande women wear black gloves and stockings, black costumes of shredded raffia fibers that cover the entire body, and black masks called *nowo* or *sowei* (**FIG. 28–7**).

With its glossy black surface, high forehead, elaborately plaited hairstyle decorated with combs, and refined facial features, the mask represents ideal female beauty. The mask is worn by a senior member of the women's Sande society whose responsibility is to prepare Sande girls for their adult roles in society including marriage and child rearing. The meanings of the mask are complex. One scholar has shown that the mask can be compared with the chrysalis of a certain African butterfly, with the creases at the base of the mask representing the segments of the chrysalis. Thus, the young woman entering adulthood is like a butterfly emerging from its cocoon. The comparison extends even further, for just as the butterfly feeds on the toxic sap of the milkweed to make itself poisonous to predatory birds, so the medicine of Sande is believed to protect the young women from danger. The creases may additionally refer to the concentric waves that radiate outward as the initiate emerges from the river to take her place as a member of the adult community.

BWAMI ASSOCIATION AMONG THE LEGA. A ceremony of initiation may accompany the achievement of other types of membership as well. Among the Lega people, who live in the dense forests between the headwaters of the Congo River and the

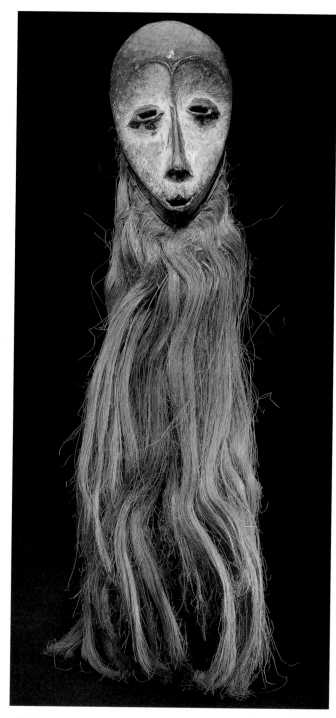

28–8 | *BWAMI* **MASK (LUKWAKONGO)**
Wood, plant fiber, and pigment, height: 22¾" (57.5 cm).
UCLA Fowler Museum of Cultural History, Los Angeles.

great lakes of East Africa, the political system is based on a voluntary association called *bwami*, which comprises six levels or grades. Some 80 percent of all male Lega belong to *bwami*, and all aspire to the highest grade. Women can belong to *bwami* as well, although not at a higher grade than their husbands.

Promotion from one grade of *bwami* to the next takes many years. It is based not only on a candidate's character but also on his or her ability to pay the initiation fees, which increase dramatically with each grade. No candidate for any

level of *bwami* can pay the fees alone; all must enlist the help of relatives to provide the necessary payment that may include cowrie shells, goats, wild game, palm oil, clothing, and trade goods. Thus, the ambition to move from one level of *bwami* to the next encourages a harmonious community, for all must stay on good terms with other members of the community if they are to advance.

Bwami initiations into advanced grades are held in the plaza at the center of the community in the presence of all members. Dances and songs are performed, and the values and ideals of the appropriate grade are explained through proverbs and sayings. These standards are illustrated by natural or crafted objects, which are presented to the initiate as signs of membership. At the highest two levels of *bwami*, such objects include exquisitely made small masks and sculpted figures.

The mask in FIGURE 28–8 is associated with *yananio*, the second-highest grade of *bwami*. Typical of Lega masks, the head is fashioned as an oval into which is carved a concave, heart-shaped face with narrow, raised features. The masks are often colored white with clay and fitted with a long beard made of plant fibers. Too small to cover the face, they are displayed in other ways—held in the palm of a hand, for example, or attached to a thigh. Each means of display recalls a different value or saying, so that one mask may convey a variety of meanings. Generally, the masks symbolize continuity between the ancestors and the living community and are thought to be direct links to deceased relatives and past members of bwami.

The Spirit World

While African religious beliefs have been influenced by Christianity and Islam for hundreds of years, many African peoples still rely on traditional customs and belief systems to find the answers to universal human problems. Why does one child fall ill and die while another remains healthy? Why does one year bring rain and a bountiful crop, while the next brings drought and famine? People everywhere confront these fundamental and troubling questions. In many African belief systems a supreme creator god is usually thought not to be fundamentally involved in the daily lives of humans. Instead, numerous subordinate spirit forces are said to be ever present and involved in human affairs. For instance, such spirits may inhabit agricultural fields, the river that provides fish, the forest that is home to game, or the land that must be cleared in order to build a new village. Families, too, may acknowledge the existence of ancestral spirits. These spirits control success and failure in life, and if a proper relationship is not maintained with the spirits, harm in the form of illness or misfortune can befall an individual, his family, or the entire community.

To communicate with these all-important spirits, many African societies rely on a specialist, such as a diviner who serves as a link between the supernatural and human worlds, opening the lines of communication through such techniques as prayer, sacrifice, offerings, ritual performance, and divination. Sometimes art plays a role in the diviner's dealings with the spirit world, giving visible identity and personality to what is imaginary and intangible.

KONGO *NKISI NKONDE*. Among the most potent images of power in African art are the *nkisi*, or spirit figures that were made by the Kongo and Songye peoples of Congo. The best known are the large wooden *nkonde*, which bristle with nails, pins, blades, and other sharp objects (FIG. 28–9). An *nkisi nkonde* begins its life as a simple, unadorned wooden figure that may be purchased from a carver at a market or commissioned by a diviner on behalf of a client who has encountered some adversity or faces an important turning point. Drawing on specialized knowledge, the diviner prescribes magical/medicinal ingredients, called *bilongo*, specific to the client's problem. These *bilongo* are added to the figure, either mixed with white clay and plastered directly onto the body or suspended in a packet from the neck or waist.

The *bilongo* transform the *nkonde* into a powerful agent, ready to attack the forces of evil on behalf of a human client. *Bilongo* ingredients are drawn from plants, animals, and minerals, and may include human hair, nail clippings, and other materials. Each ingredient has a unique role. Some bring the figure to life by embodying the spirit of an ancestor or a soul trapped by a malevolent power. Others endow the figure with distinctive powers or focus the powers in a particular direction, often through metaphor. For example, the Kongo admire the quickness and agility of a particular species of mouse. Tufts of this mouse's hair included in the *bilongo* act as a metaphor for quickness, ensuring that the *nkisi nkonde* will act rapidly when its powers are activated.

To activate the powers, clients drive in a nail or other pointed object to get the *nkonde*'s attention and provoke it to action. An *nkisi nkonde* may serve many private and public functions. Two warring communities might agree to end their conflict by swearing an oath of peace in the presence of the *nkonde* and then driving a nail into it to seal the agreement. Two merchants might agree to a partnership by driving two small nails into the figure side by side and then make their pact binding by wrapping the nails together with a cord. Someone accused of a crime might swear his innocence and drive in a nail, asking the *nkonde* to destroy him if he has lied. A mother might invoke the power of the *nkonde* to heal her sick child.

The word *nkonde* shares a stem with *konda*, meaning "to hunt," for the figure is quick to hunt down a client's enemies and destroy them. The *nkonde* here stands in a pose called *pakalala*, a stance of alertness like that of a wrestler challenging an opponent in the ring. Other *nkonde* figures hold a knife or spear in an upraised hand, ready to strike or attack.

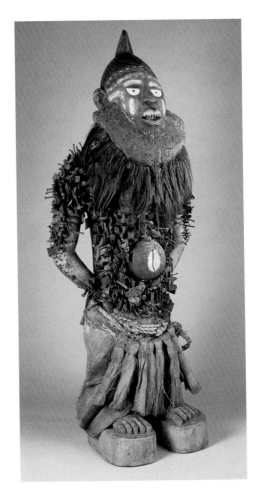

28–9 | POWER FIGURE (*NKISI NKONDE*)
Democratic Republic of Congo (Zaire). Kongo culture, 19th century. Wood, nails, pins, blades, and other materials, height 44″ (111.7 cm). The Field Museum, Chicago.
Acquisition A109979c

Nkisi nkonde provide a dramatic example of the ways in which works of African sculpture are transformed by use. When first carved, the figure is "neutral," with no particular significance or use. Magical materials applied by a diviner transform the figure into a powerful being, at the same time modifying its form. Each client who activates that power further modifies the statue. Nails may also be added as part of a healing or oath-taking process. And when the figure's particular powers are no longer needed, the additions may all be stripped away to be replaced with different magical materials that give the same figure a new function. The result is that many hands play a role in creating the *nkisi nkonde* we see in a museum. The person we are likely to label as the "artist" is only the initial creator. Many others modify the work, and in their hands the figure becomes a visual document of the history of the conflicts and afflictions that have threatened members of the community.

SPIRIT SPOUSE OF THE BAULE. Some African peoples conceive of the spirit world as a parallel realm in which spirits may have families, live in villages, attend markets, and possess personalities complete with faults and virtues. The Baule people in Côte d'Ivoire believe that each of us lived in the spirit world before we were born. While there, we had a spirit spouse, whom we left behind when we entered this life. A person who has difficulty assuming his or her gender-specific role as an adult Baule—a man who has not married or achieved his expected status in life, for example, or a woman who has not borne children—may dream of his or her spirit spouse.

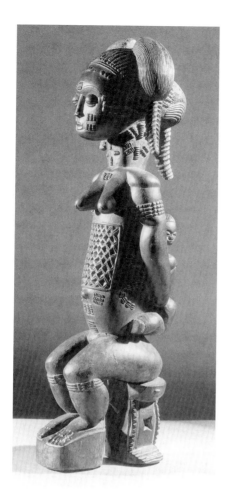

28–10 | SPIRIT SPOUSE (BLOLO BLA)
Côte d'Ivoire. Baule culture. Early 20th century.
Wood, height 17⅛″ (43.5 cm). University of Pennsylvania
Museum of Archeology and Anthropology, Philadelphia.

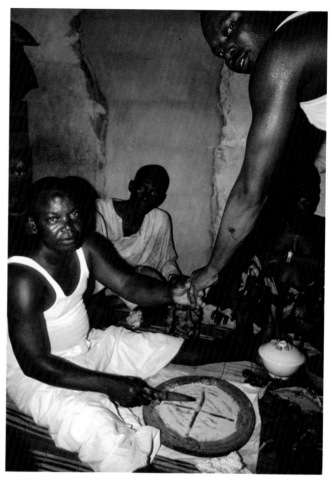

28–11 | IFA DIVINATION SESSION
Yoruba culture, Nigeria. Photograph by Margaret Drewal.
National Museum of African Art, Smithsonian Institution,
Washington, D.C.
Eliot Elisofon Photographic Archives

For such a person, the diviner may prescribe the carving of an image of the spirit spouse (FIG. 28–10). A man has a *blolo bla* (otherworld wife) and a woman has a *blolo bian* (otherworld husband) carved. The figures display the most admired and desirable marks of beauty so that the spirit spouses may be encouraged to enter and inhabit them. Spirit spouse figures are broadly naturalistic, with swelling, fully rounded musculature and careful attention to details of hairstyle, jewelry, and scarification patterns. They may be carved standing in a quiet, dignified pose or seated on a stool. The owner keeps the figure in his or her room, dressing it in beautiful textiles and jewelry, washing it, anointing it with oil, feeding it, and caressing it. Over time, the surface of the figure softens as it takes on a glossy sheen indicating the attention it has been given. The Baule hope that by caring for and pleasing his or her spirit spouse a balance may be restored that will free the individual's human life to unfold smoothly.

YORUBA DIVINATION. While spirit beings are often portrayed in African art, major deities are generally considered to be far removed from the everyday lives of humans and are thus rarely depicted. Such is the case with Olodumare, the creator god of the Yoruba people of southwestern Nigeria.

The Yoruba have a sizable pantheon of lesser, but still important, gods, or *orisha*. Two *orisha* are principal mediators: Orunmila who represents certainty, fate, order, and equilibrium; and his counterpart Eshu who represents uncertainty, disorder, and chance. Commonly represented in art, Eshu is a capricious and mischievous trickster who loves nothing better than to disrupt things that appear to be going well. The opposing forces of order and disorder are mediated through the agency of a diviner *(babalawo)* who employs a divination board *(opon ifa)* and its paraphernalia to reveal the causes of a client's problems (FIG. 28–11). The divination board is sprinkled with a white wood dust and the *orisha* Orunmila and Eshu are called to the divination by tapping the board with a special tapper. The *babalawo* throws sixteen palm nuts and after each toss the *babalawo* records the way the palm nuts have landed in the white wood dust on the divination board. Each configuration of the palm nuts relates to particular verses from a complex oral tradition also known as Ifa. As the selected verses are recited by the diviner, the client relates the verses to his or her own particular problems or concerns.

Eshu's image often appears on divination objects and in shrines employed by his worshipers. His image always appears at the top of the divination board, while other images along the edge of the board relate symbolically to the world of Ifa divination. Eshu is associated with two eternal sources of human conflict, sex and money, and is usually portrayed with a long hairstyle, because the Yoruba consider long hair to represent excess libidinous energy and unrestrained sexuality. Figures of Eshu are usually adorned with long strands of cowrie shells, a traditional African currency. Shrines to Eshu are erected wherever there is the potential for encounters that lead to conflict, especially at crossroads, in markets, or in front of banks. Eshu's followers hope that their offerings will persuade the god to spare them the pitfalls he places in front of others.

Leadership

As in societies throughout the world, art in Africa is used to identify those who hold power, to validate their right to their authority as representatives of the family or community, and to communicate the rules for moral behavior that must be obeyed by all members of the society. The gold-and-wood spokesperson's staff with which this chapter opened is an example of the art of leadership (SEE FIG. 28–1). It belongs to the culture of the Ashanti peoples of Ghana, in West Africa. The Ashanti greatly admire fine language—one of their adages is, "We speak to the wise man in proverbs, not in plain speech"—and consequently their governing system includes the special post of spokesperson to the ruler. Since about 1900 these advisers have carried staffs of office such as the one pictured here. The carved figure at the top illustrates a story that may have multiple meanings when told by a witty owner. This staff was probably carved in the 1960s or 1970s by Kojo Bonsu. The son of Osei Bonsu (1900–76), a famous carver, Kojo Bonsu lives in the Ashanti city of Kumasi and continues to carve prolifically.

The Ashanti use gold not only for objects, such as the staff, that are reserved for the use of rulers, but also for jewelry, as do other peoples of the region. But for the Ashanti, who live in the middle of the richest gold fields of West Africa, gold was long a major source of power; for centuries, they traded it, first via intermediaries across the Sahara to the Mediterranean world, then later directly to Europeans on the West African coast.

KENTE CLOTH. The Ashanti are also renowned for the beauty of their woven textiles, called *kente* (FIG. 28–12).

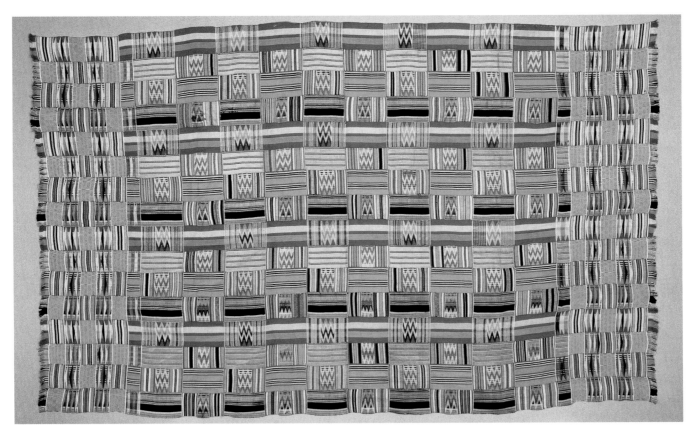

28–12 | *KENTE* CLOTH
Ashanti culture, Ghana. 20th century. Silk, 6'10⁹⁄₁₆" × 4'3⁹⁄₁₆" (2.09 × 130 m). National Museum of African Art and National Museum of Natural History, Smithsonian Institution, Washington, D.C.
Purchased with funds provided by the Smithsonian Collections Acquisition Program, 1983-85, (EJ 10583)

Weaving was introduced in Ghana sometime during the seventeenth century from neighboring regions of West Africa. The weavers were, traditionally, men. Ashanti weavers work on small, light, horizontal looms that produce long, narrow strips of cloth. They begin by laying out the long **warp** threads in brightly colored stripes. Today the threads are likely to be rayon. Formerly, however, they were cotton and later silk, which the Ashanti first procured in the seventeenth century by unraveling silk cloth obtained through European trade. **Weft** threads are woven through the warp to produce complex patterns that are named after the warp-faced patterns or weft designs. The long strips produced by the loom are then cut to size and sewn together to form large rectangles of finished *kente* cloth.

Kente cloth was originally reserved for state regalia. A man wore a single piece, about 6 to 7 feet by 12 to 13 feet, wrapped like a toga with no belt and the right shoulder bare. Women wore two pieces—a skirt and a shawl. The *kente* cloth shown here began with a warp pattern that alternates red, green, and yellow. The pattern is known as *oyokoman ogya da mu*, meaning "there is a fire between two factions of the Oyoko clan," and refers to the civil war that followed the death of the Ashanti king Osei Tutu in about 1730. Tradition-

ally, only the king of the Ashanti was allowed to wear this pattern. Other complex patterns were reserved for the royal family or members of the court.

THE KUBA NYIM. The Kuba people of the Democratic Republic of Congo produce elaborate and sophisticated arts tied to leadership. At the pinnacle of the hierarchy sits the Kuba paramount ruler (*nyim*) whose residence was located approximately in the center of the Kuba region. The current *nyim* can trace his predecessors back to the founding of the kingdom in the seventeenth century. At the installation of a new monarch, a new capital city (*Nsheng*) is built including the residence of the *nyim*, his wives and children, as well as areas for other governmental functions, all surrounded by a high palisade.

Titled individuals will often lavish elaborate surface decoration on objects that belong to them to indicate their rank and prestige within the political and social hierarchy. This is exemplified in the geometric woven decoration on the walls of royal buildings (FIG. 28–13) and decorated mats, and on the intricate carved decoration of wooden drums, boxes, and other objects. It is also seen on the variety of embroidered textiles for men and women and on regalia such as

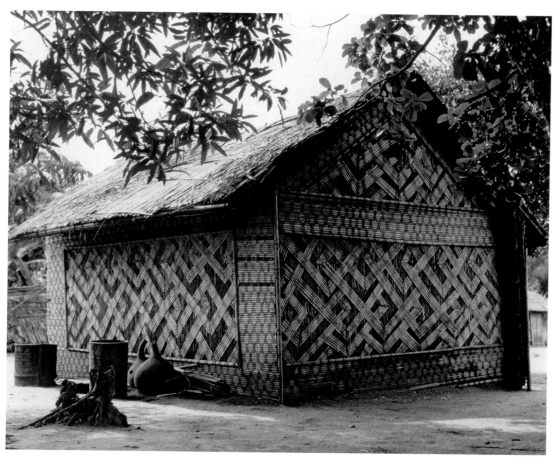

28–13 | **DECORATED BUILDING (SLEEPING ROOM FOR *NYIM*) IN THE ROYAL COMPOUND OF THE KUBA NYIM**
Nsheng, Democratic Republic of the Congo. Photograph by Angelo Turconi.

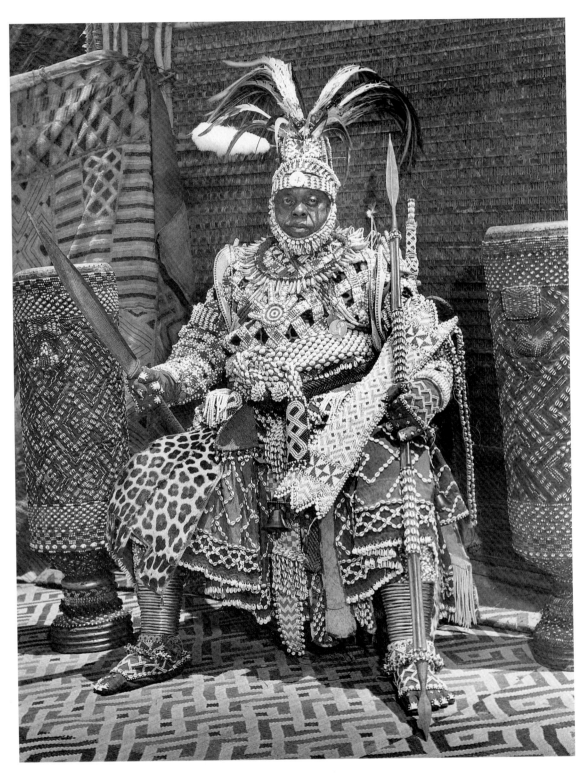

28–14 | **MBOP MABIINC MAMBEKY**
Paramount ruler (*nyim*) of Kuba peoples (reigned 1939–69). Prestige attire worn by the *nyim* for receiving important guests. The costume includes elements made from copper, brass, cowrie shells, beads, leopard skin, and eagle and parrot feathers. Photograph by Eliot Elisofon, 1947. National Museum of African Art, Smithsonian Institution, Washington, D.C.

Eliot Elisofon Photographic Archives

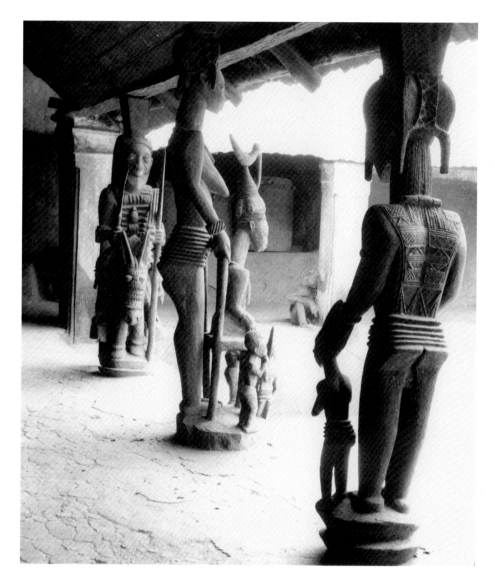

28–15 | Olowe of Ise
VERANDA POSTS
Ikere Palace, Ikere, Nigeria. 1910–14.
Wood and pigment. Photograph by
William Fagg, 1959. Royal Anthro-
pological Institute of Great Britain
and Ireland, London.

headdresses and jewelry that serve as prestige and festive attire for celebratory occasions. An eagle feather chief (*kumaphong*) displays sumptuous adornment at his investiture. Each element of regalia signifies a prerogative of an individual's titled position relative to the position of others within a complicated system of titleholding. Naturally the most extravagant adornment is worn by the paramount ruler, as can be seen in the photograph taken by Eliot Elisofon of the Kuba *nyim* in 1947 (FIG. 28–14). Textile display is also an essential aspect of funeral rituals where textiles are worn at celebratory dances and displayed on the body of the deceased. The textiles are subsequently buried with the deceased, where the Kuba believe an individual remains for a period of time before being reborn (see "Death and Ancestors," page 932).

YORUBA PALACE ART. The kings of the Yoruba people of Nigeria also manifested their authority and power through the large palaces in which they lived. In a typical palace plan,

the principal rooms opened onto a veranda with elaborately carved posts facing a courtyard (FIG. 28–15). Elaborate carving also covered the palace doors. Among the most important Yoruba artists of the early twentieth century was Olowe of Ise (d. 1938), who carved doors and veranda posts for the rulers of the Ekiti-Yoruba kingdoms in southwestern Nigeria.

The door of the royal palace in Ikere (FIG. 28–16) illustrates Olowe's artistry. Its asymmetrical composition combines narrative and symbolic scenes in horizontal rectangular panels. Tall figures carved in profile end in heads facing out to confront the viewer. Their long necks and elaborate hairstyles make them appear even taller, unlike typical Yoruba sculpture, which uses short, static figures. The figures are in such high relief that the upper portions are actually carved in the round. The figures move energetically against an underlying decorative pattern, and the entire surface of the doors is also painted.

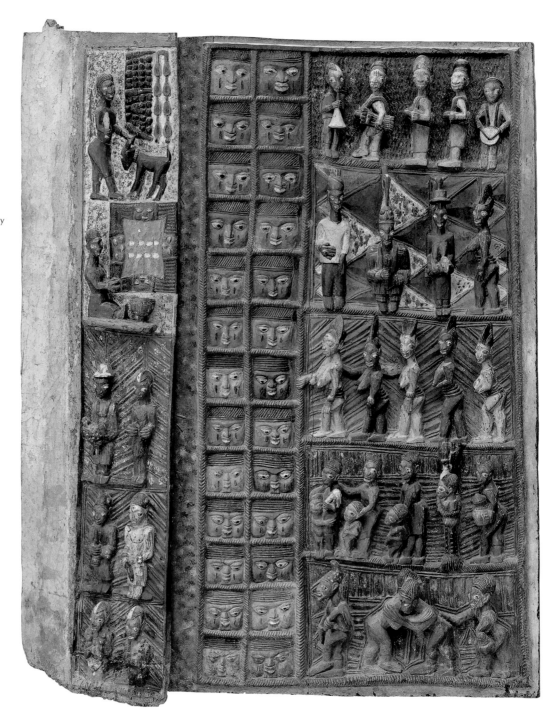

28–16 | Olowe of Ise
**DOOR FROM ROYAL
PALACE IN IKERE,
NIGERIA**
Yoruba culture. c. 1925.
Wood, pigment, height
72″ (182.9 cm).
The Detroit Institute of
the Arts.
Gift of Bethea and Irwin Green
in honor of the 20th anniversary
of the Department of African,
Oceanic, and New World
Cultures (1997.80.A)

The doors commemorate celebrations honoring the *orisha* of divination, Orunmila. In the left-hand panel, the future will be foretold by reading oracles. At the top is a man with sacrificial animal and palm nuts. Below him, a diviner sits with a divination board and the ceremonial cup for the palm nuts and lower still are messengers and assistants. On the right, two rows of faces introduce the court. The king is represented in the second panel seated between his guard and two royal wives; the chief wife wears a European top hat, a symbol of power. Above the royals, musicians perform, while below royal wives dance. The bottom two registers depict the people—farm workers and a pair of wrestlers.

Olowe seems to have worked from the early 1900s until his death in 1938. Although he was famous throughout Yorubaland and called upon by patrons as distant as 60 miles from his home, few records of his activities remain, and only one European, Philip Allison, wrote of meeting him and watching him work. Allison described Olowe carving the iron-hard African oak "as easily as [he would] a calabash [gourd]."

Death and Ancestors

In the view of many African peoples, death is not an end but a transition—the leaving behind of one phase of life and the beginning of another. Just as ceremonies mark the initiation of young men and women into the community of adults, so too they mark the initiation of the newly dead into the community of spirits. Like the rites of initiation into adulthood, death begins with a separation from the community, in this case the community of the living. A period of isolation and trial follows, during which the newly dead spirit may, for example, journey to the land of ancestors. Finally, the deceased is reintegrated into a community, this time the community of ancestral spirits. The living who preserve the memory of the deceased may appeal to his or her spirit to intercede on their behalf with nature spirits or to prevent the spirits of the dead from using their powers to harm.

DOGON FUNERARY DAMA. Among the Dogon people of Mali, in West Africa, a collective funeral rite with masks, called "dama," is held every twelve to thirteen years (FIG. 28–17). During *dama*, a variety of different masks perform to the sound of gunfire to drive the souls of the deceased from the village. Among the most common masks to perform is the *kanaga*, whose rectangular face supports a superstructure of planks that depict a woman, bird, or lizard with splayed legs.

For a deceased man, men from the community later engage in a mock battle on the roof of his home and participate in ritual hunts; for a deceased woman, the women of the community smash her cooking vessels on the threshold of her home. These portions of *dama* are reminders of human activities the deceased will no longer engage in. The *dama* may last as long as six days and include the performance of hundreds of masks. Because a *dama* is so costly, it is performed for several deceased elders at the same time. However, in certain Dogon communities frequented by tourists, *dama* performances have become more frequent as new masked characters are invented, including masks representing tourists

holding wooden cameras or anthropologists holding notebooks in their hands. In response to tourists, Dogon maskmakers produce additional masks that are offered for sale to tourists at the conclusion of the performance.

KUBA FUNERARY RITES. The Kuba people of the Democratic Republic of Congo do not hold elaborate rituals to honor ancestral spirits because the Kuba believe that after a generation or two individuals are reincarnated. Instead, they perform funerary masquerades to honor deceased members of the men's initiation society and high-ranking individuals who belonged to the community council of elders.

In the southern Kuba region, funeral rites for initiated men are often accompanied by the appearance of one or more masquerade figures on the day of interment of the deceased. For senior title holders, more elaborate preparations and the participation of the entire community is required. The most important masquerade figure in the southern Kuba region is Inuba, who appears at the funerals of senior titleholders (FIG. 28–18). Inuba's appearance requires the participation and attendance of all initiated men and community titleholders as well as the community to prepare for the masquerade on the day preceding and on the day of the funeral just prior to burial.

After touring the community on the day of the funeral, Inuba enters the shelter where the deceased has been placed into a coffin. The masked figure taps on top of the coffin to call the spirit of the deceased. Inuba speaks directly to the spirit and tells it that Inuba is performing to honor the deceased. At the same time Inuba admonishes the spirit not to be angry or harm anyone in the community because he has died. The recitation is believed to help lessen the anger of the deceased's spirit and to encourage it to leave the community peacefully. Once the recitation is concluded the deceased

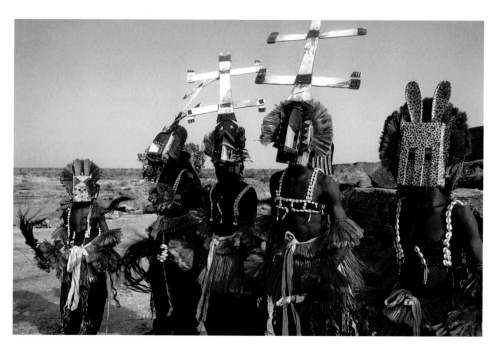

28–17 ┊ KANAGA AND RABBIT MASQUERADE FIGURES AT DAMA
Dogon culture, Mali. Performance photograph by Eliot Elisofon, 1959. National Museum of African Art, Smithsonian Institution, Washington, D.C.
Eliot Elisofon Photographic Archives. (EEPA 3502)

THE ⊙BJECT SPEAKS

AFRICAN ART CONFRONTING THE WEST

During the late nineteenth and early twentieth century, Nkanu peoples residing in the Democratic Republic of the Congo and Angola created brightly painted figurative sculpture and decorated wall panels adorned with human and animal figures to celebrate the completion of initiation rites (*nkanda*). These artworks were displayed in a three-sided roofed enclosure, called a *kikaku*, which was built at a crossroads nearby the initiation campground. These displays were made to reinforce the values taught during *nkanda* and to announce to the community that initiation was coming to a close and that their children would soon be home.

The *kikaku* resembled a stage. Wall panels were carved, painted, and attached to the back and sides of the *kikaku*, and sculpted figures were placed in front of the wall panels on the floor of the structure. The *kikaku* wall panels were accentuated with brightly colored and symbolically charged patterns that conveyed specific meanings associated with the coming of age ritual. Nkanu initiation art was left to decay after the close of *nkanda*, and only a few individual pieces were collected during the colonial era—there is no extant example of an entire *kikaku* in any museum collection.

European colonial officials were a favorite subject in *kikaku*. Their depictions were considered "portraits" of specific individuals, and included distinguishing characteristics such as costume and hair style. Nkanu artists seem to have singled out specific colonial officials whom they especially despised for their cruelty or whom they wanted to ridicule because of their dalliances with Nkanu women. These caricatures became a means of confronting colonial domination without openly attacking colonial officials, which would have undoubtedly led to severe repercussions.

In these wall panels, the central figure represents a colonial administrator. He is flanked by two figures representing Congolese men who are members of the "Force Publique," the Belgian colonial military force. One soldier is depicted wearing an ammunition belt, while the other assumes the awkward stance of an initiate who must balance on one leg. Both the stance and the painted patterns on the panels symbolically relate to the virility and procreative capacity of the initiate upon the successful completion of *nkanda*.

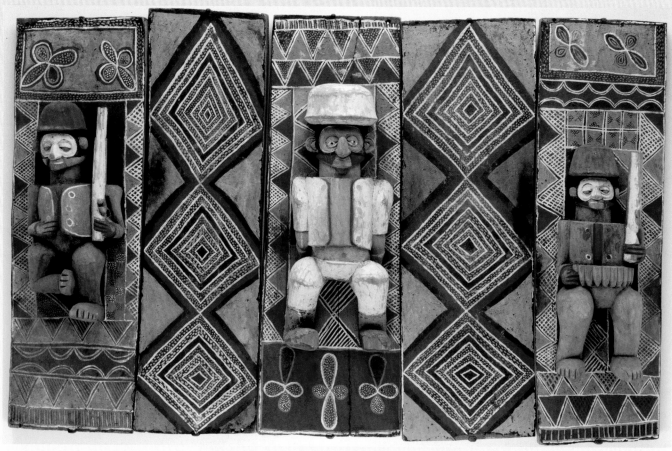

INITIATION WALL PANELS

Nkanu peoples. Democratic Republic of the Congo. Early 20th century. Wood, pigment, height 33⅜" (84.8 cm). National Museum of African Art, Smithsonian Institution, Washington, D.C.
Museum purchase, 99-2-1

arms. Frequent applications of cleansing and purifying palm oil produce a rich, glossy black surface.

The strong symmetry of the statue is especially notable. The layout of Fang villages is also symmetrical, with pairs of houses facing each other across a single long street. At each end of the street is a large public meetinghouse. The Fang immigrated to the area they now occupy during the early nineteenth century. The experience was disruptive and disorienting, and Fang culture thus emphasizes the necessity of imposing order on a disorderly world. Many civilizations have recognized the power of symmetry to express permanence and stability.

Internally, the Fang strive to achieve a balance between the opposing forces of chaos and order, male and female, pure and impure, powerful and weak. They value an attitude of quiet composure, of reflection and tranquility. These qualities are embodied in the symmetry of the *nlo byeri*, which communicates the calm and wisdom of the ancestor while also instilling awe and fear in those not initiated into the Fang religion.

IRON MEMORIAL SCULPTURE OF THE FON. In the early twentieth century, Fon peoples living in coastal Ouidah, in the Republic of Benin, created a distinctive style of iron memorial sculpture (*asen*) that were kept in a special building located in a family's courtyard. The various figurative and

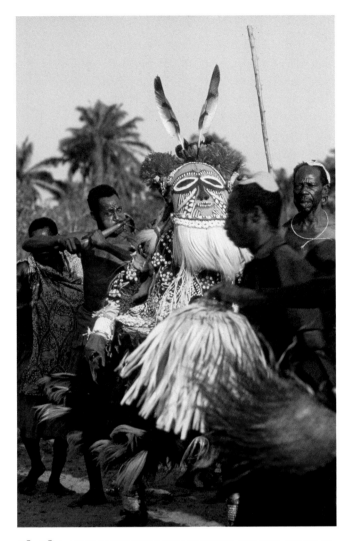

28–18 | **INUBA ENTERING THE COMMUNITY FOR FUNERAL PERFORMANCE IN THE COMPANY OF SENIOR TITLEHOLDERS**
Southern Kuba peoples, Democratic Republic of the Congo. Photograph by David A. Binkley & Patricia J. Darish, 1981.

is immediately taken to the cemetery for burial while Inuba and initiated men dance for the assembled family members and visitors until dusk.

FANG ANCESTOR GUARDIAN. The Fang people, who live near the Atlantic coast from southern Cameroon through Rio Muni and into northern Gabon, followed an ancestral religion in which bones and skulls of ancestors who have performed great deeds are collected after burial and placed together in a cylindrical bark container called *nsekh o byeri*, which a family would carry when it migrated. Deeds thus honored include killing an elephant, being the first to trade with Europeans, bearing an especially large number of children, or founding a particular lineage or community. On top of the container the Fang place a wooden figure called *nlo byeri*, which represents the ancestors and which guards their relics from malevolent spirit forces **(FIG. 28–19)**. *Nlo byeri* are often carved in a naturalistic style, with carefully arranged hairstyles, fully rounded torsos, and heavily muscled legs and

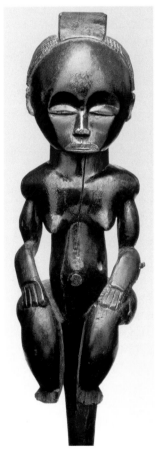

28–19 | **RELIQUARY GUARDIAN (*NLO BYERI*)**
Gabon. Fang culture. 19th century. Wood, height 16⅞" (43 cm). Musée Dapper, Paris.

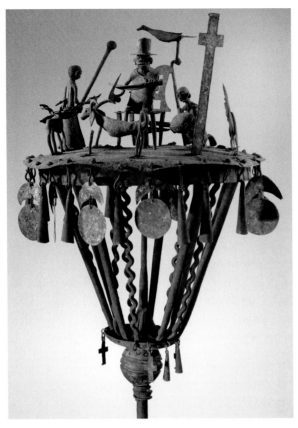

28–20 | ALTAR (ASEN)
Fon peoples, Ouidah, Republic of Benin. Iron, wood, paint traces, height 44½″ (113 cm). National Museum of African Art, Smithsonian Institution, Washington D.C.

Gift of Monique and Jean Paul Barbier-Mueller 93-2-2.

other motifs placed on top of an *asen* related to the life and achievements of a particular ancestor. Each family maintained a number of *asen*. Collectively, the *asen* served as points of contact with the ancestral spirits during annual and periodic commemorative ceremonies. Through these ceremonies the ancestors were acknowledged and their aid was sought to help in the ongoing life of the family.

The *asen* in FIGURE 28–20 is a particularly complex example. The large disk supported by iron posts serves as a circular stage onto which are attached iron figures and animals. A central seated figure holding a sword presents the deceased as a person of authority. He is surrounded by figures who pay homage to him, including a kneeling female figure holding a lidded gourd that would contain an offering of water or food for the deceased. The images of animals such as the goat, chickens, bullock, and pig represent the animals that were sacrificed to honor the deceased at his funeral or at a commemorative ceremony. Other animals such as the bird on top of a millet stalk may refer to proverbs that acknowledge the responsibility of the living to honor their ancestors. The cross on the *asen* could be a Christian symbol or (more probably) a symbol of Mawu, who is considered the female half of the creator couple.

CONTEMPORARY ART

The photographs of rituals and ceremonies in this chapter show ways that African traditional arts have continued during the modern era. All of these photographs are somewhat dated, and yet, even today, performances are staged in which the same types of masks will most likely appear. Many African communities continue to re-create artforms according to their traditions. But Africa is ever-changing, and as new experiences pose new challenges and offer new opportunities, African art changes over time.

Perhaps the most obvious change in traditional African art has been in the adaptation of modern materials to traditional forms. Some Yoruba, for example, have used photographs and bright-colored, imported plastic children's dolls in place of the traditional *ere ibeji*, the images of twins shown in FIGURE 28–4. The Guro people of Côte d'Ivoire continue to commission delicate masks dressed with costly textiles and other materials, but now they paint them with brilliantly colored oil-based enamel paints. The Baule create brightly painted versions of spirit spouse figures dressed as businessmen or soccer players.

Throughout the colonial period and especially during the years following World War II, many African artists trained in the techniques of European art. In the postcolonial era, numerous African artists have studied in Europe and the United States, and many have become known internationally through exhibits of their work in galleries and museums. Yet, the diversity of influences on contemporary Africa makes it impossible to render a homogeneous view of what constitutes a contemporary African art. As the art historian and curator Salah Hassan (1999:224) writes: "The development of a modern idiom in African art is closely linked to modern Africa's search for identity. Most contemporary works have apparent ties to traditional African folklore, belief systems and imagery. The only way to interpret or understand these works is in the light of the dual experience of colonialism and assimilation into Western culture in Africa. They reflect the search for a new identity."

EL ANATSUI OF GHANA. This search for identity inspired a desire to affirm Africa's rich legacy of tradition-based art in the work of El Anatsui. Born in Ghana in 1944, Anatsui studied art in Kumasi where he took course work he describes as predominantly Western in orientation. He found the emphasis on Western traditions irrelevant while Ghana's own rich legacy was ignored and, following his own inclinations, he began to study Ghanaian surface design traditions as produced by Ewe and Asante textile artists. In 1975, Anatsui took a position in the Fine Arts Department of the University of Nigeria at Nsukka. There he found a like-minded spirit in Uche Okeke, who was intensely interested in revitalizing *uli*, an important Igbo surface design system. Anatsui began to create what would

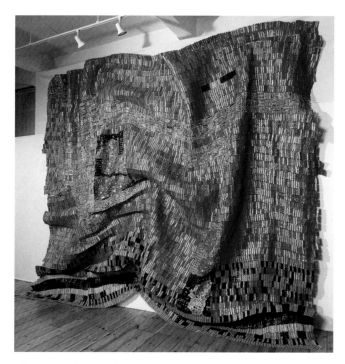

28–21 | El Anatsui **FLAG FOR A NEW WORLD POWER**
2004. Aluminum bottle tops, copper wire, 196 × 177"
(500 × 450 cm). Courtesy October Gallery, London

Myth and Religion
DIVINATION AMONG THE CHOKWE

Chokwe peoples of the Democratic Republic of the Congo and Angola consult diviners (*nganga*) to disclose the sources of problems such as death, illness, impotence, sterility, and theft. As the mediator between this world and the supernatural, the diviner's role is to ascertain the true meaning and underlying cause of an affliction or misfortune, and whether it is due to a conflict with human protagonists or with spirit forces. The diviner's ability to uncover the cause of a client's problems comes through the agency of powerful spirit forces and the efficacy of divinatory paraphernalia. A Chokwe *nganga*, utilizing a rattle to call the spirits to the divination, begins to shake a shallow covered basket (*ngombo ya kusekula*) containing a variety of natural objects including small antelope horns, seeds, and minerals. The basket also contains a number of carved wooden objects representing humans (in various symbolic poses), animals, and other objects such as small models of masks and masked figures. The objects in the basket are tossed about as the basket is shaken and when finished the cover is removed to reveal the arrangement of the objects as they came to rest below. The *nganga* interprets the results of multiple tosses to disclose the underlying cause of the client's problem and suggests what steps need to be taken to remedy the situation.

become a large body of work inspired by *uli* and other graphic systems using tools such as chainsaws and blow torches. More recently, while still concerned with the survival and transmission of inherited traditions, Anatsui began to appropriate cast-off objects he found in and around Nsukka, including broken and discarded mortars, large coconut graters, and liquor-bottle caps, to create revelatory art forms in a variety of media. These include visually stunning immense wall sculptures that fold and undulate like textiles but are made from metal bottle caps sewn together with copper wire (FIG. 28–21).

While living in Nigeria, El Anatsui, like many contemporary African artists, also participates in international art events—including international workshops, symposia, biennial exhibitions, and art festivals that dramatically invigorate our global visual culture. On the other hand, many other African artists have moved permanently to major European and American cities, which offer them increased opportunities for exposure to art dealers, museum curators, art critics, and the expanding base of public and private collectors of African contemporary art.

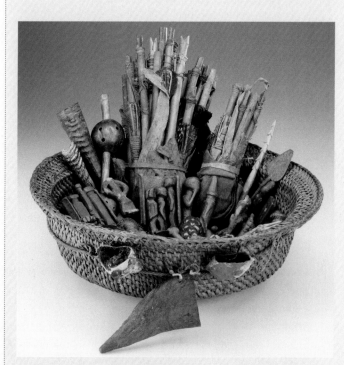

DIVINATION BASKET (*NGOMBO*)
Chokwe peoples, Democratic Republic of the Congo and Angola. Mid-19th–early 20th century. Plant fiber, seed, stone, horn, shell, bone, metal, feather, camwood, depth 12¹⁄₁₆" (30.7 cm).
National Museum of African Art, Smithsonian Institution, Washington, D.C.
Museum purchase (86-12-17.1)

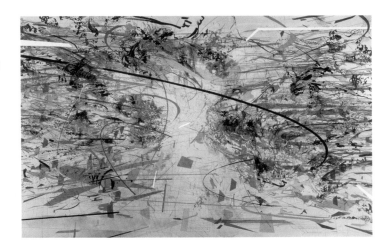

28–22 | Julie Mehretu **DISPERSION**
2002. Ink and acrylic on canvas,
90 × 144″ (228.6 × 365.8 cm).
Collection of Nicolas and Jeanne
Greenberg Rohatyn, New York.

AFRICAN ARTISTS IN DIASPORA While many African artists are primarily influenced by their own culture and traditions, others—especially some who no longer live on the continent—seem entirely removed from African stylistic influences and yet still express the search for a new African identity in revelatory ways. Their experiences of movement, accommodation, and change often become important elements in their art making and form an additional basis for the interpretation of their work. Julie Mehretu (FIG. 28–22) is an eminent example of this kind of African artist.

Born in Ethiopia in 1970, but having lived as well in Senegal and the United States, and now in New York City, Julie Mehretu makes large-scale paintings and wall drawings that exude intense energy. Her works speak not only to her own history of movement and change, but also to the transnational movement of myriad others uprooted by choice or by force as they create new identities in this increasingly turbulent period of globalization and change.

The underpinnings of her intricately layered canvases are architectural plans of airports, passenger terminals, and other places where people congregate and pass through during their lives. Layered and at times obscuring these architectural elements are an immense inventory of signs and markings influenced by cartography, weather maps, Japanese and Chinese calligraphy, tattooing, graffiti, and various stylized forms suggesting smoke and explosions borrowed from cartoons, comic books, and anime. Occasionally architectural details such as arches, stairways, and columns reminiscent of Dürer or Piranesi can also be discerned. The ambiguous reading of the paintings as either implosion and chaos or explosion and regeneration gives the works visual and conceptual complexity. Mehretu explains that she is not interested in describing or mapping specific locations but "in the multifaceted layers of place, space, and time that impact the formation of personal and communal identity" (quoted in Fogle 2003:5). Mehretu's

concerns echo those of other contemporary African artists whose identification with the continent becomes increasingly complex as they move from Africa and enter a global arena.

IN PERSPECTIVE

Africans today create both tradition-based art and contemporary art. Tradition-based African art appears in an immense variety of forms, ranging from complete naturalism to total abstraction. These artworks are often directly related to the commemoration of significant rites of passage such as procreation and birth, initiation to adulthood, socialization in adult life, and death. In these contexts, art is often intended to help mediate aid and support from a supernatural world of ancestors and other spirit forces.

Generally, the full meaning of a tradition-based work of art can only be realized in the context of its use. For instance, when masked dancers perform within a specific ceremonial event, the mask itself (which we may later see as an artwork in a museum) is only a part of a process that most fully reveals its meaning in performance.

While political leaders throughout the world use art to express their authority and status, in Africa community leaders are thought to connect the living community with the spirit world. In this regard, African art often especially idealizes the spirits of community leaders and deceased persons, who are expected to mediate between the temporal and supernatural worlds to help achieve well-being both for themselves and for the entire community.

Increasingly, contemporary African artists are creating and exhibiting their work with an international art audience in mind. In searching for ways to express an African identity in art, some of these artists are continuing to draw inspiration from indigenous traditions, while others are seeking new meanings in radically modern forms.

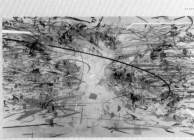

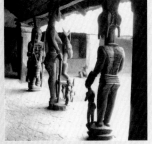

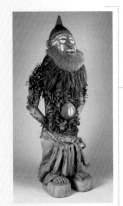

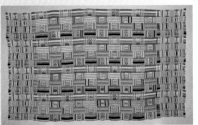

CHOWKE DIVINATION BASKET
MID 19TH–EARLY 20TH CENTURY

KONGO NKISI NKONDE
19TH CENTURY

OLOWE OF ISE
VERANDAH POSTS
1910–14

KENTE CLOTH
20TH CENTURY

MEHRETU
DISPERSION
2002

1400

1500

1600

1700

1800

1900

2000

ART OF AFRICA IN THE MODERN ERA

◄ **Europeans Establish Contact with Coastal Sub-Saharan Africa** c. 1400

◄ **Portuguese First Encounter Congo Culture** 1482

◄ **Cordial Relations Established between Benin and Portugal** 1485

◄ **British Sack and Burn Benin Royal Palace** 1897

◄ *Oba* of Benin Return from Exile 1914

◄ **Most of Africa Under Foreign Control** c. 1914

◄ **Colonies Gain Independence** 1950s–mid1970s

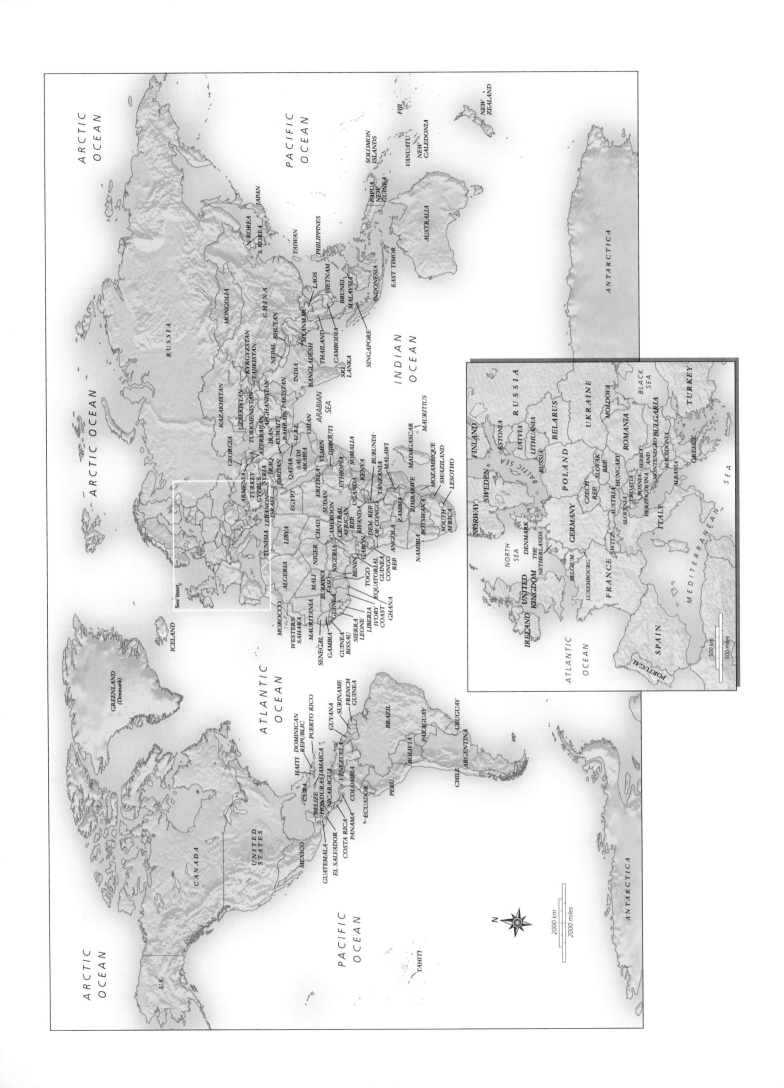

GLOSSARY

abacus The flat slab at the top of a **capital**, directly under the **entablature**.

absolute dating A method of assigning a precise historical date to periods and objects based on known and recorded events in the region as well as technically extracted physical evidence (such as carbon-14 disintegration). See also **radiometric dating, relative dating**.

abstract, abstraction Any art that does not represent observable aspects of nature or transforms visible forms into a stylized image. Also: the formal qualities of this process.

acropolis The **citadel** of an ancient Greek city, located at its highest point and housing temples, a treasury, and sometimes a royal palace. The most famous is the Acropolis in Athens.

acroterion (acroteria) An ornament at the corner or peak of a roof.

adobe Sun-baked blocks made of clay mixed with straw. Also: the buildings made with this material.

adyton The back room of a Greek temple. At Delphi, the place where the **oracles** were delivered. More generally, a very private space or room.

aedicula (aediculae) A decorative architectural frame, usually found around a niche, door, or window. An aedicula is made up of a **pediment** and **entablature** supported by **columns** or **pilasters**.

agora An open space in a Greek town used as a central gathering place or market. See also forum.

aisle Passage or open corridor of a church, hall, or other building that parallels the main space, usually on both sides, and is delineated by a row, or **arcade**, of **columns** or piers. Called side aisles when they flank the **nave** of a church.

album A book consisting of a series of painting or prints (album leaves) mounted into book form.

all'antica Meaning, "in the ancient manner."

allegory In a work of art, an image (or images) that symbolically illustrates an idea, concept, or principle, often moral or religious.

alloy A mixture of metals; different metals melted together.

amalaka In Hindu architecture, the circular or square-shaped element on top of a spire (*shikhara*), often crowned with a **finial**, symbolizing the cosmos.

ambulatory The passage (walkway) around the **apse** in a basilican church or around the **central space in a central-plan building**.

amphiprostyle Term describing a building, usually a temple, with **porticoes** at each end but without **columns** along the other two sides.

amphora An ancient Greek jar for storing oil or wine, with an egg-shaped body and two curved handles.

aniconic A symbolic representation without images of human figures, very often found in Islamic art.

animal interlace Decoration made of interwoven animals or serpents, often found in Celtic and early medieval Northern European art.

ankh A looped cross signifying life, used by ancient Egyptians.

appropriation Term used to describe an artist's practice of borrowing from another source for a new work of art. While in previous centuries artists often copied one another's figures, motifs, or compositions, in modern times the sources for appropriation extend from material culture to works of art.

apse, apsidal A large semicircular or polygonal (and usually vaulted) niche protruding from the end wall of a building. In the Christian church, it contains the altar. Apsidal is an adjective describing the condition of having such a space.

arabesque A type of linear surface decoration based on foliage and **calligraphic** forms, usually characterized by flowing lines and swirling shapes.

arcade A series of **arches**, carried by **columns** or **piers** and supporting a common wall or lintel. In a blind arcade, the arches and supports are engaged (attached to the wall) and have a decorative function.

arch In architecture, a curved structural element that spans an open space. Built from wedge-shaped stone blocks called **voussoirs**, which, when placed together and held at the top by a trapezoidal **keystone**, form an effective space-spanning and weight-bearing unit. Requires buttresses at each side to contain the outward thrust caused by the weight of the structure. **Corbel** arch: arch or **vault** formed by **courses** of stones, each of which projects beyond the lower course until the space is enclosed; usually finished with a **capstone**. Horseshoe arch: an arch of more than a half-circle; typical of western Islamic architecture. Ogival arch: a pointed arch created by S curves. Relieving arch: an arch built into a heavy wall just above a post-and-lintel structure (such as a gate, door, or window) to help support the wall above by transferring the load to the side walls.

archaic smile The curved lips of an ancient Greek statue, usually interpreted as an attempt to animate the features.

architrave The bottom element in an **entablature**, beneath the **frieze** and the **cornice**.

art brut French for "raw art." Term introduced by Jean Dubuffet to denote the often vividly **expressionistic** art of children and the insane, which he considered uncontaminated by culture.

articulated Joined; divided into units; in architecture, divided intoparts tomake spatial organization intelligible.

ashlar A highly finished, precisely cut block of stone. When laid in even **courses**, ashlar masonry creates a uniform face with fine joints. Often used as a facing on the visible exterior of a building, especially as a veneer for the **façade**. Also called **dressed stone**.

assemblage Artwork created by gathering and manipulating two and/or three-dimensional found objects.

astragal A thin convex decorative **molding**, often found on classical **entablatures**, and usually decorated with a continuous row of beadlike circles.

atelier The studio or workshop of a master artist or craftsperson, often including junior associates and apprentices.

atmospheric perspective See **perspective**.

atrial cross The cross placed in the atrium of a church. In Colonial America, used to mark a gathering and teaching place.

atrium An unroofed interior courtyard or room in a Roman house, sometimes having a pool or garden, sometimes surrounded by columns. Also: the open courtyard in front of a Christian church; or an entrance area in modern architecture.

automatism A technique whereby the usual intellectual control of the artist over his or her brush or pencil is foregone. The artist's aim is to allow the subconscious to create the artwork without rational interference.

avant-garde Term derived from the French military word meaning "before the group," or "vanguard." Avant-garde denotes those artists or concepts of a strikingly new, experimental, or radical nature for the time.

axis mundi A concept of an "axis of the world," which marks sacred sites and denotes a link between the human and celestial realms. For example, in Buddhist art, the axis mundi can be marked by monumental freestanding decorative pillars.

baldachin A canopy (whether suspended from the ceiling, projecting from a wall, or supported by columns) placed over an honorific or sacred space such as a throne or church altar.

bargeboards Boards covering the rafters at the gable end of a building; bargeboards are often carved or painted.

barrel vault See **vault**.

bar tracery See **tracery**.

bas-de-page French: bottom of the page; a term used in manuscript studies to indicate pictures below the text, literally at the bottom of the page.

base Any support. Also: masonry supporting a statue or the **shaft** of a **column**.

basilica A large rectangular building. Often built with a **clerestory**, side **aisles** separated from the center **nave** by **colonnades**, and an **apse** at one or both ends. Roman centers for administration, later adapted to Christian church use. Constantine's architects added a transverse aisle at the end of the nave called a **transept**.

bay A unit of space defined by architectural elements such as **columns**, **piers**, and walls.

beehive tomb A **corbel-vaulted** tomb, conical in shape like a beehive, and covered by an earthen mound.

Benday dots In modern printing and typesetting, the individual dots that, together with many others, make up lettering and images. Often machine- or computer-generated, the dots are very small and closely spaced to give the effect of density and richness of tone.

bestiary A book describing characteristics, uses, and meaning illustrated by moralizing tales about real and imaginary animals, especially popular during the Middle Ages in western Europe.

bi A jade disk with a hole in the center.

biomorphic Adjective used to describe forms that resemble or suggest shapes found in nature.

black-figure A style or technique of ancient Greek pottery in which black figures are painted on a red clay ground. See also **red-figure**.

bodhisattva In Buddhism, a being who has attained enlightenment but chooses to remain in this world in order to help others advance spiritually. Also defined as a potential Buddha.

boss A decorative knoblike element. Bosses can be found in many places, such as at the intersection of a Gothic vault rib. Also buttonlike projections in decorations and metalwork.

bracket, bracketing An architectural element that projects from a wall to support a horizontal part of a building, such as beams or the eaves of a roof.

brandea An object, such as a linen strip, having contact with a relic and taking on the power of the relic.

buon fresco *See* **fresco**.

cairn A pile of stones or earth and stones that served both as a prehistoric burial site and as a marker of underground tombs.

calligraphy Handwriting as an art form.

calyx krater *See* **krater**.

came (cames) A lead strip used in the making of leaded or **stained-glass** windows. Cames have an indented vertical groove on the sides into which the separate pieces of glass are fitted to hold the design together.

cameo Gemstone, clay, glass, or shell having layers of color, carved in **low relief** to create an image and ground of different colors.

camera obscura An early cameralike device used in the Renaissance and later for recording images of nature. Made from a dark box (or room) with a hole in one side (sometimes fitted with a lens), the camera obscura operates when bright light shines through the hole, casting an upside-down image of an object outside onto the inside wall of the box.

canon of proportions A set of ideal mathematical ratios in art based on measurements of the human body.

capital The sculpted block that tops a **column**. According to the conventions of the orders, capitals include different decorative elements. See **order**. Also: a historiated capital is one displaying a narrative.

capriccio A painting or print of a fantastic, imaginary landscape, usually with architecture.

capstone The final, topmost stone in a **corbel arch** or vault, which joins the sides and completes the structure.

cartoon A full-scale drawing used to transfer the outline of a design onto a surface (such as a wall, canvas, panel, or tapestry) to be painted, carved, or woven.

cartouche A frame for a **hieroglyphic** inscription formed by a rope design surrounding an oval space. Used to signify a sacred or honored name. Also: in architecture, a decorative device or plaque, usually with a plain center used for inscriptions or epitaphs.

caryatid A sculpture of a draped female figure acting as a column supporting an **entablature**.

catacomb A subterranean burial ground consisting of tunnels on different levels, having niches for urns and **sarcophagi** and often incorporating rooms (cubiculae).

celadon A high-fired, transparent **glaze** of pale bluish-green hue whose principal coloring agent is an oxide of iron. In China and Korea, such glazes typically were applied over a pale gray **stoneware** body, though Chinese potters some-

times applied them over **porcelain** bodies during the Ming (1368-1644) and Qing (1644-1911) dynasties. Chinese potters invented celadon glazes and initiated the continuous production of celadon-glazed wares as early as the third century CE.

cella The principal interior room at the center of a Greek or Roman temple within which the cult statue was usually housed. Also called the **naos**.

cenotaph A funerary monument commemorating an individual or group buried elsewhere.

centering A temporary structure that supports a masonry **arch** and **vault** or **dome** during construction until the mortar is fully dried and the masonry is self-sustaining.

centrally planned building Any structure designed with a primary central space surrounded by symmetrical areas on each side. For example, **Greek-cross plan** (equal-armed cross).

ceramics A general term covering all types of wares made from fired clay, including **porcelain** and **terra cotta**.

chaitya A type of Buddhist temple found in India. Built in the form of a hall or **basilica**, a chaitya hall is highly decorated with sculpture and usually is carved from a cave or natural rock location. It houses a sacred shrine or stupa for worship.

chamfer The slanted surface produced when an angle is trimmed or beveled, common in building and metalwork.

chasing Ornamentation made on metal by incising or hammering the surface.

chattri (*chattris*) A decorative pavilion with an umbrella-shaped **dome** in Indian architecture.

chevron A decorative or heraldic motif of repeated Vs; a zigzag pattern.

chiaroscuro An Italian word designating the contrast of dark and light in a painting, drawing, or print. Chiaroscuro creates spatial depth and volumetric forms through gradations in the intensity of light and shadow.

chiton A thin sleeveless garment, fastened at waist and shoulders, worn by men and women in ancient Greece.

citadel A fortress or defended city, if possible placed in a high, commanding location.

clapboard Horizontal overlapping planks used as protective siding for buildings, particularly houses in North America.

clerestory The topmost zone of a wall with windows in a **basilica** extending above the **aisle** roofs. Provides direct light into the central interior space (the **nave**).

cloisonné An enamel technique in which metal wire or strips are affixed to the surface to form the design. The resulting areas (cloisons) are filled with enamel (colored glass).

cloister An open space, part of a monastery, surrounded by an **arcaded** or **colonnaded** walkway, often having a fountain and garden, and dedicated to nonliturgical activities and the secular life of the religious. Members of a cloistered order do not leave the monastery or interact with outsiders.

codex (codices) A book, or a group of **manuscript** pages (folios), held together by stitching or other binding on one side.

coffer A recessed decorative panel that is used to reduce the weight of and to decorate ceilings or **vaults**. The use of coffers is called coffering.

colonnade A row of **columns**, supporting a straight lintel (as in a **porch** or **portico**) or a series of arches (an **arcade**).

colophon The data placed at the end of a book listing the book's author, publisher, illuminator, and other information related to its production. Also, in East Asian handscrolls, the inscriptions which follow the painting are called colophons.

column An architectural element used for support and/or decoration. Consists of a rounded or polygonal vertical **shaft** placed on a **base** and topped by a decorative **capital**. In classical architecture, built in accordance with the rules of one of the architectural **orders**. Columns can be freestanding or attached to a background wall (**engaged**).

complementary color The primary and secondary colors across from each other on the color wheel (red and green, blue and orange, yellow and purple). When juxtaposed, the intensity of both colors increases. When mixed together, they negate each other to make a neutral gray-brown.

Composite order *See* **order**.

cong A square or octagonal jade tube with a cylindrical hole in the center. A symbol of the earth, it was used for ritual worship and astronomical observations in ancient China.

connoisseurship A term derived from the French word connoisseur, meaning "an expert," and signifying the study and evaluation of art based primarily on formal, visual, and stylistic analysis. A connoisseur studies the style and technique of an object to deduce its relative quality and possible maker. This is done through visual association with other, similar objects and styles. See also **contextualism**; **formalism**.

contextualism An interpretive approach in art history that focuses on the culture surrounding an art object. Unlike **connoisseurship**, contextualism utilizes the literature, history, economics, and social developments (among other things) of a period, as well as the object itself, to explain the meaning of an artwork. See *also* **connoisseurship**.

contrapposto An Italian term meaning "set against," used to describe the twisted pose resulting from parts of the body set in opposition to each other around a central axis.

corbel, corbeling An early roofing and **arching** technique in which each course of stone projects slightly beyond the previous layer (a corbel) until the uppermost corbels meet. Results in a high, almost pointed **arch** or **vault**. A corbel table is a ledge supported by corbels.

corbeled vault *See* **vault**.

Corinthian order *See* **order**.

cornice The uppermost section of a Classical **entablature**. More generally, a horizontally projecting element found at the top of a building wall or **pedestal**. A raking cornice is formed by the junction of two slanted cornices, most often found in **pediments**.

course A horizontal layer of stone used in building.

crenellation Alternating high and low sections of a wall, giving a notched appearance and creating permanent defensive shields in the walls of fortified buildings.

crockets A stylized leaf used as decoration along the outer angle of spins, pinnacles, gables, and around **capitals** in Gothic architecture.

cuneiform An early form of writing with wedge-shaped marks impressed into wet clay with a stylus, primarily used by ancient Mesopotamians.

curtain wall A wall in a building that does not support any of the weight of the structure. Also: the freestanding outer wall of a castle, usually encircling the inner bailey (yard) and keep (primary defensive tower).

cyclopean construction or **masonry** A method of building using huge blocks of rough-hewn stone. Any large-scale, monumental building project that impresses by sheer size. Named after the Cyclopes (sing. Cyclops) one-eyed giants of legendary strength in Greek myths.

cylinder seal A small cylindrical stone decorated with incised patterns. When rolled across soft clay or wax, the resulting raised pattern or design (**relief**) served in Mesopotamian and Indus Valley cultures as an identifying signature.

dado (dadoes) The lower part of a wall, differentiated in some way (by a **molding** or different coloring or paneling) from the upper section.

daguerreotype An early photographic process that makes a positive print on a light-sensitized copperplate; invented and marketed in 1839 by Louis-Jacques-Mandé Daguerre.

demotic writing The simplified form of ancient Egyptian hieratic writing, used primarily for administrative and private texts.

dharmachakra Sanskrit for "wheel" (*chakra*) and "law" or "doctrine" (*dharma*); often used in Buddhist iconography to signify the "wheel of the law."

diptych Two panels of equal size (usually decorated with paintings or reliefs) hinged together.

dogu Small human figurines made in Japan during the Jomon period. Shaped from clay, the figures have exaggerated expressions and are in contorted poses. They were probably used in religious rituals.

dolmen A prehistoric structure made up of two or more large upright stones supporting a large, flat, horizontal slab or slabs.

dome A round **vault**, usually over a circular space. Consists of a curved masonry vault of shapes and cross sections that can vary from hemispherical to bulbous to ovoidal. May use a supporting vertical wall (**drum**), from which the vault springs, and may be crowned by an open space (**oculus**) and/or an exterior **lantern**. When a dome is built over a square space, an intermediate element is required to make the transition to a circular drum. There are two types: A dome on **pendentives** (spherical triangles) incorporates **arched**, sloping intermediate sections of wall that carry the weight and thrust of the dome to heavily buttressed supporting **piers**. A dome on **squinches** uses an arch built into the wall (squinch) in the upper corners of the space to carry the weight of the dome across the corners of the square space below. A half-dome or conch may cover a semicircular space.

domino construction System of building construction introduced by the architect Le Corbusier in which reinforced concrete floor slabs are floated on six freestanding posts placed as if at the positions of the six dots on a domino playing piece.

Doric order See **order**.

dressed stone See **ashlar**.

drum The wall that supports a **dome**. Also: a segment of the circular **shaft** of a **column**.

drypoint An **intaglio** printmaking process by which a metal (usually copper) plate is directly inscribed with a pointed instrument (**stylus**). The resulting design of scratched lines is inked, wiped, and printed. Also: the print made by this process.

earthenware A low-fired, opaque **ceramic** ware that is fired in the range of 800 to 900 degrees Celsius. Earthenware employs humble clays that are naturally heat resistant; the finished wares remain porous after firing unless **glazed**. Earthenware occurs in a range of earth-toned colors, from white and tan to gray and black, with tan predominating.

echinus A cushionlike circular element found below the **abacus** of a Doric **capital**. Also: a similarly shaped **molding** (usually with egg-and-dart motifs) underneath the **volutes** of an Ionic **capital**.

electron spin resonance techniques Method that uses magnetic field and microwave irradiation to date material such as tooth enamel and its surrounding soil.

emblema (emblemata) In a mosaic, the elaborate central motif on a floor, usually a self-contained unit done in a more refined manner, with smaller **tesserae** of both marble and semiprecious stones.

encaustic A painting technique using pigments mixed with hot wax as a medium.

engaged column A **column** attached to a wall. See also column.

engraving An intaglio printmaking process of inscribing an image, design, or letters onto a metal or wood surface from which a print is made. An engraving is usually drawn with a sharp implement (burin) directly onto the surface of the plate. Also: the print made from this process.

entablature In the **Classical orders**, the horizontal elements above the **columns** and **capitals**. The entablature consists of, from bottom to top, an **architrave**, a **frieze**, and a **cornice**.

entasis A slight swelling of the **shaft** of a Greek column. The optical illusion of entasis makes the column appear from afar to be straight.

exedra (exedrae) In architecture, a semicircular niche. On a small scale, often used as decoration, whereas larger exedrae can form interior spaces (such as an **apse**).

expressionism, expressionistic Terms describing a work of art in which forms are created primarily to evoke subjective emotions rather than to portray objective reality.

façade The face or front wall of a building.

faience Type of **ceramic** covered with colorful, opaque glazes that form a smooth, impermeable surface. First developed in ancient Egypt.

fang ding A square or rectangular bronze vessel with four legs. The fang ding was used for ritual offerings in ancient China during the Shang dynasty.

fête galante A subject in painting depicting well-dressed people at leisure in a park or country setting. It is most often associated with eighteenth-century French Rococo painting.

filigree Delicate, lacelike ornamental work.

fillet The flat ridge between the carved out flutes of a **column shaft**. See also **fluting**.

finial A knoblike architectural decoration usually found at the top point of a spire, pinnacle, canopy, or gable. Also found on furniture; also the ornamental top of a staff.

fluting In architecture, evenly spaced, rounded parallel vertical grooves **incised** on **shafts** of **columns** or columnar elements (such as **pilasters**).

foreshortening The illusion created on a flat surface in which figures and objects appear to recede or project sharply into space. Accomplished according to the rules of **perspective**.

formal analysis See **formalism**.

formalism, formalist An approach to the understanding, appreciation, and valuation of art based almost solely on considerations of form. This approach tends to regard an artwork as independent of its time and place of making. See also **connoisseurship**.

four-iwan mosque See **iwan** and **mosque**.

fresco A painting technique in which waterbased pigments are applied to a surface of wet plaster (called **buon fresco**). The color is absorbed by the plaster, becoming a permanent part of the wall. **Fresco secco** is created by painting on dried plaster, and the color may flake off. Murals made by both these techniques are called frescoes.

fresco secco See **fresco**.

frieze The middle element of an **entablature**, between the **architrave** and the **cornice**. Usually decorated with sculpture, painting, or **moldings**. Also: any continuous flat band with **relief sculpture** or painted decorations.

frottage A design produced by laying a piece of paper over a textured surface and rubbing with charcoal or other soft medium.

fusuma Sliding doors covered with paper, used in traditional Japanese construction. Fusuma are often highly decorated with paintings and colored backgrounds.

galleria See **gallery**.

gallery In church architecture, the story found above the side **aisles** of a church, usually open to and overlooking the nave. Also: in secular architecture, a long room, usually above the ground floor in a private house or a public building used for entertaining, exhibiting pictures, or promenading. *Also:* a building or hall in which art is displayed or sold. Also: *galleria*.

garbhagriha From the Sanskrit word meaning "womb chamber," a small room or shrine in a Hindu temple containing a holy image.

genre A type or category of artistic form, subject, technique, style, or medium. See also genre painting.

gesso A ground made from glue, gypsum, and/or chalk forming the ground of a wood panel or the priming layer of a canvas. Provides a smooth surface for painting.

gilding The application of paper-thin **gold leaf** or gold pigment to an object made from another medium (for example, a sculpture or painting). Usually used as a decorative finishing detail.

giornata (giornate) Adopted from the Italian term meaning "a day's work," a giornata is the section of a **fresco** plastered and painted in a single day.

glaze See **glazing**.

glazing An outermost layer of vitreous liquid (**glaze**) that, upon firing, renders **ceramics** waterproof and forms a decorative surface. In painting, a technique particularly used with oil mediums in which a transparent layer of paint (**glaze**) is laid over another, usually lighter, painted or glazed area.

gloss A type of clay **slip** used in **ceramics** by ancient Greeks and Romans that, when fired, imparts a colorful sheen to the surface.

golf foil A thin sheet of gold.

gold leaf Paper-thin sheets of hammered gold that are used in **gilding**. In some cases (such as Byzantine **icons**), also used as a ground for paintings.

gopura The towering gateway to an Indian Hindu temple complex. A temple complex can have several different gopuras.

Grand Manner An elevated style of painting popular in the eighteenth century in which the artist looked to the ancients and to the Renaissance for inspiration; for portraits as well as history painting, the artist would adopt the poses, compositions, and attitudes of Renaissance and antique models.

Grand Tour Popular during the eighteenth and nineteenth centuries, an extended tour of cultural sites in southern Europe intended to finish the education of a young upper-class person from Britain or North America.

grattage A pattern created by scraping off layers of paint from a canvas laid over a textured surface. See also *frottage*.

Greek-cross plan See **centrally planned building**.

Greek-key pattern A continuous rectangular scroll often used as a decorative border. Also called a **meander pattern**.

grid A system of regularly spaced horizontally and vertically crossed lines that gives regularity to an architectural plan. Also: in painting, a grid enables designs to be enlarged or transferred easily.

grisaille A style of monochromatic painting in shades of gray. Also: a painting made in this style.

groin vault See **vault**.

guild An association of craftspeople. The medieval guild had great economic power, as it set standards and controlled the selling and marketing of its members' products, and as it provided economic protection, group solidarity, and training in the craft to its members.

hall church A church with a **nave** and **aisles** of the same height, giving the impression of a large, open hall.

handscroll A long, narrow, horizontal painting or text (or combination thereof) common in Chinese and Japanese art and of a size intended for individual use. A handscroll is stored wrapped tightly around a wooden pin and is unrolled for viewing or reading.

hanging scroll In Chinese and Japanese art, a vertical painting or text mounted within sections of silk. At the top is a semicircular rod; at the bottom is a round dowel. Hanging scrolls are kept rolled and tied except for special occasions, when they are hung for display, contemplation, or commemoration.

haniwa Pottery forms, including cylinders, buildings, and human figures, that were placed on top of Japanese tombs or burial mounds.

hemicycle A semicircular interior space or structure.

henge A circular area enclosed by stones or wood posts set up by Neolithic peoples. It is usually bounded by a ditch and raised embankment.

hieratic In painting and sculpture, a formalized style for representing rulers or sacred or priestly figures.

hieratic scale The use of different sizes for significant or holy figures and those of the everyday world to indicate importance. The larger the figure, the greater the importance.

high relief Relief sculpture in which the image projects strongly from the background. See also **relief sculpture**.

himation In ancient Greece, a long loose outer garment.

historicism The strong consciousness of and attention to the institutions, themes, styles, and forms of the past, made accessible by historical research, textual study, and archaeology.

history painting Paintings based on historical, mythological, or biblical narratives. Once considered the noblest form of art, history paintings generally convey a high moral or intellectual idea and are often painted in a grand pictorial style.

hollow-casting See **lost-wax casting**.

hypostyle hall A large interior room characterized by many closely spaced **columns** that support its roof.

icon An image in any material representing a sacred figure or event in the Byzantine, and later in the Orthodox, Church. Icons were venerated by the faithful, who believed them to have miraculous powers to transmit messages to God.

iconoclasm The banning or destruction of images, especially icons and religious art. Iconoclasm in eighth- and ninth-century Byzantium and sixteenth- and seventeenth-century Protestant territories arose from differing beliefs about the power, meaning, function, and purpose of imagery in religion.

iconographic See **iconography**.

iconography The study of the significance and interpretation of the subject matter of art.

iconostasis The partition screen in a Byzantine or Orthodox church between the **sanctuary** (where the Mass is performed) and the body of the church (where the congregation assembles). The iconostasis displays **icons**.

idealism *See* idealization.

idealization A process in art through which artists strive to make their forms and figures attain perfection, based on pervading cultural values and/or their own mental image of beauty.

ideograph A written character or symbol representing an idea or object. Many Chinese characters are ideographs.

ignudi Heroic figures of nude young men.

illumination A painting on paper or **parchment** used as illustration and/or decoration for **manuscripts** or **albums**. Usually done in rich colors, often supplemented by gold and other precious materials. The illustrators are referred to as illuminators. Also: the technique of decorating manuscripts with such paintings.

impasto Thick applications of pigment that give a painting a palpable surface texture.

impost, impost block A block, serving to concentrate the weight above, imposed between the **capital** of a **column** and the springing of an arch above.

in antis Term used to describe the position of columns set between two walls, as in a **portico** or a **cella**.

incising A technique in which a design or inscription is cut into a hard surface with a sharp instrument. Such a surface is said to be incised.

ink painting A monochromatic style of painting developed in China using black ink with gray **washes**.

inlay To set pieces of a material or materials into a surface to form a design. *Also:* material used in or decoration formed by this technique.

installation art Artworks created for a specific site, especially a gallery or outdoor area, that create a total environment.

intaglio Term used for a technique in which the design is carved out of the surface of an object, such as an engraved seal stone. In the graphic arts, intaglio includes **engraving**, etching, and **drypoint**—all processes in which ink transfersto paper from incised, ink-filled lines cut into a metal plate.

intarsia Decoration formed through wood **inlay**.

intuitive perspective See **perspective**.

Ionic order See **order**.

iwan A large, **vaulted** chamber in a **mosque** with a monumental arched opening on one side.

jamb In architecture, the vertical element found on both sides of an opening in a wall, and supporting an **arch** or lintel.

japonisme A style in French and American nineteenth-century art that was highly influenced by Japanese art, especially prints.

jasperware A fine-grained, unglazed, white **ceramic** developed by Josiah Wedgwood, often colored by metallic oxides with the raised designs ramaining white.

jataka **tales** In Buddhism, stories associated with the previous lives of Shakyamuni, the historical Buddha.

joined-wood sculpture A method of constructing large-scale wooden sculpture developed in Japan. The entire work is constructed from smaller hollow blocks, each individually carved, and assembled when complete. The joined-wood technique allowed the production of larger sculpture, as the multiple joints alleviate the problems of drying and cracking found with sculpture carved from a single block.

joggled voussoirs Interlocking voussoirs in an arch or lintel, often of contrasting materials for colorful effect.

kantharos A type of Greek vase or goblet with two large handles and a wide mouth.

key block A key block is the master block in the production of a colored **woodblock print**, which requires different blocks for each color. The key block is a flat piece of wood with the entire design carved or drawn on its surface. From this, other blocks with partial drawings are made for printing the areas of different colors.

keystone The topmost **voussoir** at the center of an **arch**, and the last block to be placed. The pressure of this block holds the arch together. Often of a larger size and/or decorated.

kiln An oven designed to produce enough heat for the baking, or firing, of clay.

kinetic art Artwork that contains parts that can be moved either by hand, air, or motor.

kondo The main hall inside a Japanese Buddhist temple where the images of Buddha are housed.

kore (korai) An Archaic Greek statue of a young woman.

kouros (kouroi) An Archaic Greek statue of a young man or boy.

krater An ancient Greek vessel for mixing wine and water, with many subtypes that each have a distinctive shape. **Calyx krater:** a bell-shaped vessel with handles near the base that resemble a flower calyx. Volute krater: a type of krater with handles shaped like scrolls.

kufic An ornamental, angular Arabic script.

kylix A shallow Greek vessel or cup, used for drinking, with a wide mouth and small handles near the rim.

lacquer A type of hard, glossy surface varnish used on objects in East Asian cultures, made from the sap of the Asian sumac or from shellac, a resinous secretion from the lac insect. Lacquer can be layered and manipulated or combined with pigments and other materials for various decorative effects.

lakshana Term used to designate the thirtytwo marks of the historical Buddha. The lakshana include, among others, the Buddha's golden body, his long arms, the wheel impressed on his palms and the soles of his feet, and his elongated earlobes.

lamassu Supernatural guardian-protector of ancient Near Eastern palaces and throne rooms, often represented sculpturally as a combination of the bearded head of a man, powerful body of a lion or bull, wings of an eagle, and the horned headdress of a god, and usually possessing five legs.

lancet A tall narrow window crowned by a sharply pointed **arch**, typically found in Gothic architecture.

lantern A turretlike structure situated on a roof, **vault**, or **dome**, with windows that allow light into the space below.

lekythos (lekythoi) A slim Greek oil vase with one handle and a narrow mouth.

limner An artist, particularly a portrait painter, in England during the sixteenth and seventeenth centuries and in New England during the seventeenth and eighteenth centuries.

lingam shrine A place of worship centered on an object or representation in the form of a phallus (the lingam), which symbolizes the power of the Hindu god Shiva.

literati The English word used for the Chinese wenren or the Japanese bunjin, referring to well-educated artists who enjoyed literature, **calligraphy**, and painting as a pastime. Their painting are termed **literati painting**.

literati painting A style of painting that reflects the taste of the educated class of East Asian intellectuals and scholars. Aspects include an appreciation for the antique, small scale, and an intimate connection between maker and audience.

lithograph See **lithography**.

lithography Process of making a print (**lithograph**) from a design drawn on a flat stone block with greasy crayon. Ink is applied to the wet stone and adheres only to the greasy areas of the design.

loggia Italian term for a covered open-air. **gallery**. Often used as a corridor between buildings or around a courtyard, loggias usually have **arcades** or **colonnades**.

lost-wax casting A method of casting metal, such as bronze, by a process in which a wax mold is covered with clay and plaster, then fired, melting the wax and leaving a hollow form. Molten metal is then poured into the hollow space and slowly cooled. When the hardened clay and plaster exterior shell is removed, a solid metal form remains to be smoothed and polished.

low relief Relief sculpture whose figures project slightly from the background. See also **relief sculpture**.

lunette A semicircular wall area, framed by an arch over a door or window. Can be either plain or decorated.

lusterware Ceramic pottery decorated with metallic **glazes**.

madrasa An Islamic institution of higher learning, where teaching is focused on theology and law.

maenad In ancient Greece, a female devotee of the wine god Dionysos who participated in orgiastic rituals. She is often depicted with swirling drapery to indicate wild movement or dance. (Also called a Bacchante, after Bacchus, the Roman name of Dionysos.)

majolica Pottery painted with a tin glaze that, when fired, gives a lustrous and colorful surface.

mandala An image of the cosmos represented by an arrangement of circles or concentric geometric shapes containing diagrams or images. Used for meditation and contemplation by Buddhists.

mandapa In a Hindu temple, an open hall dedicated to ritual worship.

mandorla Light encircling, or emanating from, the entire figure of a sacred person.

manuscript A handwritten book or document.

maqsura An enclosure in a Muslim mosque, near the mihrab, designated for dignitaries.

martyrium (martyria) In Christian architecture, a church, chapel, or shrine built over the grave of a martyr or the site of a great miracle.

mastaba A flat-topped, one-story structure with slanted walls over an ancient Egyptian underground tomb.

matte Term describing a smooth surface that is without shine or luster.

mausoleum A monumental building used as a tomb. Named after the tomb of Mausolos erected at Halikarnassos around 350 BCE.

meander See **Greek-key pattern**.

medallion Any round ornament or decoration. Also: a large medal.

megalith A large stone used in prehistoric building. Megalithic architecture employs such stones.

megaron The main hall of a Mycenaean palace or grand house, having a columnar **porch** and a room with a central fireplace surrounded by four **columns**.

memento mori From Latin for "remember that you must die." An object, such as a skull or extinguished candle, typically found in a *vanitas* image, symbolizing the transience of life.

memory image An image that relies on the generic shapes and relationships that readily spring to mind at the mention of an object.

menorah A Jewish lamp-stand with seven or nine branches; the nine-branched menorah is used during the celebration of Hanukkah. Representations of the seven-branched menorah, once used in the Temple of Jerusalem, became a symbol of Judaism.

metope The carved or painted rectangular panel between the **triglyphs** of a **Doric frieze**.

mihrab A recess or niche that distinguishes the wall oriented toward Mecca (*qibla*) in a **mosque**.

minaret A tall slender tower on the exterior of a mosque from which believers are called to prayer.

minbar A high platform or pulpit in a **mosque**.

miniature Anything small. In painting, miniatures may be illustrations within **albums** or **manuscripts** or intimate portraits.

mirador In Spanish and Islamic palace architecture, a very large window or room with windows, and sometimes balconies, providing views to interior courtyards or the exterior landscape.

mithuna The amorous male and female couples in Buddhist sculpture, usually found at the entrance to a sacred building. The mithuna symbolize the harmony and fertility of life.

moat A large ditch or canal dug around a castle or fortress for military defense. When filled with water, the moat protects the walls of the building from direct attack.

mobile A sculpture made with parts suspended in such a way that they move in a current of air.

modeling In painting, the process of creating the illusion of three-dimensionality on a two-dimensional surface by use of light and shade. In sculpture, the process of molding a three-dimensional form out of a malleable substance.

module A segment or portion of a repeated design. Also: a basic building block.

molding A shaped or sculpted strip with varying contours and patterns. Used as decoration on architecture, furniture, frames, and other objects.

monolith A single stone, often very large.

mortise-and-tenon joint A method of joining two elements. A projecting pin (tenon) on one element fits snugly into a hole designed for it (mortise) on the other. Such joints are very strong and flexible.

mosaic Images formed by small colored stone or glass pieces (tesserae), affixed to a hard, stable surface.

mosque An edifice used for communal Muslim worship.

mudra A symbolic hand gesture in Buddhist art that denotes certain behaviors, actions, or feelings.

mullion A slender vertical element or **colonnette** that divides a window into subsidiary sections.

muqarnas Small nichelike components stacked in tiers to fill the transition between differing vertical and horizontal planes.

naos The principal room in a temple or church. In ancient architecture, the **cella**. In a Byzantine church, the **nave** and **sanctuary**.

narthex The vestibule or entrance porch of a church.

naturalism, naturalistic A style of depiction that seeks to imitate the appearance of nature. A naturalistic work appears to record the visible world.

nave The central space of a **basilica**, two or three stories high and usually flanked by **aisles**.

necking The molding at the top of the **shaft** of the **column**.

necropolis A large cemetery or burial area; literally a "city of the dead."

nemes headdress The royal headdress of Egypt.

niello A metal technique in which a black sulfur alloy is rubbed into fine lines engraved into a metal (usually gold or silver). When heated, the alloy becomes fused with the surrounding metal and provides contrasting detail.

nishiki-e A multicolored and ornate Japanese print.

nocturne A night scene in painting, usually lit by artificial illumination.

nonrepresentational art An **abstract** art that does not attempt to reproduce the appearance of objects, figures, or scenes in the natural world. Also called nonobjective art.

oculus (oculi) In architecture, a circular opening. Oculi are usually found either as windows or at the apex of a **dome**. When at the top of a dome, an oculus is either open to the sky or covered by a decorative exterior lantern.

ogee An S-shaped curve. See **arch**.

olpe Any Greek vase or jug without a spout.

one-point perspective See **perspective**.

opithodomos In greek temples, the entrance porch or room at the back.

oracle A person, usually a priest or priestess, who acts as a conduit for divine information. Also: the information itself or the place at which this information is communicated.

orant The representation of a standing figure praying with outstretched and upraised arms.

orchestra The circular performance area of an ancient Greek theater. In later architecture, the section of seats nearest the stage or the entire main floor of the theater.

order A system of proportions in Classical architecture that includes every aspect of the building's plan, elevation, and decorative system. Composite: a combination of the Ionic and the Corinthian orders. The **capital** combines acanthus leaves with **volute** scrolls. **Corinthian:** the most ornate of the orders, the Corinthian includes a **base**, a fluted **column shaft** with a capital elaborately decorated with acanthus leaf carvings. Its **entablature** consists of an **architrave** decorated with **moldings**, a **frieze** often containing **sculptured reliefs**, and a **cornice** with dentils. Doric: the column shaft of the Doric order can be fluted or smooth-surfaced and has no base. The Doric capital consists of an undecorated **echinus** and **abacus**. The Doric entablature has a plain architrave, a frieze with **metopes** and **triglyphs**, and a simple cornice. Ionic: the column of the Ionic order has a base, a fluted shaft, and a capital decorated with volutes. The Ionic entablature consists of an architrave of three panels and moldings, a frieze usually containing sculpted relief ornament, and a cornice with dentils. **Tuscan:** a variation of Doric characterized by a smooth-surfaced column shaft with a base, a plain architrave, and an undecorated frieze. A colossal order is any of the above built on a large scale, rising through several stories in height and often raised from the ground by a **pedestal**.

orthogonal Any line running back into the represented space of a picture perpendicular to the imagined picture plane. In linear perspective, all orthogonals converge at a single **vanishing point** in the picture and are the basis for a **grid** that maps out the internal space of the image. An orthogonal plan is any plan for a building or city that is based exclusively on right angles, such as the grid plan of many modern cities.

pagoda An East Asian **reliquary** tower built with successively smaller, repeated stories. Each story is usually marked by an elaborate projecting roof.

palace complex A group of buildings used for living and governing by a ruler and his or her supporters, usually fortified.

palmette A fan-shaped ornament with radiating leaves.

parapet A low wall at the edge of a balcony, bridge, roof, or other place from which there is a steep drop, built for safety. A parapet walk is the passageway, usually open, immediately behind the uppermost exterior wall or battlement of a fortified building.

parchment A writing surface made from treated skins of animals. Very fine parchment is known as **vellum**.

parterre An ornamental, highly regimented flowerbed. An element of the ornate gardens of seventeenth-century palaces and châteaux.

pastel Dry pigment, chalk, and gum in stick or crayon form. Also: a work of art made with pastels.

pedestal A platform or **base** supporting a sculpture or other monument. Also: the block found below the base of a Classical **column** (or **colonnade**), serving to raise the entire element off the ground.

pediment A triangular gable found over major architectural elements such as Classical Greek **porticoes**, windows, or doors. Formed by an **entablature** and the ends of a sloping roof or a raking **cornice**. A similar architectural element is often used decoratively above a door or window, sometimes with a curved upper **molding**. A broken pediment is a variation on the traditional pediment, with an open space at the center of the topmost angle and/or the horizontal cornice.

pendentive The concave triangular section of a **vault** that forms the transition between a square or polygonal space and the circular base of a **dome**.

peplos A loose outer garment worn by women of ancient Greece. A cloth rectangle fastened on the shoulders and belted below the bust or at the waist.

peripteral A term used to describe any building (or room) that is surrounded by a single row of columns. When such **columns** are engaged instead of freestanding, called pseudo-peripteral.

peristyle A surrounding **colonnade** in Greek architecture. A peristyle building is surrounded on the exterior by a colonnade. Also: a peristyle court is an open colonnaded courtyard, often having a pool and garden.

perspective A system for representing three-dimensional space on a two-dimensional surface. **Atmospheric** perspective: A method of rendering the effect of spatial distance by subtle variations in color and clarity of representation. **Intuitive perspective:** A method of giving the impression of recession by visual instinct, not by the use of an overall system or program. Oblique perspective: An intuitive spatial system in which a building or room is placed with one corner in the picture plane, and the other parts of the structure recede to an imaginary vanishing point on its other side. Oblique perspective is not a comprehensive, mathematical system. **One-point** and multiple-point **perspective** (also called linear, scientific or mathematical perspective): A method of creating the illusion of three-dimensional space on a two-dimensional surface by delineating a horizon line and multiple orthogonal lines. These recede to meet at one or more points on the horizon (called **vanishing** points), giving the appearance of spatial depth. Called scientific or mathematical because its use requires some knowledge of geometry and mathematics, as well as optics. **Reverse perspective:** A Byzantine perspective theory in which the orthogonals or rays of sight do not converge on a vanishing point in the picture, but are thought to originate in the viewer's eye in front of the picture. Thus, in reverse perspective the image is constructed with orthogonals that diverge, giving a slightly tipped aspect to objects.

photomontage A photographic work created from many smaller photographs arranged (and often overlapping) in a composition.

picture plane The theoretical spatial plane corresponding with the actual surface of a painting.

picture stone A medieval northern European memorial stone covered with figural decoration. See also **rune stone**.

picturesque A term describing the taste for the familiar, the pleasant, and the pretty, popular in the eighteenth and nineteenth centuries in Europe. When contrasted with the sublime, the picturesque stood for all that was ordinary but pleasant.

piece-mold casting A casting technique in which the mold consists of several sections that are connected during the pouring of molten metal, usually bronze. After the cast form has hardened, the pieces of the mold are disassembled, leaving the completed object.

pier A masonry support made up of many stones, or rubble and concrete (in contrast to a **column shaft** which is formed from a single stone or a series of **drums**), often square or rectangular in plan, and capable of carrying very heavy architectural loads.

pietra dura Italian for "hard stone." Semiprecious stones selected for color variation and cut in shapes to form ornamental designs such as flowers or fruit.

pietra serena A gray Tuscan limestone used in Florence.

pilaster An **engaged** columnar element that is rectangular in format and used for decoration in architecture.

pillar In architecture, any large, freestanding vertical element. Usually functions as an important weight-bearing unit in buildings.

plate tracery See **tracery**.

plinth The slablike **base** or **pedestal** of a **column**, statue, wall, building, or piece of furniture.

pluralism A social structure or goal that allows members of diverse ethnic, racial, or other groups to exist peacefully within the society while continuing to practice the customs of their own divergent cultures. Also: an adjective describing the state of having many valid contemporary styles available at the same time to artists.

podium A raised platform that acts as the foundation for a building, or as a platform for a speaker.

polychrome See **polychromy**.

polychromy The multicolored painted decoration applied to any part of a building, sculpture, or piece of furniture.

polyptych An altarpiece constructed from multiple panels, sometimes with hinges to allow for movable wings.

porcelain A high-fired, vitrified, translucent, white **ceramic** ware that employs two specific clays—kaolin and petuntse—and that is fired in the range of 1,300 to 1,400 degrees Celsius. The relatively high proportion of silica in the body clays renders the finished porcelains translucent. Like **stonewares**, porcelains are glazed to enhance their aesthetic appeal and to aid in keeping them clean. By definition, porcelain is white, though it may be covered with a **glaze** of bright color or subtle hue. Chinese potters were the first in the world to produce porcelain, which they were able to make as early as the eighth century.

porch   The covered entrance on the exterior of a building. With a row of **columns** or **colonnade**, also called a **portico**.

portal   A grand entrance, door, or gate, usually to an important public building, and often decorated with sculpture.

portico   In architecture, a projecting roof or porch supported by columns, often marking an entrance. See also porch.

post-and-lintel construction   An architectural system of construction with two or more vertical elements (posts) supporting a horizontal element (lintel).

potassium-argon dating   Technique used to measure the decay of a radioactive potassium isotope into a stable isotope of argon, an inert gas.

potsherd   A broken piece of ceramic ware.

Praire Style   A style of architecture initiated by the American Frank Lloyd Wright (1867-1959), in which he sought to integrate his structures in an "organic" way into the surrounding natural landscape, often having the lines of the building follow the horizontal contours of the land. Since Wright's early buildings were built in the Prairie States of the Midwest, this type of architecture became known as the Prairie Style.

primitivism   The borrowing of subjects or forms usually from non-Western or prehistoric sources by Western artists. Originally practiced by Western artists as an attempt to infuse their work with the naturalistic and expressive qualities attributed to other cultures, especially colonized cultures, primitivism also borrowed from the art of children and the insane.

pronaos   The enclosed vestibule of a Greek or Roman temple, found in front of the **cella** and marked by a row of **columns** at the entrance.

proscenium   The stage of an ancient Greek or Roman theater. In modern theater, the area of the stage in front of the curtain. Also: the framing **arch** that separates a stage from the audience.

psalter   In Jewish and Christian scripture, a book containing the psalms, or songs, attributed to King David.

punchwork   Decorative designs that are stamped onto a surface, such as metal or leather, using a punch (a handheld metal implement).

putto (putti)   A plump, naked little boy, often winged. In classical art, called a cupid; in Christian art, a cherub.

pylon   A massive gateway formed by a pair of tapering walls of oblong shape. Erected by ancient Egyptians to mark the entrance to a temple complex.

qibla   The mosque wall oriented toward Mecca indicated by the mihrab.

quatrefoil   A four-lobed decorative pattern common in Gothic art and architecture.

quincunx   A building in which five **domed** bays are arranged within a square, with a central unit and four corner units. (When the central unit has similar units extending from each side, the form becomes a **Greek cross**.)

quoin   A stone, often extra large or decorated for emphasis, forming the corner of two walls. A vertical row of such stones is called quoining.

radiometric dating   A method of dating prehistoric works of art made from organic materials, based on the rate of degeneration of radiocarbons in these materials. *See also* **relative dating, absolute dating**.

raigo   A painted image that depicts the Amida Buddha and other Buddhist deities welcoming the soul of a dying worshiper to paradise.

raku   A type of **ceramic** pottery made by hand, coated with a thick, dark **glaze**, and fired at a low heat. The resulting vessels are irregularly shaped and glazed, and are highly prized for use in the Japanese tea ceremony.

readymade   An object from popular or material culture presented without further manipulation as an artwork by the artist.

realism   In art, a term first used in Europe around 1850 to designate a kind of **naturalism** with a social or political message, which soon lost its didactic import and became synonymous with naturalism.

red-figure   A style and technique of ancient Greek vase painting characterized by red clay-colored figures on a black background. (The figures are reversed against a painted ground and details are drawn, not engraved, as in black-figure style.) See also **black-figure**.

register   A device used in systems of spatial definition. In painting, a register indicates the use of differing **groundlines** to differentiate layers of space within an image. In sculpture, the placement of self-contained bands of **reliefs** in a vertical arrangement. In printmaking, the marks at the edges used to align the print correctly on the page, especially in multiple-block color printing.

registration marks   In Japanese **woodblock** printing, these were two marks carved on the blocks to indicate proper alignment of the paper during the printing process. In multicolor printing, which used a separate block for each color, these marks were essential for achieving the proper position or registration of the colors.

relative dating   See also **radiometric dating**.

relief sculpture   A three-dimensional image or design whose flat background surface is carved away to a certain depth, setting off the figure. Called high or **low (bas) relief** depending upon the extent of projection of the image from the background. Called **sunken relief** when the image is carved below the original surface of the background, which is not cut away.

reliquary   A container, often made of precious materials, used as a repository to protect and display sacred relics.

repoussé   A technique of hammering metal from the back to create a protruding image. Elaborate reliefs are created with wooden armatures against which the metal sheets are pressed and hammered.

reverse perspective   See **perspective**.

rhyton   A vessel in the shape of a figure or an animal, used for drinking or pouring liquids on special occasions.

rib vault   See **vault**.

ridgepole   A longitudinal timber at the apex of a roof that supports the upper ends of the rafters.

rosette   A round or oval ornament resembling a rose.

rotunda   Any building (or part thereof) constructed in a circular (or sometimes polygonal) shape, usually producing a large open space crowned by a **dome**.

round arch   See **arch**.

roundel   Any element with a circular format, often placed as a decoration on the exterior of architecture.

rune stone   A stone used in early medieval northern Europe as a commemorative monument, which is carved or inscribed with runes, a writing system used by early Germanic peoples.

running spirals   A decorative motif based on the shape formed by a line making a continuous spiral.

rustication   In building, the rough, irregular, and unfinished effect deliberately given to the exterior facing of a stone edifice. Rusticated stones are often large and used for decorative emphasis around doors or windows, or across the entire lower floors of a building. Also, masonry construction with conspicuous, often beveled joints.

salon   A large room for entertaining guests; a periodic social or intellectual gathering, often of prominent people; a hall or **gallery** for exhibiting works of art.

sanctuary   A sacred or holy enclosure used for worship. In ancient Greece and Rome, consisted of one or more temples and an altar. In Christian architecture, the space around the altar in a church called the chancel or presbytery.

sarcophagus (sarcophagi)   A stone coffin. Often rectangular and decorated with **relief sculpture**.

scarab   In Egypt, a stylized dung beetle associated with the sun and the god Amun.

scarification   Ornamental decoration applied to the surface of the body by cutting the skin for cultural and/or aesthetic reasons.

school of artists   An art historical term describing a group of artists, usually working at the same time and sharing similar styles, influences, and ideals. The artists in a particular school may not necessarily be directly associated with one another, unlike those in a workshop or **atelier**.

scribe   A writer; a person who copies texts.

scriptorium (scriptoria)   A room in a monastery for writing or copying manuscripts.

scroll painting   A painting executed on a rolled support. Rollers at each end permit the horizontal scroll to be unrolled as it is studied or the vertical scroll to be hung for contemplation or decoration.

seals   Personal emblems usually carved of stone in **intaglio** or **relief** and used to stamp a name or legend onto paper or silk. They traditionally employ the archaic characters appropriately known as "seal script," of the Zhou or Qin. Cut in stone, a seal may state a formal givem name, or it may state any of the numerous personal names that China's painters and writers adopted throughout their lives. A treasured work of art often bears not only the seal of its maker but also those of collectors and admirers through the centuries. In the Chinese view, these do not disfigure the work but add another layer of interest.

seraph (seraphim) An angel of the highest rank in the Christian hierarchy.

serdab In Egyptian tombs, the small room in which the ka statue was placed.

sfumato Italian term meaning "smoky," soft, and mellow. In painting, the effect of haze in an image. Resembling the color of the atmosphere at dusk, sfumato gives a smoky effect.

sgraffito Decoration made by incising or cutting away a surface layer of material to reveal a different color beneath.

shaft The main vertical section of a column between the capital and the base, usually circular in cross section.

shaftgrave A deep pit used for burial.

shikhara In the architecture of northern India, a conical (or pyramidal) spire found atop a Hindu temple and often crowned with an *amalaka*.

shoji A standing Japanese screen covered in translucent rice paper and used in interiors.

sinopia The preparatory design or underdrawing of a **fresco**. Also: a reddish chalklike earth pigment.

site-specific sculpture A sculpture commissioned and/or designed for a particular spot.

slip A mixture of clay and water applied to a **ceramic** object as a final decorative coat. Also: a solution that binds different parts of a vessel together, such as the handle and the main body.

spandrel The area of wall adjoining the exterior curve of an arch between its **springing** and the **keystone**, or the area between two arches, as in an **arcade**.

springing The point at which the curve of an arch or vault meets with and rises from its support.

squinch An **arch** or lintel built across the upper corners of a square space, allowing a circular or polygonal **dome** to be more securely set above the walls.

stained glass Molten glass is given a color that becomes intrinsic to the material. Additional colors may be fused to the surface (flashing). Stained glass is most often used in windows, for which small pieces of differently colored glass are precisely cut and assembled into a design, held together by **cames**. Additional painted details may be added to create images.

stele (stelae) A stone slab placed vertically and decorated with inscriptions or reliefs. Used as a grave marker or memorial.

stereobate A foundation upon which a Classical temple stands.

still life A type of painting that has as its subject inanimate objects (such as food, dishes, fruit, or flowers).

stoa In Greek architecture, a long roofed walkway, usually having columns on one long side and a wall on the other.

stoneware A high-fired, vitrified, but opaque **ceramic** ware that is fired in the range of 1,100 to 1,200 degrees Celsius. At that temperature, particles of silica in the clay bodies fuse together so that the finished vessels are impervious to liquids, even without **glaze**. Stoneware pieces are glazed to enhance their aesthetic appeal and to aid in keeping them clean (since unglazed ceramics are easily soiled). Stoneware occurs in a range of earth-toned colors, from white and tan to gray and black, with light gray predominating. Chinese potters were the first in the world to produce stoneware, which they were able to make as early as the Shang dynasty.

stucco A mixture of lime, sand, and other ingredients into a material that can be easily molded or modeled. When dry, produces a very durable surface used for covering walls or for architectural sculpture and decoration.

stupa In Buddhist architecture, a bell-shaped or pyramidal religious monument, made of piled earth or stone, and containing sacred relics.

stylobate In Classical architecture, the stone foundation on which a temple **colonnade** stands.

stylus An instrument with a pointed end (used for writing and printmaking), which makes a delicate line or scratch. Also: a special writing tool for **cuneiform** writing with one pointed end and one triangular wedge end.

sublime Adjective describing a concept, thing, or state of high spiritual, moral, or intellectual value; or something awe-inspiring. The sublime was a goal to which many nineteenth-century artists aspired in their artworks.

sunken relief See **relief sculpture**.

syncretism In religion or philosophy, the union of different ideas or principles.

taotie A mask with a dragon or animal-like face common as a decorative motif in Chinese art.

tapestry Multicolored pictorial or decorative weaving meant to be hung on a wall or placed on furniture.

tatami Mats of woven straw used in Japanese houses as a floor covering.

tempera A painting medium made by blending egg yolks with water, pigments, and occasionally other materials, such as glue.

tenebrism The use of strong **chiaroscuro** and artificially illuminated areas to create a dramatic contrast of light and dark in a painting.

terra cotta A medium made from clay fired over a low heat and sometimes left unglazed. Also: the orange-brown color typical of this medium.

tessera (tesserae) The small piece of stone, glass, or other object that is pieced together with many others to create a mosaic.

tetrarchy Four-man rule, as in the late Roman Empire, when four emperors shared power.

thatch A roof made of plant materials.

thermo-luminescence dating A technique that measures the irradiation of the crystal structure of material such as flint or pottery and the soil in which it is found, determined by luminescence produced when a sample is heated.

tholos A small, round building. Sometimes built underground, as in a Mycenaean tomb.

thrust The outward pressure caused by the weight of a vault and supported by buttressing. See **arch**.

tierceron In **vault** construction, a secondary rib that arcs from a **springing** point to the rib that runs lengthwise through the vault, called the ridge rib.

tokonoma A niche for the display of an art object (such as a screen, scroll, or flower arrangement) in a Japanese hall or tearoom.

tondo A painting or **relief sculpture** of circular shape.

torana In Indian architecture, an ornamented gateway arch in a temple, usually leading to the stupa.

toron In West African **mosque** architecture, the wooden beams that project from the walls. Torons are used as support for the scaffolding erected annually for the replastering of the building.

tracery Stonework or woodwork applied to wall surfaces or filling the open space of windows. In **plate tracery**, opening are cut through the wall. In **bar tracery**, **mullions** divide the space into vertical segments and form decorative patterns at the top of the opening or panel.

transept The arm of a cruciform church, perpendicular to the **nave**. The point where the nave and transept cross is called the crossing. Beyond the crossing lies the **sanctuary**, whether **apse**, choir, or chevet.

travertine A mineral building material similar to limestone, typically found in central Italy.

trefoil An ornamental design made up of three rounded lobes placed adjacent to one another.

triglyph Rectangular block between the **metopes** of a **Doric frieze**. Identified by the three carved vertical grooves, which approximate the appearance of the end of a wooden beam.

triptych An artwork made up of three panels. The panels may be hinged together so the side segments (**wings**) fold over the central area.

trompe l'oeil A manner of representation in which the appearance of natural space and objects is re-created with the express intention of fooling the eye of the viewer, who may be convinced that the subject actually exists as three-dimensional reality.

trumeau A column, pier, or post found at the center of a large portal or doorway, supporting the lintel.

tugra A calligraphic imperial monogram used in Ottoman courts.

Tuscan order *See* **order**.

twisted perspective A convention in art in which every aspect of a body or object is represented from its most characteristic viewpoint.

ukiyo-e A Japanese term for a type of popular art that was favored from the sixteenth century, particularly in the form of color **woodblock prints**. Ukiyo-e prints often depicted the world of the common people in Japan, such as courtesans and actors, as well as landscapes and myths.

urna In Buddhist art, the curl of hair on the forehead that is a characteristic mark of a buddha. The urna is a symbol of divine wisdom.

ushnisha In Asian art, a round turban or tiara symbolizing royalty and, when worn by a buddha, enlightenment.

vanishing point In a **perspective** system, the point on the horizon line at which **orthogonals** meet. A complex system can have multiple vanishing points.

vanitas An image, especially popular in Europe during the seventeenth century, in which all the objects symbolize the transience of life. Vanitas paintings are usually of **still lifes** or **genre** subjects.

vault An **arched** masonry structure that spans an interior space. Barrel or tunnel vault: an elongated or continuous semicircular vault, shaped like a half-cylinder. **Corbeled** vault: a vault made by projecting courses of stone. **Groin** or cross vault: a vault created by the intersection of two barrel vaults of equal size which creates four side compartments of identical size and shape. Quadrant or half-barrel vault: as the name suggests, a half-barrel vault. Rib vault: ribs (extra masonry) demarcate the junctions of a groin vault. Ribs may function to reinforce the groins or may be purely decorative. See also **corbeling**.

veduta (vedute) Italian for "vista" or "view."

Paintings, drawings, or prints often of expansive city scenes or of harbors.

vellum A fine animal skin prepared for writing and painting. See also parchment.

veneer In architecture, the exterior facing of a building, often in decorative patterns of fine stone or brick. In decorative arts, a thin exterior layer of finer material (such as rare wood, ivory, metal, and semiprecious stones) laid over the form.

verism A style in which artists concern themselves with capturing the exterior likeness of an object or person, usually by rendering its visible details in a finely executed, meticulous manner.

vihara From the Sanskrit term meaning "for wanderers." A vihara is, in general, a Buddhist monastery in India. It also signifies monks' cells and gathering places in such a monastery.

vimana The main element of a Southern Indian Hindu temple, usually in the shape of a pyramidal or tapering tower raised on a **plinth**.

volute A spiral scroll, as seen on an Ionic **capital**.

votive figure An image created as a devotional offering to a god or other deity.

voussoirs The oblong, wedge-shaped stone blocks used to build an **arch**. The topmost voussoir is called a **keystone**.

warp The vertical threads in a weaver's loom. Warp threads make up a fixed framework that provides the structure for the entire piece of cloth, and are thus often thicker than **weft** threads. See also **weft**.

wash A diluted watercolor or ink. Often washes are applied to drawings or prints to add tone or touches of color.

wattle and daub A wall construction method combining upright branches, woven with twigs (wattles) and plastered or filled with clay or mud (daub).

weft The horizontal threads in a woven piece of cloth. Weft threads are woven at right angles to and through the **warp** threads to make up the bulk of the decorative pattern. In carpets, the weft is often completely covered or formed by the rows of trimmed knots that form the carpet's soft surface. See also **warp**.

white-ground A type of ancient Greek pottery in which the background color of the object is painted with a slip that turns white in the firing process. Figures and details were added by painting on or **incising** into this **slip**. White-ground wares were popular in the Classical period as funerary objects.

wing A side panel of a **triptych** or **polyptych** (usually found in pairs), which was hinged to fold over the central panel. Wings often held the depiction of the donors and/or subsidiary scenes relating to the central image.

woodblock print A print made from one or more carved wooden blocks. In Japan, woodblock prints were made using multiple blocks carved in relief, usually with a block for each color in the finished print. See also **woodcut**.

woodcut A type of print made by carving a design into a wooden block. The ink is applied to the block with a roller. As the ink remains only on the raised areas between the carved-away lines, these carved-away areas and lines provide the white areas of the print. Also: the process by which the woodcut is made.

x-ray style In Aboriginal art, a manner of representation in which the artist depicts a figure or animal by illustrating its outline as well as essential internal organs and bones.

yaksha, yakshi The male (yaksha) and female (yakshi) nature spirits that act as agents of the Hindu gods. Their sculpted images are often found on Hindu temples and other sacred places, particularly at the entrances.

ziggurat In Mesopotamia, a tall stepped tower of earthen materials, often supporting a shrine.

BIBLIOGRAPHY

Susan V. Craig

This bibliography is composed of books in English that are appropriate "further reading" titles. Most items on this list are available in good libraries, whether college, university, or public institutions. I have emphasized recently published works so that the research information would be current. There are three classifications of listings: general surveys and art history reference tools, including journals and Internet directories; surveys of large periods that encompass multiple chapters (ancient art in the Western tradition, European medieval art, European Renaissance through eighteenth-century art, modern art in the West, Asian art, and African and Oceanic art and art of the Americas); and books for individual chapters 1 through 32.

General Art History Surveys and Reference Tools

Adams, Laurie Schneider. *Art across Time*. 2nd ed. New York: McGraw-Hill, 2002.

Barnet, Sylvan. *A Short Guide to Writing about Art*. 8th ed. New York: Pearson/Longman, 2005.

Boströöm, Antonia. *Encyclopedia of Sculpture*. 3 vols. New York: FitzroyDearborn, 2004.

Broude, Norma, and Garrard, Mary D., eds. *Feminism and Art History: Questioning the Litany*. Icon Editions. New York: Harper & Row, 1982.

Chadwick, Whitney. *Women, Art, and Society*. 3rd ed. New York: Thames and Hudson, 2002.

Chilvers, Ian, ed. *The Oxford Dictionary of Art*. 3rd ed. New York: Oxford Univ. Press, 2004.

Curl, James Stevens. *A Dictionary of Architecture and Landscape Architecture*. 2nd ed. Oxford: Oxford Univ. Press, 2006.

Davies, Penelope J.E., et al. *Janson's History of Art: The Western Tradition*. 7th ed. Upper Saddle River, NJ: Prentice Hall, 2006.

Dictionary of Art, The. 34 vols. New York: Grove's Dictionaries, 1996.

Encyclopedia of World Art. 16 vols. New York: McGraw-Hill, 1972–83.

Frank, Patrick, Duane Preble, and Sarah Preble. *Preble's Artforms*. 8th ed. Upper Saddle River, NJ: Prentice Hall, 2006.

Gardner, Helen. *Gardner's Art through the Ages*. 12th ed. Ed. Fred S. Kleiner & Christin J. Mamiya. Belmont, CA: Thomson/Wadsworth, 2005.

Gaze, Delia, ed. *Dictionary of Women Artists*. 2 vols. London: Fitzroy Dearborn Publishers, 1997.

Griffiths, Antony. *Prints and Printmaking: An Introduction to the History and Techniques*. 2nd ed. London: British Museum Press, 1996.

Hadden, Peggy. *The Quotable Artist*. New York: Allworth Press, 2002.

Hall, James. *Illustrated Dictionary of Symbols in Eastern and Western Art*. New York: Icon Editions, 1994.

Holt, Elizabeth Gilmore, ed. *A Documentary History of Art*. 3 vols. New Haven: Yale Univ. Press, 1986.

Honour, Hugh, and John Fleming. *The Visual Arts: A History*. 7th ed. Upper Saddle River, NJ: Prentice Hall, 2005.

Hults, Linda C. *The Print in the Western World: An Introductory History*. Madison: Univ. of Wisconsin Press, 1996.

Johnson, Paul. *Art: A New History*. New York: HarperCollins, 2003.

Kaltenbach. G. E. *Pronunciation Dictionary of Artists' Names*. 3rd ed. Rev. Debra Edelstein. Boston: Little, Brown, and Co., 1993.

Kemp, Martin. *The Oxford History of Western Art*. Oxford: Oxford Univ. Press, 2000.

Kostof, Spiro. *A History of Architecture: Settings and Rituals*. 2nd ed. Rev. Greg Castillo. New York: Oxford Univ. Press, 1995.

Mackenzie, Lynn. *Non-Western Art: A Brief Guide*. 2nd ed. Upper Saddle River, NJ: Prentice Hall, 2001.

Marmor, Max, and Alex Ross, eds. *Guide to the Literature of Art History 2*. Chicago: American Library Association, 2005.

Onians, John, ed. *Atlas of World Art*. New York: Oxford Univ. Press, 2004.

Roberts, Helene, ed. *Encyclopedia of Comparative Iconography: Themes Depicted in Works of Art*. 2 vols. Chicago: Fitzroy Dearborn, 1998.

Rogers, Elizabeth Barlow. *Landscape Design: A Cultural and Architectural History*. New York: Harry N. Abrams, 2001.

Sayre, Henry M. *Writing about Art*. 5th ed. Upper Saddle River, NJ: Pearson/Prentice Hall, 2006.

Sed-Rajna, Gabrielle. *Jewish Art*. Trans. Sara Friedman and Mira Reich. New York: Abrams, 1997.

Slatkin, Wendy. *Women Artists in History: From Antiquity to the Present*. 4th ed. Upper Saddle River, NJ: Prentice Hall, 2000.

Sutton, Ian. *Western Architecture: From Ancient Greece to the Present*. World of Art. New York: Thames and Hudson, 1999.

Trachtenberg, Marvin, and Isabelle Hyman. *Architecture: From Prehistory to Postmodernity*. 2nd ed. Upper Saddle River, NJ: Prentice Hall, 2001.

Tufts, Eleanor. *Our Hidden Heritage: Five Centuries of Women Artists*. New York: Paddington Press, 1974.

West, Shearer. *Portraiture*. Oxford History of Art. Oxford: Oxford Univ. Press, 2004.

Wilkins, David G., Bernard Schultz, and Katheryn M. Linduff. *Art Past, Art Present*. 5th ed. Upper Saddle River, NJ: Prentice Hall, 2005.

Watkin, David. *A History of Western Architecture*. 4th ed. New York: Watson-Guptill Publications, 2005.

Art History Journals: A Select List of Current Titles

African Arts. Quarterly. Los Angeles: Univ. of California at Los Angeles, James S. Coleman African Studies Center, 1967–

American Art: The Journal of the Smithsonian American Art Museum. 3/year. Chicago: Univ. of Chicago Press, 1987–

American Indian Art Magazine, Quarterly. Scottsdale, AZ: American Indian Art Inc, 1975–

American Journal of Archaeology. Quarterly. Boston: Archaeological Institute of America, 1885–

Antiquity: A Periodical of Archaeology. Quarterly. Cambridge, UK: Antiquity Publications Ltd, 1927–

Apollo: The International Magazine of the Arts. Monthly. London: Apollo Magazine Ltd, 1925–

Architectural History. Annually. Farnham, UK: Society of Architectural Historians of Great Britain, 1958–

Archives of American Art Journal. Quarterly. Washington, D.C.: Archives of American Art, Smithsonian Institution, 1960–

Archives of Asian Art. Annually. New York: Asia Society, 1945–

Ars Orientalis: The Arts of Asia, Southeast Asia, and Islam. Annually. Ann Arbor: Univ. of Michigan Dept. of Art History, 1954–

Art Bulletin. Quarterly. New York: College Art Association, 1913–

Art History: Journal of the Association of Art Historians. 5/year. Oxford: Blackwell Publishing Ltd, 1978–

Art in America. Monthly. New York: Brant Publications Inc, 1913–

Art Journal. Quarterly. New York: College Art Association, 1960–

Art Nexus. Quarterly. Bogata, Colombia: Arte en Colombia Ltda, 1976–

Art Papers Magazine. Bi-monthly. Atlanta: Atlanta Art Papers Inc, 1976–

Artforum International. 10/year. New York: Artforum International Magazine Inc, 1962–

Artnews. 11/year. New York: Artnews LLC, 1902–

Bulletin of the Metropolitan Museum of Art. Quarterly. New York: Metropolitan Museum of Art, 1905–.

Burlington Magazine. Monthly. London: Burlington Magazine Publications Ltd, 1903–

Dumbarton Oaks Papers. Annually. Locust Valley, NY: J. J. Augustin Inc, 1940–

Flash Art International. Bimonthly. Trevi, Italy: Giancarlo Politi Editore, 1980–

Gesta. Semiannually. New York: International Center of Medieval Art, 1963–

History of Photography. Quarterly. Abingdon, UK: Taylor & Francis Ltd, 1976–

International Review of African American Art. Quarterly. Hampton, VA: International Review of African American Art, 1976–

Journal of Design History. Quarterly. Oxford: Oxford Univ. Press, 1988–

Journal of Egyptian Archaeology. Annually. London: Egypt Exploration Society, 1914–

Journal of Hellenic Studies. Annually. London: Society for the Promotion of Hellenic Studies, 1880–

Journal of Roman Archaeology. Annually. Portsmouth, RI: Journal of Roman Archaeology LLC, 1988–

Journal of the Society of Architectural Historians. Quarterly. Chicago: Society of Architectural Historians, 1940–

Journal of the Warburg and Courtauld Institutes. Annually. London: Warburg Institute, 1937–

Leonardo: Art, Science and Technology. 6/year. Cambridge, MA: MIT Press, 1968–

Marg. Quarterly. Mumbai, India: Scientific Publishers, 1946–

Master Drawings. Quarterly. New York: Master Drawings Association, 1963–

October. Cambridge, MA: MIT Press, 1976–

Oxford Art Journal. 3/year. Oxford: Oxford Univ. Press, 1978–

Parkett. 3/year. Züürich, Switzerland: Parkett Verlag AG, 1984–

Print Quarterly. Quarterly. London: Print Quarterly Publications, 1984–

Simiolus: Netherlands Quarterly for the History of Art. Quarterly. Apeldoorn, Netherlands: Stichting voor Nederlandse Kunsthistorische Publicaties, 1966–

Woman's Art Journal. Semiannually. Philadelphia: Old City Publishing Inc, 1980–

Internet Directories for Art History Information

ARCHITECTURE AND BUILDING

http://library.nevada.edu/arch/rsrce/webrsrce/contents.html

A directory of architecture websites collected by Jeanne Brown at the Univ. of Nevada at Las Vegas. Topical lists include architecture, building and construction, design, history, housing, planning, preservation, and landscape architecture. Most entries include a brief annotation and the last date the link was accessed by the compiler.

ART HISTORY RESOURCES ON THE WEB

http://witcombe.sbc.edu/ARTHLinks.html

Authored by Christopher L. C. E. Witcombe of Sweet Briar College in Virginia since 1995, the site includes an impressive number of links for various art historical eras as well as links to research resources, museums, and galleries. The content is frequently updated.

ART IN FLUX: A DIRECTORY OF RESOURCES FOR RESEARCH IN CONTEMPORARY ART

http://www.boisestate.edu/art/artinflux/intro.html

Cheryl K. Shutleff of Boise State Univ. in Idaho has authored this directory, which includes sites selected according to their relevance to the study of national or international contemporary art and artists. The subsections include artists, museums, theory, reference, and links.

ARTCYCLOPEDIA: THE FINE ARTS SEARCH ENGINE

With over 2,100 art sites and 75,000 links, this is one of the most comprehensive web directories for artists and art topics.

The primary searching is by artist's name but access is also available by artistic movement, nation, timeline and medium.

MOTHER OF ALL ART HISTORY LINKS PAGES

http://www.art-design.umich.edu/mother/

Maintained by the Dept. of the History of Art at the Univ. of Michigan, this directory covers art history departments, art museums, fine arts schools and departments as well as links to research resources. Each entry includes annotations.

VOICE OF THE SHUTTLE

http://vos.ucsb.edu

Sponsored by Univ. of California, Santa Barbara, this directory includes over 70 pages of links to humanities and humanities-related resources on the Internet. The structured guide includes specific sub-sections on architecture, on art (modern & contemporary), and on art history. Links usually include a one sentence explanation and the resource is frequently updated with new information.

YAHOO! ARTS>ART HISTORY
http://dir.yahoo.com/Arts/Art_History/
Another extensive directory of art links organized into subdivisions with one of the most extensive being "Periods and Movements." Links include the name of the site as well as a few words of explanation.

Asian Art, General

Addiss, Stephen, Gerald Groemer, and J. Thomas Rimer, eds. *Traditional Japanese Arts and Culture: An Illustrated Sourcebook*. Honolulu: Univ. of Hawai'i Press, 2006.

Barnhart, Richard M. Three *Thousand Years of Chinese Painting*. New Haven: Yale Univ. Press, 1997.

Blunden, Caroline, and Mark Elvin. *Cultural Atlas of China*. 2nd ed. New York: Checkmark Books, 1998.

Brown, Kerry, ed. *Sikh Art and Literature*. New York: Routledge in collaboration with the Sikh Foundation, 1999.

Bussagli, Mario. *Oriental Architecture*. History of World Architecture. 2 vols. New York: Electa/Rizzoli, 1989.

Chang, Leon Long-Yien, and Peter Miller. *Four Thousand Years of Chinese Calligraphy*. Chicago: Univ. of Chicago Press, 1990.

Chung, Yang-mo. *Arts of Korea*. Ed. Judith G. Smith. New York: Metropolitan Museum of Art, 1998.

Clark, John. *Modern Asian Art*. Honolulu: Univ. of Hawaii Press, 1998.

Clunas, Craig. *Art in China*. Oxford History of Art. Oxford: Oxford Univ. Press, 1997.

Collcutt, Martin, Marius Jansen, and Isao Kumakura. *Cultural Atlas of Japan*. New York: Facts on File, 1988.

Craven, Roy C. *Indian Art: A Concise History*. Rev. ed. World of Art. New York: Thames and Hudson, 1997.

Dehejia, Vidya. *Indian Art*. Art & Ideas. London: Phaidon Press, 1997.

Fisher, Robert E. *Buddhist Art and Architecture*. World of Art. New York: Thames and Hudson, 1993.

Fu, Xinian. *Chinese Architecture*. Ed. & exp. Nancy S. Steinhardt. The Culture & Civilization of China. New Haven: Yale Univ. Press, 2002.

Hearn, Maxwell K., and Judith G. Smith, eds. *Arts of the Sung and Yüüan: Papers Prepared for an International Symposium*. New York: Dept. of Asian Art, Metropolitan Museum of Art, 1996.

Heibonsha Survey of Japanese Art. 31 vols. New York: Weatherhill, 1972–80.

Hertz, Betti-Sue. *Past in Reverse: Contemporary Art of East Asia*. San Diego: San Diego Museum of Art, 2004.

Japanese Arts Library. 15 vols. New York: Kodansha International, 1977–87.

Kerlogue, Fiona. *Arts of Southeast Asia*. World of Art. New York: Thames & Hudson, 2004.

Khanna, Balraj, and George Michell. *Human and Divine: 2000 Years of Indian Sculpture*. London: Hayward Gallery Pub., 2000.

Lee, Sherman E. *A History of Far Eastern Art*. 5th ed. Ed. Naomi Noble Richards. New York: Abrams, 1994.

———. *China, 5000 Years: Innovation and Transformation in the Arts*. New York: Solomon R. Guggenheim Museum, 1998.

Liu, Cary Y., and Dora C.Y. Ching, eds. *Arts of the Sung and Yüüan: Ritual, Ethnicity, and Style in Painting*. Princeton: Art Museum, Princeton Univ., 1999.

McArthur, Meher. *The Arts of Asia: Materials, Techniques, Styles*. New York: Thames & Hudson, 2005.

———. *Reading Buddhist Art: An Illustrated Guide to Buddhist Signs and Symbols*. New York: Thames & Hudson, 2002.

Mason, Penelope. *History of Japanese Art*. 2nd ed. Upper Saddle River, NJ: Pearson Prentice Hall, 2005.

Michell, George. *Hindu Art and Architecture*. World of Art. London: Thames & Hudson, 2000.

———. *The Penguin Guide to the Monuments of India*. 2 vols. New York: Viking, 1989.

Mitter, Partha. *Indian Art*. Oxford History of Art. Oxford: Oxford Univ. Press, 2001.

Nickel, Lukas, ed. *Return of the Buddha: The Qingzhou Discoveries*. London: Royal Academy of Arts, 2002.

Pak, Youngsook, and Roderick Whitfield. *Buddhist Sculpture*. Handbook of Korean Art. London: Laurence King, 2003.

Stanley-Baker, Joan. *Japanese Art*. Rev. & exp. ed. World of Art. New York: Thames and Hudson, 2000.

Sullivan, Michael. *The Arts of China*. 4th ed., Exp. & rev. Berkeley: Univ. of California Press, 1999.

Thorp, Robert L., and Richard Ellis Vinograd. *Chinese Art & Culture*. New York: Abrams, 2001.

Topsfield, Andrew, ed. *In the Realm of Gods and Kings: Arts of India*. London: Philip Wilson, 2004.

Tucker, Jonathan. *The Silk Road: Art and History*. Chicago: Art Media Resources, 2003.

Tregear, Mary. *Chinese Art*. Rev. ed. World of Art. New York: Thames and Hudson, 1997.

Vainker S. J. *Chinese Pottery and Porcelain: From Prehistory to the Present*. London: British Museum, 1991.

Varley, H. Paul *Japanese Culture*. 4th ed., Updated & exp. Honolulu: Univ. of Hawaii Press, 2000.

African and Oceanic Art and Art of the Americas, General

Anderson, Richard L., and Karen L Field, eds. *Art in Small-Scale Societies: Contemporary Readings*. Englewood Cliffs, NJ: Prentice-Hall, 1993.

Bacquart, Jean-Baptiste. *The Tribal Arts of Africa*. New York: Thames and Hudson, 1998.

Bassani, Ezio, ed. *Arts of Africa: 7000 Years of African Art*. Milan: Skira, 2005.

Benson, Elizabeth P. *Retratos: 2,000 Years of Latin American Portraits*. San Antonio: San Antonio Museum of Art, 2004.

Berlo, Janet Catherine, and Lee Ann Wilson. *Arts of Africa, Oceania, and the Americas: Selected Readings*. Upper Saddle River, NJ: Prentice Hall, 1993.

Calloway, Colin G.. *First Peoples: A Documentary Survey of American Indian History*. Boston and New York: Bedford/St. Martin's, 2004.

Coote, Jeremy, and Anthony Shelton, eds. *Anthropology, Art, and Aesthetics*. New York: Oxford Univ. Press, 1992.

D'Azevedao, Warren L. *The Traditional Artist in African Societies*. Bloomington: Indiana Univ. Press, 1989.

Drewal, Henry, and John Pemberton III. *Yoruba: Nine Centuries of African Art and Thought*. New York: Center for African Art, 1989.

Evans, Susan Toby. *Ancient Mexico & Central America: Archaeology and Culture History*. New York: Thames & Hudson, 2004.

———, and David L. Webster, eds. *Archaeology of Ancient Mexico and Central America : An Encyclopedia*. New York: Garland Pub., 2001.

———, and Joanne Pillsbury, eds. *Palaces of the Ancient New World: A Symposium at Dumbarton Oaks, 10th and 11th October, 1998*. Washington, D.C.: Dumbarton Oaks Research Library and Collection, 2004.

Geoffroy-Schneiter, Bérééénice. *Tribal Arts*. New York: Vendome Press, 2000.

Guidoni, Enrico. *Primitive Architecture*. Trans. Robert Eric Wolf. History of World Architecture. New York: Rizzoli, 1987.

Hiller, Susan, ed. & comp. *The Myth of Primitivism: Perspectives on Art*. London: Routledge, 1991.

Mack, John, ed. *Africa, Arts and Cultures*. London: British Museum, 2000.

Mexico: Splendors of Thirty Centuries. New York: Metropolitan Museum of Art, 1990.

Murray, Jocelyn, ed. *Cultural Atlas of Africa*. Rev. ed. New York: Facts on File, 1998.

Nunley, John W., and Cara McCarty. *Masks: Faces of Culture*. New York: Abrams in assoc. with the Saint Louis Art Museum, 1999.

Perani, Judith, and Fred T. Smith. *The Visual Arts of Africa: Gender, Power, and Life Cycle Rituals*. Upper Saddle River, NJ: Prentice Hall, 1998.

Phillips, Tom. *Africa: The Art of a Continent*. London: Prestel, 1996.

Price, Sally. *Primitive Art in Civilized Places*. Chicago: Univ. of Chicago Press, 1989.

Rabineau, Phyllis. *Feather Arts: Beauty, Wealth, and Spirit from Five Continents*. Chicago: Field Museum of Natural History, 1979.

Schuster, Carl, and Edmund Carpenter. *Patterns that Connect: Social Symbolism in Ancient & Tribal Art*. New York: Abrams, 1996.

Scott, John F. *Latin American Art: Ancient to Modern*. Gainesville: Univ. Press of Florida, 1999.

Stepan, Peter. *Africa*. Trans. John Gabriel & Elizabeth Schwaiger. World of Art. London: Prestel, 2001.

Visonàà, Monica Blackmun, et al. *A History of Art in Africa*. Upper Saddle River, NJ: Prentice Hall, 2000.

CHAPTER 23
Art of India after 1200

Asher, Catherine B. *Architecture of Mughal India*. New York: Cambridge Univ. Press, 1992.

Beach, Milo Cleveland. *Mughal and Rajput Painting*. New York: Cambridge Univ. Press, 1992.

Guy, John, and Deborah Swallow, eds. *Arts of India, 1550–1900*. London: Victoria and Albert Museum, 1990.

Khanna, Balraj, and Aziz Kurtha. *Art of Modern India*. London: Thames and Hudson, 1998.

Koch, Ebba. *Mughal Art and Imperial Ideology: Collected Essays*. New Delhi: Oxford Univ. Press, 2001.

Michell, George. *Hindu Art and Architecture*. World of Art. London: Thames & Hudson, 2000.

Moynihan, Elizabeth B., ed. *The Moonlight Garden: New Discoveries at the Taj Mahal*. Asian Art & Culture. Washington, D.C.: Arthur M. Sackler Gallery, Smithsonian Institution, 2000.

Nou, Jean-Louis. *Taj Mahal*. Text by Amina Okada & M. C. Joshi. New York: Abbeville, 1993.

Pal, Pratapaditya. *Court Paintings of India, 16th-19th Centuries*. New York: Navin Kumar, 1983.

———. *The Peaceful Liberators: Jain Art from India*. New York: Thames and Hudson, 1994.

Rossi, Barbara. *From the Ocean of Painting: India's Popular Paintings, 1589 to the Present*. New York: Oxford Univ. Press, 1998.

Schimmel, Annemarie. *The Empire of the Great Mughals: History, Art and Culture*. Ed. Burzine K. Waghmar. Trans. Corinne Attwood. London: Reaktion Books, 2004.

Stronge, Susan. *Painting for the Mughal Emperor: The Art of the Book, 1560-1660*. London: V&A, 2002.

Tillotson, G. H. R. *Mughal India*. Architectural Guides for Travelers. San Francisco: Chronicle, 1990.

———, *The Rajput Palaces: The Development of an Architectural Style, 1450–1750*. New York: Oxford Univ. Press, 1999.

———. *The Tradition of Indian Architecture: Continuity, Controversy and Change since 1850*. New Haven: Yale Univ. Press, 1989.

Verma, Som Prakash. *Painting the Mughal Experience*. New York: Oxford Univ. Press, 2005.

Welch, Stuart Cary. *The Emperors' Album: Images of Mughal India*. New York: Metropolitan Museum of Art, 1987.

———. *India: Art and Culture 1300–1900*. New York: Metropolitan Museum of Art, 1985.

CHAPTER 24
Chinese and Korean Art after 1279

Andrews, Julia Frances, and Kuiyi Shen. *A Century in Crisis: Modernity and Tradition in the Art of Twentieth-Century China*. New York: Guggenheim Museum, 1998.

Barnhart, Richard M. *Painters of the Great Ming: The Imperial Court and the Zhe School*. Dallas: Dallas Museum of Art, 1993.

Barrass, Gordon S. *The Art of Calligraphy in Modern China*. London: British Museum, 2002.

Berger, Patricia Ann. *Empire of Emptiness: Buddhist Art and Political Authority in Qing China*. Honolulu: Univ. of Hawaii Press, 2003.

Bickford, Maggie. *Ink Plum: The Making of a Chinese Scholar-Painting*. New York: Cambridge Univ. Press, 1996.

Billeter, Jean Franççois. *The Chinese Art of Writing*. New York: Skira/Rizzoli, 1990.

Bush, Susan, and Hsui-yen Shih, eds. *Early Chinese Texts on Painting*. Cambridge, MA: Harvard Univ. Press, 1985.

Cahill, James. *The Distant Mountains: Chinese Painting in the Late Ming Dynasty, 1580–1644*. New York: Weatherhill, 1982.

———. *Hills beyond a River: Chinese Painting of the Y'uan Dynasty, 1279–1368*. New York: Weatherhill, 1976.

———. *Parting at the Shore: Chinese Painting of the Early and Middle Ming Dynasty 1368–1580*. New York: Weatherhill, 1978.

Chung, Anita. *Drawing Boundaries: Architectural Images in Qing China*. Honolulu: Univ. of Hawaii Press, 2004.

Clunas, Craig. *Pictures and Visualities in Early Modern China*. Princeton: Princeton Univ. Press, 1997.

Fang, Jing Pei. *Treasures of the Chinese Scholar: Form, Function and Symbolism*. Ed. J. May Lee Barrett. New York: Weatherhill, 1997.

Fong Wen C., and James C.Y. Watt. *Possessing the Past: Treasures from the National Palace Museum, Taipei*. New York: Metropolitan Museum of Art, 1996.

Fong, Wen C. *Between Two Cultures: Late-Nineteenth- and Twentieth-Century Chinese Paintings from the Robert H. Ellsworth Collection in the Metropolitan Museum of Art.* New York: Metropolitan Museum of Art, 2001.
Hearn, Maxwell K. and Judith G. Smith, eds. *Chinese Art: Modern Expressions.* New York: Dept. of Asian Art, the Metropolitan Museum of Art, 2001.
Ho, Chuimei, and Bennet Bronson. *Splendors of China's Forbidden City: The Glorious Reign of Emperor Qianlong.* Chicago: Field Museum, 2004.
Ho, Wai-kam. *The Century of Tung Ch`i-ch`ang.* 2 vols. Kansas City: Nelson-Atkins Museum of Art, 1992
Kim, Hongnam. *The Life of a Patron: Zhou Lianggong (1612-1672) and the Painters of Seventeenth-Century China.* New York: China Institute in America, 1996.
Knapp, Ronald G. *China's Vernacular Architecture: House Form and Culture.* Honolulu: Univ. of Hawaii Press, 1989.
Lee, Sherman, and Wai-Kam Ho. *Chinese Art under the Mongols: The Y'uan Dynasty, 1279–1368.* Cleveland: Cleveland Museum of Art, 1968.
Lim, Lucy. ed. *Wu Guanzhong: A Contemporary Chinese Artist.* San Francisco: Chinese Culture Foundation, 1989.
Liu, Laurence G. *Chinese Architecture.* New York: Rizzoli, 1989.
Moss, Paul. *Escape from the Dusty World: Chinese Paintings and Literati Works of Art.* London: Sydney L. Moss Ltd., 1999.
Ng, So Kam. *Brushstrokes: Styles and Techniques of Chinese Painting.* San Francisco: Asian Art Museum of San Francisco, 1993.
The Poetry [of] Ink: The Korean Literati Tradition, 1392-1910. Paris: Rééunion des Muséées Nationaux: Muséée National des Arts Asiatiques Guimet, 2005.
Smith, Karen. *Nine Lives: The Birth of Avant-Garde Art in New China.* Zurich: Scalo, 2006.
Till, Barry. *The Manchu Era (1644-1912), Arts of China's Last Imperial Dynasty.* Victoria, B.C: Art Gallery of Greater Victoria, 2004.
Vainker, S. J. *Chinese Pottery and Porcelain: From Prehistory to the Present.* London: British Museum, 1991.
Watson, William. *The Arts of China 900–1620.* Pelican History of Art. New Haven: Yale Univ. Press, 2000.
Weidner, Marsha Smith. *Views from Jade Terrace: Chinese Women Artists, 1300–1912.* Indianapolis, IN: Indianapolis Museum of Art, 1988.

Chapter 25
Japanese Art after 1392

Addiss, Stephen. *The Art of Zen: Painting and Calligraphy by Japanese Monks, 1600–1925.* New York: Abrams, 1989.
Berthier, Françços. *Reading Zen in the Rocks: The Japanese Dry Landscape Garden.* Trans. & essay Graham Parkes. Chicago: Univ. of Chicago Press, 2000.
Brinker, Helmut, and Hiroshi Kanazawa. *Zen, Masters of Meditation in Images and Writings.* Trans. Andreas Leisinger. Artibus Asiae: Supplementum, 40. Züürich: Artibus Asiae, 1996.
Calza, Gian Carlo. *Ukiyo-e.* New York: Phaidon, 2005.
Carpenter, John T. ed. *Hokusai and his Age: Ukiyo-e Painting, Printmaking and Book Illustration in Late Edo Japan.* Amsterdam: Hotei, 2005.
Clark, Timothy, et al. *The Dawn of the Floating World, 1650-1765: Early Ukiyo-e Treasures from the Museum of Fine Arts, Boston.* London: Royal Academy of Arts, 2001.
Guth, Christine. *Art of Edo Japan: The Artist and the City 1615–1868. Perspectives.* New York: Abrams, 1996.
Hickman, Money L. *Japan's Golden Age: Momoyama.* New Haven: Yale Univ. Press, 1996.
Jordan, Brenda G. and Victoria Weston, eds. *Copying the Master and Stealing his Secrets: Talent and Training in Japanese Painting.* Honolulu: Univ. of Hawaii Press, 2003.
Levine, Gregory P. A. Daitokuji: *The Visual Cultures of a Zen Monastery.* Seattle: Univ. of Washington Press, 2005.
McKelway, Matthew P. *Traditions Unbound: Groundbreaking Painters of Eighteenth-Century Kyoto.* San Francisco: Asian Art Museum—Chong-Moon Lee Center, 2005.
Miyajima, Shin´´ichi, and Sato Yasuhiro. *Japanese Ink Painting.* Ed. George Kuwayama. Los Angeles: Los Angeles County Museum of Art, 1985.
Munroe, Alexandra. *Japanese Art after 1945: Scream Against the Sky.* New York: Abrams, 1994.
Murase, Miyeko, ed. *Turning Point: Oribe and the Arts of Sixteenth-Century Japan.* New York: Metropolitan Museum of Art, 2003.
Newland, Amy Reigle, ed. *The Hotei Encyclopedia of Japanese Woodblock Prints.* 2 vols. Amsterdam: Hotei Publishing, 2005.
Parker, Joseph D. *Zen Buddhist Landscape Arts of Early Muromachi Japan (1336-1573).* SUNY Series in Buddhist Studies. Albany: State Univ. of New York Press, 1999.
Phillips, Quitman E. *The Practices of Painting in Japan, 1475-1500.* Stanford, CA: Stanford Univ. Press, 2000.
Plutschow, Herbert E. Rediscovering Rikyu and the Beginnings of the Japanese Tea Ceremony. Folkestone: Global Oriental, 2003.
Seo, Aubrey Yoshiko. *The Art of Twentieth-Century Zen: Paintings and Calligraphy by Japanese Masters.* Boston: Shambala, 1998.
Singer, Robert T., and John T. Carpenter. *Edo, Art in Japan 1615–1868.* Washington, D.C.: National Gallery of Art, 1998.
Till, Barry. *The Arts of Meiji Japan, 1868–1912: Changing Aesthetics.* Victoria, BC: Art Gallery of Victoria, 1995.

Chapter 26
Art of the Americas after 1300

Bauer, Brian S. *Ancient Cuzco: Heartland of the Inca.* Joe R. and Teresa Lozano Long Series in Latin American and Latino Art and Culture. Austin: Univ.of Texas Press, 2004.
Burger, Richard L. and Lucy C., eds. *Machu Picchu: Unveiling the Mystery of the Incas.* New Haven: Yale Univ. Press, 2004.
Berlo, Janet Catherine, and Ruth B. Phillips. *Native North American Art.* Oxford History of Art. Oxford: Oxford Univ. Pres, 1998.
Bingham, Hiram. *Lost City of the Incas: The Story of Machu Picchu and Its Builders.* London: Weidenfeld & Nicolson, 2002.
Boone, Elizabeth Hill. *The Aztec World. Exploring the Ancient World.* Washington, D.C.: Smithsonian Books, 1994.
Broder, Patricia Janis. *American Indian Painting and Sculpture.* New York: Abbeville, 1981.
——. *Earth Songs, Moon Dreams: Paintings by American Indian Women.* New York: St. Martin's Press, 1999.
Brown, Steven C. *Native Visions: Evolution in Northwest Coast Art from the Eighteenth through the Twentieth Century.* Seattle: Seattle Art Museum in assoc. with the Univ. of Washington Press, 1998.
Diaz del Castillo, Bernal. *Discovery and Conquest of Mexico, 1517-1521.* Ed. Genaro Garcíía. Trans. & notes A. P. Maudslay. New intro. Hugh Thomas. Originally published: New York: Farrar, Straus, and Cudahy, 1956. New York: DeCapo Press, 1996.
Duffek, Karen, and Charlotte Townsend-Gault, eds. *Bill Reid and Beyond: Expanding on Modern Native Art.* Vancouver: Douglas & McIntyre, 2004.
Feest, Christian F. *Native Arts of North America.* Updated ed. World of Art. New York: Thames and Hudson, 1992.
Fields, Virginia M., and Victor Zamudio-Taylor. *The Road to Aztlan: Art from a Mythic Homeland.* Los Angeles: Los Angeles County Museum of Art, 2001.
Griffin-Pierce, Trudy. *Earth is my Mother, Sky is my Father: Space, Time, and Astronomy in Navajo Sandpainting.* Albuquerque: Univ. of New Mexico Press, 1992.
Holm, Bill. *Northwest Coast Indian Art; An Analysis of Form.* Thomas Burke Memorial Washington State Museum Monograph, 1. Seattle, Univ. of Washington Press, 1965.
Hughes, Paul. *Time Warps: Ancient Andean Textiles.* London: Fine Textile Art, 1995.
Kaufman, Alice, and Christopher Selser. *The Navajo Weaving Tradition: 1650 to the Present.* New York: Dutton, 1985.
Macnair, Peter L., Robert Joseph, and Bruce Grenville. *Down from the Shimmering Sky: Masks of the Northwest Coast.* Vancouver: Douglas & McIntyre, 1998.
Matos Moctezuma, Eduardo, and Felix R. Solíís Olguíín. *Aztecs.* London: Royal Academy of Arts, 2002.
Moseley, Michael. *The Incas and Their Ancestors: The Archaeology of Peru.* London: Thames and Hudson, 1992.
Nabokov, Peter, and Robert Easton. *Native American Architecture.* New York: Oxford Univ. Press, 1989.
Rushing III, W. Jackson, ed. *Native American Art in the Twentieth Century: Makers, Meanings, Histories.* New York: Routledge, 1999
Shaw, George Everett. *Art of the Ancestors: Antique North American Indian Art.* Aspen, CO: Aspen Art Museum, 2004.
Solíís, Felipe R. *The Aztec Empire.* New York: Guggenheim Museum Publications, 2004.
Taylor, Colin F. *Buckskin & Buffalo: The Artistry of the Plains Indians.* New York: Rizzoli, 1998.
Townsend. Richard, ed. *The Aztecs.* 2nd rev. ed. Ancient Peoples and Places. London: Thames and Hudson, 2000.
Trimble, Stephen. *Talking with the Clay: The Art of Pueblo Pottery.* Santa Fe: School of American Research Press, 1987.
Wood, Nancy C. *Taos Pueblo.* New York: Knopf, 1989.

Chapter 27
Art of Pacific Cultures

Brandon, Reiko Mochinaga, and Loretta G. H. Woodard. *Hawaiian Quilts: Tradition and Transition.* Honolulu: Honolulu Academy of Arts, 2004.
Caruana, Wally. *Aboriginal Art.* World of Art. New York: Thames and Hudson, 1996.
D'Alleva, Anne. *Arts of the Pacific Islands.* Perspectives. New York: Abrams, 1998.
Herle, Anita, ed. *Pacific Art: Persistence, Change, and Meaning.* Honolulu: Univ. of Hawai'i Press, 2002.
Kaeppler, Adrienne Lois, Christian Kaufmann, and Douglas Newton. *Oceanic Art.* Trans. Nora Scott & Sabine Bouladon. New York: Abrams, 1997.
Kirch, Patrick Vinton. *The Lapita Peoples: Ancestors of the Oceanic World.* The Peoples of South-East Asia and the Pacific. Cambridge, MA: Blackwell, 1997.
Kjellgren, Eric. *Splendid Isolation: Art of Easter Island.* New York: Metropolitan Museum of Art, 2001.
Küüchler, Susanne, and Graeme Were. *Pacific Pattern.* London: Thames & Hudson, 2005.
Lilley, Ian, ed. *Archaeology of Oceania: Australia and the Pacific Islands.* Malden, MA: Blackwell, 2006.
McCulloch, Susan. *Contemporary Aboriginal Art: A Guide to the Rebirth of an Ancient Culture.* Honolulu: Univ. of Hawaii Press, 1999.
Moore, Albert C. *Arts in the Religions of the Pacific: Symbols of Life.* Religion and the Arts Series. New York: Pinter Publishers, 1995.
Morwood, M. J. *Visions from the Past: The Archaeology of Australian Aboriginal Art.* Washington, D.C.: Smithsonian Institution Press, 2002.
Neich, Roger, and Mick Pendergrast. *Traditional Tapa Textiles of the Pacific.* London: Thames and Hudson, 1997.
Newton, Douglas, ed. *Arts of the South Seas: Island Southeast Asia, Melanesia, Polynesia, Micronesia; The Collections of the Muséée Barbier-Mueller.* Trans. David Radzinowicz Howell. New York: Prestel, 1999.
Rainbird, Paul. *The Archaeology of Micronesia.* Cambridge World Archaeology. New York: Cambridge Univ. Press, 2004.
Smidt, Dirk, ed. *Asmat Art: Woodcarvings of Southwest New Guinea.* New York: George Braziller in assoc. with Rijksmuseum voor Volkenkunde, Leiden, 1993.
Starzecka, D. C., ed. *Maori Art and Culture.* London: British Museum Press, 1996.
Taylor, Luke. *Seeing the Inside: Bark Painting in Western Arnhem Land.* Oxford Studies in Social and Cultural Anthropology. New York: Oxford Univ. Press, 1996.
Thomas, Nicholas. *Oceanic Art.* World of Art. New York: Thames and Hudson, 1995.
———, Anna Cole and Bronwen Douglas, eds. *Tattoo: Bodies, Art, and Exchange in the Pacific and the West.* Durham: Duke Univ. Press, 2005.

Chapter 28
Art of Africa in the Modern Era

Anatsui, El. *El Anatsui Gawu.* Llandudno, Wales, U.K.: Oriel Mostyn Gallery, 2003.
Astonishment and Power. Washington, D.C.: National Museum of African Art, Smithsonian Institution, 1993.
Beckwith, Carol, and Angela Fisher. *African Ceremonies.* 2 vols. New York: Harry N. Abrams, 1999.
Binkley, David A. "Avatar of Power: Southern Kuba Masquerade Figures in a Funerary Context" in *Africa-Journal of the International African Institute,* v.57: 1, 1987. Pgs. 75-97.
Cameron, Elisabeth L. *Art of the Lega.* Los Angeles: UCLA Fowler Museum of Cultural History, 2001.
Cole, Herbert M., ed. *I Am Not Myself: The Art of African Masquerade.* Los Angeles: Fowler Museum of Cultural History, Univ. of California, 1985.
——. *Icons: Ideals and Power in the Art of Africa.* Washington, D.C.: National Museum of African Art, Smithsonian Institution, 1989.
A Fiction of Authenticity: Contemporary Africa Abroad. St. Louis: Contemporary Art Museum St. Louis, 2003.

Fogle, Douglas, and Olukemi Ilesanmi. *Julie Mehretu: Drawing into Painting*. Minneapolis, MN: Walker Art Center, 2003.

Gillow, John. *African Textiles*. San Francisco: Chronicle Books, 2003.

Graham, Gilbert. *Dogon Sculpture: Symbols of a Mythical Universe*. Brookville, NY: Hillwood Art Museum, Long Island Univ., C.W. Post Campus, 1997.

Hess, Janet Berry. *Art and Architecture in Postcolonial Africa*. Jefferson, NC: McFarland & Co., 2006.

Jordáán, Manuel, ed. Chokwe! *Art and Initiation Among the Chokwe and Related Peoples*. Munich: Prestel-Verlag., 1998

Kasfir, Sidney Littlefield. *Contemporary African Art*. World of Art. London: Thames and Hudson, 2000.

Morris, James, and Suzanne Preston Blier. *Butabu: Adobe Architecture of West Africa*. New York: Princeton Architectural Press, 2004.

Oguibe, Ole, and Okwui Enwezor. *Reading the Contemporary: African Art from Theory to the Marketplace*. Cambridge, MA: MIT Press, 1999.

Pemberton III, John, ed. *Insight and Artistry in African Divination*. Washington, D.C.: Smithsonian Institution Press, 2000.

Perrois, Louis, and Marta Sierra Delage. *The Art of Equatorial Guinea: The Fang Tribes*. New York: Rizzoli, 1990.

Picton, John, et al. *El Anatsui: A Sculpted History of Africa*. London: Saffron Books in conjunction with the October Gallery, 1998.

Roberts, Mary Nooter, and Allen F. Roberts, eds. *Memory: Luba Art and the Making of History*. New York: Museum for African Art, 1996.

Roy, Christopher D. *Art of the Upper Volta Rivers*. Meudon, France: Chaffin, 1987.

Schildkrout, Enid, and Curtis A. Keim. *African Reflections: Art from Northeastern Zaire*. Seattle: Univ. of Washington Press, 1990.

Sieber, Roy, and Roslyn Adele Walker. *African Art in the Cycle of Life*. Washington, D.C.: National Museum of African Art, Smithsonian Institution, 1987.

Stepan, Peter, and Iris Hahner-Herzog. *Spirits Speak: A Celebration of African Masks*. Munich. Prestel, 2005.

Van Damme, Annemieke. *Spectacular Display: The Art of Nkanu Initiation Rituals*. Washington, D.C.: Smithsonian National Museum of African Art, 2001.

Vogel, Susan Mullin. *Baule : African Art, Western Eyes*. New Haven: Yale Univ. Press, 1997.

Walker, Roslyn Adele. *O?_lo?_?_we?_?_ of Ise?_?_: A Yoruba Sculptor to Kings*. Washington, D.C.: National Museum of African Art, Smithsonian Institution, 1998.

CREDITS

Chapter 23

23-1 Steve Vidler / SuperStock, Inc; 23-2 Dirk Bakker; 23-5 Borromeo / Art Resource, NY; 23-6 Michael Flinn / Courtesy of Marilyn Stokstad; 23-7 Photo by Craig Smith; 23-8 V & A Picture Library; 23-09 Borromeo / Art Resource, NY; 23-11 © 2005 Museum of Fine Arts, Boston. All Rights Reserved; 23-12, 23-16 © David Ball / Alamy; 23-13 © 2007 Museum of Fine Arts, Boston. All Rights Reserved; 23-14 B.P. Mathur and Pierre / Dinodia Picture Agency; 23-15, 23-19 Photograph by Sexton / Dykes; 23-18 Craig Smith / Phoenix Art Museum; BOX: Katherine Wetzel / © Virginia Museum of Fine Arts, Richmond; BOXES: Reunion des Musees Nationaux / Art Resource, NY.

Chapter 24

24-2, 24-3, 24-5, 24-6, 24-7, 24-12, 24-13 The National Palace Museum; 24-4, 24-11 The Cleveland Museum of Art; 24-8 Collection of the Palace Museum, Beijing; 24-9 Panorama Stock / Robert Harding; 24-10 The Nelson-Atkins Museum of Art; 24-14 Spencer Museum of Art; 24-15 Museum of Oriental Ceramics, Osaka; 24-16 Ewha Woman's University Museum, Seoul, Korea; 24-17 Photo Courtesy of Central Library, Tenri University, Tenri, Japan; 24-18 Samsung Museum, Lee'um, Seoul, Republic of Korea; 24-20 Whanki Foundation / Whanki Museum, Seoul, Korea; 24-24 Courtesy of the Oriental Institute of the University of Chicago; BOX: The Nelson-Atkins Museum of Art, Kansas City, Missouri.

Chapter 25

25-1 Tibor Franyo / Honolulu Academy of Arts; 25-2 © 2005 Museum of Fine Arts, Boston. All Rights Reserved; 25-3, 25-13, BOX: TNM Image Archives; 25-4, 25-9 Stephen Addiss; 25-5 Michael Yamashita; 25-6 Steve Vidler / SuperStock, Inc; 25-7, 25-11 Japan National Tourist Organization / Sakamoto Manschichi Photo Research Library, Tokyo; 25-8 Myoki-an / Pacific Press Service; 25-10 Freer Gallery of Art/Smithsonian; 25-12 Spencer Museum of Art; 25-14 Photograph © 2003 Museum Associates/LACMA; 25-15 Philadelphia Museum of Art; 25-16 © Shokodo, Ltd. & Japan Artists Association, Inc. 2006; 25-17 © Miyashita Zenji / Spencer Museum of Art / University of Kansas, Kansas; 25-18 Dr. Tatsuo Yamamoto; 25-19 © 1999 Takashi Murakami / Kaikai Kiki Co., Ltd. All Rights Reserved; BOX: The Frank Lloyd Wright Archives.

Chapter 26

26-1 National Museums and Galleries on Merseyside / Walker Art Gallery / World Museum Liverpool, National Museums Liverpool; 26-2 Bodleian Library, University of Oxford; 26-3 Enrique Franco Torrijos, Mexico City / Embassy of Mexico; 26-4 Werner Forman / Art Resource, NY; 26-5 Dorling Kindersley Media Library / © Michel Zabe; 26-6 Chris Rennie / Robert Harding; 26-7 Dagli Orti / Picture Desk, Inc. / Kobal Collection; 26-8 Justin Kerr / Dumbarton Oaks, Byzantine Photograph and Fieldwork Archives, Washington, DC; 26-9 John Bigelow Taylor, NY / American Museum of Natural History; 26-10 With permission of the Royal Ontario Museum © ROM; 26-11 Smithsonian National Museum of Natural History; 26-12 Detroit Institute of Arts; 26-13 Montana Historical Society; 26-14 © 2006 Peabody Museum, Harvard University 99-12-10/53121 T4279; 26-15 Denver Art Museum, 26-16 Stephen S. Meyers / Courtesy Dept. of Library Services, American Museum of Natural History; 26-17 Amon Carter Museum / © Laura Gilpin Collection; 26-18 Museum of Indian Arts & Culture; 26-20 The Heard Museum; 26-21 Embassy of Canada ; 26-22 J. Scott Applewhite / AP Photo; 26-29 The Philbrook Museum of Art; BOX: Courtesy Curtis Library, Northwestern University Library; BOX: Courtesy University of British Columbia Museum of Anthropology; BOX: The Philbrook Museum of Art.

Chapter 27

27-1 Jeffrey Dykes / Peabody Essex Museum; 27-2 Australian Tourist Commission; 27-3 E. Brandl / Courtesy AIATSIS Pictorial Collection; 27-4 Kluge-Ruhe / Aboriginal Art Collection / University of Virginia Library; 27-5 Marilyn Stokstad / Photo Courtesy Anthony Forge; 27-6 Photograph © 2007 The Metropolitan Museum of Art, NY; 27-7 R. Berle Clay; 27-8 Federated States of Micronesia; 27-9 James Balog / Black Star; 27-10 Peabody Essex Museum; 27-11 By permission of The British Library; 27-12 Robert Newcombe / The Nelson-Atkins Museum of Art; 27-13 Museum of New Zealand Te Papa Tongarewa; 27-14 Bishop Museum; 27-15 Dr. Joyce D. Hammond; 27-16 Art Gallery of South Australia; BOX: Bishop Museum MAP: Prehistoric Architecture in Micronesia, William N. Morgan , p. 60, ©1988. BOX: Otago Museum, Dunedin.

Chapter 28

28-1 Sarah DaVanzo Collection; 28-2 Margaret Courtney-Clarke / Corbis / Bettmann; 28-03 Igor Delmas; 28-4 University of Iowa Museum of Art; 28-5, 28-11 Margaret Thompson Drewal / Eliot Elisofon Photographic Archives / National Museum of African Art / Smithsonian Institution; 28-6 Charles & Josette Lenars / Corbis-NY; 28-7 Frederick John Lamp; 28-8 Photo by Don Cole; 28-9 The Field Museum; 28-10 University of Pennsylvania Museum of Archaeology and Anthropology, Philadelphia; 28-12, 28-20, BOXES: Franko Khoury /National Museum of African Art / Smithsonian Institution; 28-13 © Angelo Turconi; 28-14, 28-17 Eliot Elisofon / Eliot Elisofon Photographic Archives / National Museum of African Art / Smithsonian Institution; 28-15 Royal Anthropological Institute of Great Britain and Ireland; 28-16 Detroit Institute of Arts; 28-18 © David A. Binkley / Patricia Darish; 28-19 Hughes Dubois / Musee Dapper; 28-21 Photograph Courtesy October Gallery, London; 28-22 Courtesy The Project, New York.

INDEX

Notes